Intergenerational transmission
of criminal and violent behaviour

Sidestone Press

Intergenerational transmission
of criminal and violent behaviour

Sytske Besemer

Dissertation submitted for the Degree of *Doctor of Philosophy*, 8 March 2012

Institute of Criminology, University of Cambridge | http://www.crim.cam.ac.uk

Jesus College, Cambridge | http://www.jesus.cam.ac.uk

Netherlands Institute for the Study of Crime and Law Enforcement (NSCR) | http://www.nscr.

Supervised by
Professor David P. Farrington
Professor Catrien C.J.H. Bijleveld

© 2012 S. Besemer

Published by Sidestone Press, Leiden
   www.sidestone.com
   Sidestone registration number: SSP130500001

ISBN 978-90-8890-101-0

Photograph cover: Chalabala | Dreamstime.com
Cover design: K. Wentink, Sidestone Press
Lay-out: S. Besemer

Printing and publishing of this dissertation was made possible with financial support from the J.E. Jurriaanse Stichting and the Netherlands Institute for the Study of Crime and Law Enforcement (NSCR).

This dissertation was written in LaTeX.

Preface

This dissertation is the result of my own work and contains nothing which is the outcome of work done in collaboration with others, except where specifically indicated in the text. This dissertation, including footnotes, does not exceed the permitted length.

Although this work is my own, I do want to acknowledge a number of people who supported me throughout my time as a Ph.D. student. I have had an extremely rewarding, stimulating and also personally inspiring experience. I am grateful for the opportunities I have had and for the wonderful people I have met along the way.

First, I am grateful to both my supervisors, David Farrington and Catrien Bijleveld. I had never thought of doing a Ph.D. when Catrien, some five years ago, suggested that I should apply to do a Ph.D. Thank you for your confidence and enthusiasm, for being critical and wonderfully down-to-earth. David, I feel lucky that you were immediately enthusiastic when I suggested to conduct Ph.D. research using your data. Thank you for your trust, your warm personality, your expertise, for being critical in such an encouraging manner and for teaching me to look at my own work like that.

For the work in my dissertation, I collaborated with two other people to whom I am grateful: Joe Murray and Victor van der Geest. Thank you for starting with me on my Ph.D. journey by working on our article and for encouraging me throughout my Ph.D. I have conducted my research at the Institute of Criminology as well as at the NSCR and feel lucky to be part of two stimulating communities. The NSCR not only provided for a professional research environment when I was in the Netherlands, but also a social community. There are too many names to mention, but I want to thank you for always making me feel welcome when I was in my Dutch life. Peter and Ariena were always happy to help.

Similarly, I want to thank the staff at the Institute of Criminology - Joanne, Alex, Matt, Jordi, Mary and Stuart in particular - for their invaluable help in administrative, statistical, computer and library issues. Working at the IoC was a daily pleasure also thanks to my fellow Ph.D. students. Particularly, I want to thank my office mates Jake, Anton, and Esther for being my living grammar test, making me laugh so often, and for discussing Dutch crime policies.

Sheena Bridgman at Jesus College made my experience of Cambridge memorable and welcoming. I am proud to be one of her first Ph.D. babies to graduate. I am also thankful to Friedrich Lösel, Manuel Eisner, and Barak Ariel for their thoughtful feedback on my first- and second-year reports.

I was fortunate to have been funded throughout my Ph.D. research and was able to attend several conferences and summer schools. I am grateful to the Gates Cambridge Trust, Prins Bernhard Cultuurfonds, VSB Fonds, Jesus College Doctoral Research Fund, Institute of Criminology Ph.D. fund, the Cambridge Philosophical Society and the Yorke Fund for this.

In terms of intergenerational transmission, I clearly show some discontinuity since I am the first one pursuing an academic 'career' in my family. There are also similarities and I thank my parents for never pushing us, but for encouraging us to do what we are interested in. And for the endless support, visits and driving me over to Cambridge. Similarly, I want to thank my own generation, my sisters (and brother!) and my friends for their support and welcome escape out of the bubble. Thank you (and in particular Chris, Corina, Kirst, Laura, Maikel, Renate, Rogier, Sander, Simon, and Wouter) also for wanting to discuss and reflect on my research and proofread my chapters. Life is not just work and because my life outside work was particularly enjoyable, I was able to do this research.

Wouter, thank you for being there, for feeding me, for showing me how to finish, for helping me with the nerdy bits of the dissertation, for being wonderful and for never ever complaining about the fact that I was more than often on the other side of the pond.

Sytske Besemer
Cambridge/Leiden, January 2012

Contents

Preface	iii
List of Tables	ix
List of Figures	xi

1		**Introduction**	1
1.1		Definitions	2
	1.1.1	Intergenerational transmission	2
	1.1.2	Crime	2
	1.1.3	Aggressive and violent behaviour	3
1.2		Mechanisms explaining intergenerational transmission	3
	1.2.1	Risk factors: a criminogenic environment	4
	1.2.2	Social learning	6
	1.2.3	Genetic or biological transmission	6
	1.2.4	Official bias against certain families	7
	1.2.5	Assortative mating	7
	1.2.6	Interactional theory of intergenerational transmission	8
1.3		Research questions and outline of the dissertation	9
	1.3.1	Outline	9
	1.3.2	Intergenerational specialisation in violence	9
	1.3.3	Timing and frequency of parental crime in the child's life and risk factors	10
	1.3.4	Intergenerational continuity of conviction trajectories	11
	1.3.5	Official bias and labelling	11
	1.3.6	Parental imprisonment	12
1.4		Methodology	12
	1.4.1	Cross-national comparison: England and the Netherlands	12
	1.4.2	England: The Cambridge Study in Delinquent Development	13
	1.4.3	The Netherlands: The NSCR Transfive Study	13
	1.4.4	Measures	15
	1.4.5	Data Analytic Approach	16
1.5		Summary	17

2	**Specialised versus versatile intergenerational transmission of violence**	**19**
2.1	Introduction	19
2.2	Theories of specialisation in intergenerational transmission	22
2.3	Hypotheses	24
2.4	Method	25
	2.4.1 Sample	25
	2.4.2 Measures	25
	2.4.3 Analytic Approach	26
2.5	Results	28
	2.5.1 Traditional approach	28
	2.5.2 Latent Class Analysis	30
2.6	Discussion	34
2.7	Summary	37
3	**The impact of timing and frequency of parental criminal behaviour and risk factors on offspring offending**	**39**
3.1	Introduction	39
3.2	Theoretical Background	40
3.3	Hypotheses	44
3.4	Method	46
	3.4.1 Sample	46
	3.4.2 Measures	46
	3.4.3 Analytic Approach	48
3.5	Results	49
	3.5.1 Parents' frequency of convictions	49
	3.5.2 Timing of parents' crime in the child's life	50
3.6	Discussion	54
3.7	Summary	58
4	**Intergenerational transmission of criminal behaviour: conviction trajectories of fathers and their offspring**	**59**
4.1	Introduction	59
4.2	Hypotheses	62
4.3	Method	62
	4.3.1 Sample	62
	4.3.2 Measures	62
	4.3.3 Analytic Approach	63
4.4	Results	65
	4.4.1 Fathers' conviction trajectories - England	65
	4.4.2 Fathers' conviction trajectories - the Netherlands	66
	4.4.3 Offspring offending behaviour per father trajectory group	68
	4.4.4 Sons' conviction trajectories - England	68
	4.4.5 Sons' conviction trajectories - the Netherlands	70
	4.4.6 Daughters' conviction trajectories - England	72
	4.4.7 Intergenerational resemblance of conviction trajectories	72
4.5	Discussion	76
4.6	Summary	79

Contents

5	**Official bias in intergenerational transmission and the impact of labelling on criminal behaviour**	**81**
5.1	Introduction	81
5.2	Previous research on official bias and labelling	83
5.3	Hypotheses	86
5.4	Method	88
	5.4.1 Sample	88
	5.4.2 Measures	88
	5.4.3 Analytic Approach	90
5.5	Results	92
	5.5.1 Impact of biasing variables on self-reported offending versus official convictions	92
	5.5.2 Relationship between biasing variables and offspring convictions while controlling for self-reported offending	92
	5.5.3 The impact of a conviction on subsequent offending	97
	5.5.4 Interaction between labelling and convicted parent	97
5.6	Discussion	99
5.7	Summary	103
6	**The relationship between parental imprisonment and offspring offending in England and the Netherlands**	**105**
6.1	Introduction	105
6.2	Theoretical Background	107
	6.2.1 Unfavourable impact	108
	6.2.2 No impact	109
	6.2.3 Favourable impact	109
	6.2.4 Moderators	110
	6.2.5 Hypotheses	112
6.3	Method	112
	6.3.1 Sample	112
	6.3.2 Measures	113
	6.3.3 Data analysis	113
6.4	Results	113
	6.4.1 Moderators	115
	6.4.2 Multivariate Regression Analyses	119
6.5	Discussion	121
6.6	Summary	127
7	**Discussion**	**129**
7.1	What we know now	129
	7.1.1 Intergenerational specialisation of violence	129
	7.1.2 Timing and frequency of parental crime in the child's life and risk factors	130
	7.1.3 Intergenerational continuity of conviction trajectories	130
	7.1.4 Official bias and labelling	131
	7.1.5 Parental imprisonment	131
	7.1.6 Cross-national comparison: England and the Netherlands	132

7.2	Implications for theories on intergenerational transmission		133
	7.2.1	Risk factors: a criminogenic environment	134
	7.2.2	Social learning: imitating behaviour	135
	7.2.3	Genetic or biological transmission	136
	7.2.4	The impact of sentencing of parents on intergenerational transmission	136
7.3	Strengths and limitations of the present research		138
	7.3.1	Strengths	139
	7.3.2	Limitations	139
7.4	Implications for future research		141
	7.4.1	Intergenerational transmission with self-reported offending behaviour	141
	7.4.2	Intergenerational transmission for females	142
	7.4.3	Intergenerational specialisation of violence	142
	7.4.4	Intergenerational resemblance of conviction trajectories	143
	7.4.5	Experimental designs	143
	7.4.6	Reciprocal relationships	144
	7.4.7	Peers and school environment	145
	7.4.8	Other settings	145
7.5	Implications for policy and politics		146
7.6	Conclusion		149

References 151

Summary 169

Appendix 171

Subject Index 173

Author Index 175

List of Tables

2.1	Sons' general and violent offending for violent and non-violent fathers	29
2.2	Overview of results and criteria for the LCA models - fathers - England	31
2.3	Overview of results and criteria for the LCA models - fathers - the Netherlands	31
2.4	Describing the two-class model for fathers - conditional item probabilities - England	32
2.5	Describing the two-class model for fathers - conditional item probabilities - the Netherlands	32
2.6	Sons' offending for the two latent classes for fathers: violence/other versus theft	33
3.1	Impact of parental conviction (when parent aged 12-39) on offspring's conviction rate 12-39	49
3.2	Impact of *number of* parental convictions (when parent aged 12-39) on offspring's conviction rate 12-39	49
3.3	Impact of the number of parental convictions (when parent aged 12-39) on offspring's conviction rate for parents who had at least one conviction	50
3.4	The impact of timing of parents' convictions on offspring's conviction rate	50
3.5	Comparing offspring's conviction rate for children whose parents had only been convicted before the child's birth versus those whose parents had never been convicted up until the child's 19th birthday and the impact of risk factors	51
3.6	Comparing offspring's conviction rate for children whose parents had only been convicted before the child's birth versus those whose parents had been convicted between the child's birth and 19th birthday and the impact of risk factors	52
3.7	The impact of the timing of parents' convictions in the child's life on offspring's conviction rate	53
4.1	Offspring conviction rate between 12th and 40th birthdays per father trajectory group	69
4.2	Resemblance between fathers and sons: percentages of group membership for fathers and sons - England	73

4.3	Resemblance between fathers' and sons' groups: proportion of sons per father group and Adjusted Standardised Residuals - England	73
4.4	Resemblance between fathers and sons: percentages of group membership for fathers and sons - the Netherlands	74
4.5	Resemblance between fathers' and sons' groups: proportion of sons per father group and Adjusted Standardised Residuals - the Netherlands	74
4.6	Resemblance between fathers and daughters: percentages of group membership for fathers and daughters	75
4.7	Resemblance between fathers' and daughters' groups: proportion of daughters per father group and Adjusted Standardised Residuals	75
5.1	Overview of variables	90
5.2	Percentage of offspring with a conviction versus self-reported offending in relation to biasing variables.	93
5.3	Percentage of offspring with a conviction versus self-reported offending in relation to biasing variables.	94
5.4	Partial odds ratios for the relationship between offspring convictions and biasing variables while controlling for self-reported offending.	96
5.5	The impact of a conviction between ages 19-26 (time 2) for offspring with no previous convictions on level of self-reported offending between ages 27-32 (time 3) while controlling for the level of self-reported offending between ages 15-18 (time 1) and the interaction with parental conviction.	98
5.6	Interaction effect of parental conviction and offspring conviction on self-reported offending.	98
6.1	Parental imprisonment and parental conviction versus offspring conviction rate - England and the Netherlands	114
6.2	Impact of paternal versus maternal imprisonment on offspring offending - England	116
6.3	Sons' age at parental imprisonment and sons' conviction rate - England	117
6.4	Number and length of parental imprisonment - England	118
6.5	Parental imprisonment and parental conviction for violent and non-violent parents versus sons' conviction rate - England	119
6.6	Multivariate regression analyses predicting sons' conviction rate by parental imprisonment controlling for parental convictions and violence - England	120
6.7	Multivariate regression analyses predicting sons' conviction rate by parental imprisonment controlling for risk factors - England	121
1	Bayesian Information Criterion (BIC) Values per model	171

List of Figures

1.1	Transmission of a criminogenic environment	5
4.1	Age-crime curves for fathers' convictions - England	66
4.2	Age-crime curves for fathers' convictions - the Netherlands	67
4.3	Age-crime curves for sons' convictions - England	70
4.4	Age-crime curves for sons' convictions - the Netherlands	71
4.5	Age-crime curves for daughters' convictions - England	72
5.1	Percentages of offspring with a conviction between ages 15-18 and/or 27-32, at different levels of self-reported offending with and without biasing variable.	95
5.2	Interaction effect of parental conviction and offspring conviction on self-reported offending.	98
6.1	Number of parental imprisonments and son's conviction rate 19-39 - England	118

Chapter 1

Introduction

'She's going to end up like me. I do not want her to live that life. I do not want her to be out there making money or using drugs or running in and out of jail.'

(Giordano, 2010, p. 152)

Children whose parents exhibit criminal behaviour have an increased risk of becoming criminal themselves.[1] Criminal or antisocial parents appear to be the strongest family factor predicting offending (Farrington, 2011). Similarly with aggression, children of aggressive parents tend to become aggressive (Avakame, 1998a,b; Conger, Neppl, Jeong Kim & Scaramella, 2003). Although many studies have shown the existence of this phenomenon, little research has focused on the mechanisms underlying this transmission. This dissertation investigates mechanisms that might explain intergenerational transmission of criminal and violent behaviour.

Crime and violent behaviour is widespread in our society: in the Netherlands as well as in England and Wales about twenty-five per cent of the population become victims of a crime every year, and between three to five per cent experience a violent offence (Chaplin, Flatley & Smith, 2011; Kalidien & De Heer-de Lange, 2011). It is increasingly recognised that especially being victimised by a violent crime can have long-term physical, emotional, practical and financial consequences (Zedner, 2002). Because of these profound negative consequences for those who are often the most vulnerable members of society, such as children, it is important to design effective interventions to reduce violent and criminal behaviour. To do this, a more comprehensive

---

[1] See for example Besjes & Van Gaalen (2008); Bijleveld & Wijkman (2009); Farrington, Barnes & Lambert (1996); Farrington, Jolliffe, Loeber, Stouthamer-Loeber & Kalb (2001); Farrington (2011); Giordano (2010); Gorman-Smith, Tolan, Loeber & Henry (1998); Jaffee, Moffitt, Caspi & Taylor (2003); Kim, Capaldi, Pears, Kerr & Owen (2009); Nijhof, Engels, Wientjes & Kemp (2007); Rowe & Farrington (1997); Thornberry (2009); Thornberry, Freeman-Gallant, Lizotte, Krohn & Smith (2003); Thornberry, Freeman-Gallant & Lovegrove (2009); Van de Rakt, Nieuwbeerta & Apel (2009).

understanding of the aetiology of such behaviour is necessary. This study contributes to that effort by providing knowledge about the development of violent and criminal behaviour and pointing to relevant factors and mechanisms that a prevention program could tackle. In addition, most intervention programs are targeted at individual offenders. A greater understanding of the mechanisms that cause children of violent or criminal parents to become violent or criminal themselves would enable interventions that would operate not only at the level of the offender, but at his or her entire family system.

Although little empirical research has been carried out on mechanisms explaining intergenerational transmission, theoretical knowledge exists on these mechanisms. In this introduction, after giving definitions of some of the key concepts used in this dissertation, I will first discuss mechanisms that could explain intergenerational transmission. Subsequently I will present an outline of this dissertation and discuss the research questions this dissertation aims to answer. This will be followed by a discussion of the methodology employed to examine these questions, including a description of the data used and methods of analysis.

1.1 Definitions

1.1.1 Intergenerational transmission

Intergenerational transmission does not literally mean that something physical is transmitted, such as a car or money, but means that some characteristic or behaviour is seen in both the parent and the child (Liefbroer, 2005). Intergenerational transmission is also referred to as intergenerational continuity. Intergenerational transmission of behaviour can be wide-ranging, from socioeconomic status (e.g. Bowles & Gintis, 2002; Bailey, Hill, Oesterle & Hawkins, 2009; Sharkey, 2008; Solon, 1992), education (e.g. Gamoran, 2001, mental health status (e.g. Serbin et al., 1998), parenting behaviours (e.g. Bailey et al., 2009; Capaldi, Pears, Patterson & Owen, 2003; Shaffer, Hurt, Obradović, Herbers & Masten, 2009), substance use (e.g. Bailey, Hill, Oesterle & Hawkins, 2006; Bailey et al., 2009), to criminal behaviour. This dissertation focuses on the transmission of criminal and violent offending.

1.1.2 Crime

Common definitions of criminal behaviour include 'behaviour which is prohibited by the criminal code' (Michael & Adler, 1933, p. 2) and 'any act committed in violation of a law that prohibits it and authorizes punishment for its commission' (J. Q. Wilson & Herrnstein, 1985, p. 22). Criminal behaviour can be defined in several ways, depending on the perspective taken and it is impossible to find one general definition of crime. These two definitions also face problems, because laws change over time and place, thereby showing that crime is not an empirically derived concept that we can unequivocally measure as the same in all times and places. Nevertheless, there is a great deal of consistency among Western industrialised countries and over time in what is defined as crime. In this dissertation criminal behaviour is operationalised as behaviour prohibited by criminal law and measured by official convictions. One chapter (5) also includes measures of self-reported offending, but these are also based on the criminal law infriction definition.

1.1.3 Aggressive and violent behaviour

Aggression is often defined as 'behaviour intended to injure another person or animal' (*Shorter Oxford English Dictionary*, 2002). In the *Compact Oxford English Dictionary of Current English* (2005) aggression is defined as 'hostile or violent behaviour or attitudes'. In this same dictionary, violence is defined as 'behaviour involving physical force intended to hurt, damage, or kill'. The intention involved in this definition is problematic: how do you know if someone intends to hurt another person or not? If it were possible to read someone's mind, this would be the most valid way of measuring intention; since this is not possible, most research relies on an observer's opinion about whether the behaviour was intended or not. Moreover, anger and fear can sometimes lead to impulsive reactions, which were not intended. Because it is problematic to determine whether the harmful behaviour was intended, Loeber and Stouthamer-Loeber (1998, p. 242) defined aggression as 'those acts that inflict bodily or mental harm on others'. Aggression is generally perceived as socially undesirable. As Tremblay (2000, p. 130) has pointed out, in some situations aggression can be desirable: 'Most parents would be proud to hear their child described as an aggressive tennis player. Most sales managers want aggressive salesmen. Most political parties want leaders who can be aggressive when needed.' Although one could argue that violence and aggression are not exactly the same, the concepts are clearly related. When using the term *violence* in this thesis, this refers to the undesirable behaviour defined above. I will mainly focus on the legal outcomes of this behaviour: convictions for violent offences, ranging from threats, assault, robbery, rape to murder.

1.2 Mechanisms explaining intergenerational transmission

Farrington (2011) describes six explanations for the intergenerational transmission of criminal behaviour: (a) intergenerational exposure to multiple risk factors, (b) mediation through environmental risk factors, (c) teaching and co-offending, (d) genetic mechanisms, (e) official (police and justice) bias, and (f) assortative mating. These explanations are not mutually exclusive and they are empirically intertwined; a combination of these mechanisms could explain intergenerational transmission. After discussing these mechanisms, I will present Thornberry's intergenerational extension of his Interactional Theory of Offending (Thornberry, 2005; Thornberry & Krohn, 2001, 2005).

1.2.1 Risk factors: a criminogenic environment

The first two explanations both involve risk factors. A risk factor is 'a characteristic, experience, or event that, if present, is associated with an increase in the probability (risk) of a particular outcome over the base rate of the outcome in the general (unexposed) population' (Kazdin, Kraemer, Kessler, Kupfer & Offord, 1997, p. 377). A risk factor is more than a correlate. If a variable is a correlate, it is associated with the outcome. Risk factors are correlates that also *predict* criminal behaviour. To be a risk factor, a variable needs to precede the outcome (Murray, Farrington, Sekol & Olsen, 2009).

We can distinguish between risk factors, causal risk factors and risk markers (Kraemer et al., 1997; Kraemer, Stice, Kazdin, Offord & Kupfer, 2001; Murray, 2006). The difference between these types of factors lies in the knowledge about causation. Predictors are called *risk factors* when there is no knowledge about whether the predictor causes the outcome. If research has demonstrated that the predictor causes the outcome, it is labelled a *causal risk factor*. When, conversely, research has shown that there is no causal relationship, the predictor is termed a *risk marker*. A risk marker shows that the predictor and dependent variable are correlated, but other (confounding) factors can explain the relationship between the two. A classical example is the relationship between people carrying matches and lung cancer. These two are correlated, but smoking is the causal variable: smokers are more likely to carry matches and they also have a higher chance of developing lung cancer. Carrying matches, in this case, is a risk marker for developing lung cancer, but it is in no way the causal factor.

Farrington describes how crime 'seems to be only one element of a larger syndrome of anti-social behaviour which arises in childhood and usually persists into adulthood' (1997, p. 363). People who offend also exhibit problems in other areas of their life, such as unemployment, drug use, heavy alcohol use and unstable living accommodation. Farrington's (2011) first explanation describes how these circumstances are transmitted from parents to children. Successive generations 'may be entrapped in poverty, have disrupted family lives, may experience single and teenage parenting, and may live in the most deprived neighborhoods' (Farrington, 2011, p. 132). He does not distinguish between the three types of risk factors described above, but his explanation can be interpreted in two different ways, depending on whether the circumstances are *causal risk factors* or *risk markers*. Assuming they are risk markers, the process pictured in figure 1.1(a) is representative. 'The antisocial syndrome' (Farrington, 1997, p. 363) is transmitted from parents to children, and one element of this syndrome can be criminal behaviour.

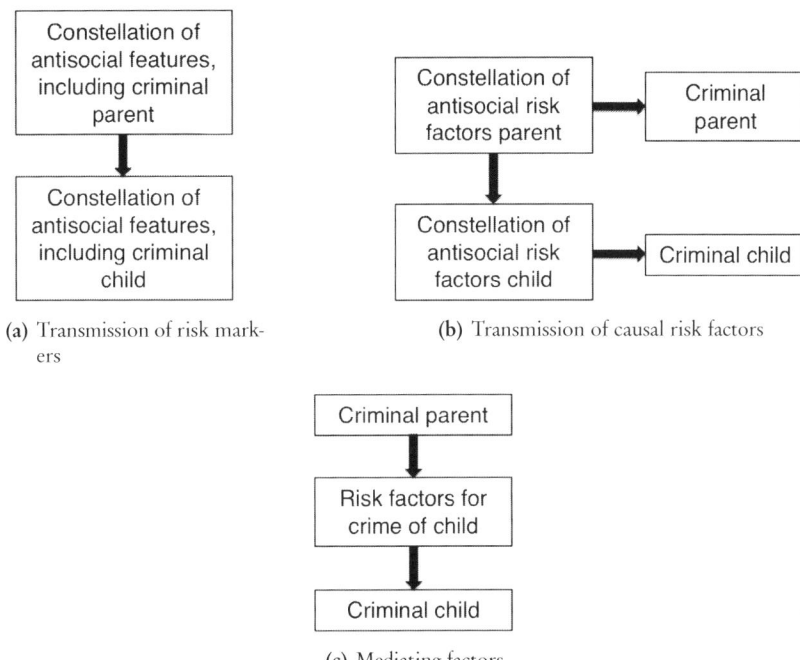

Figure 1.1: Transmission of a criminogenic environment

If, instead, we assume the circumstances are causal risk factors, the process pictured in figure 1.1(b) is exhibited. In this case, *antisocial* features are similarly transmitted from parents to children, but instead of being one element of an antisocial syndrome, crime is caused by the criminogenic factors that are transmitted. In both cases crime is not directly transmitted from parents to children, but rather through continuity of a constellation of antisocial features or 'a larger cycle of deprivation and antisocial behaviour' (Farrington, 2011, p. 133).

Farrington's second mechanism is connected to the first, because it also concerns criminogenic or risk factors. Here, these features are neither causal risk factors nor risk markers, but mediating factors. A mediator is 'the generative mechanism through which the focal independent variable is able to influence the dependent variable of interest' (R. M. Baron & Kenny, 1986, p. 1173). Parental criminality causes the mediating factor and this mediating factor causes the child's criminality. Mediating factors can be the same risk factors as mentioned above, such as poverty, living in a bad neighbourhood, poor parenting practices, and so on. The mediator is a link in the causal chain between parents' and children's criminality as pictured in figure 1.1(c).

1.2.2 Social learning

A third possible mechanism is that parents may teach their children (how) to commit crime and may possibly offend together with their offspring (Farrington, 2011). This relates to theories about social learning. In his Differential Association Theory, Sutherland hypothesizes that people learn behaviour through interaction with other people such as their parents (Lanier & Henry, 2004; Sutherland & Cressey, 1955). Children will develop similar attitudes to their parents. An individual will commit delinquent acts when he/she has learned (more) motivations to break rather than to follow the law. Bandura (1973, 1977) posits that children learn behaviour through observation and imitation of role models. Parents are important role models; if they are aggressive, children will copy their aggression. Furthermore, children's antisocial or violent behaviour might be reinforced by their parents and they might observe their parents' antisocial behaviour being reinforced (Bandura, 1971; Black, Sussman & Unger, 2010). According to these two theories children with aggressive parents will imitate aggressive behaviour and will learn that it is acceptable to engage in such behaviour. Previous analyses with the *Cambridge Study in Delinquent Development* demonstrated that co-offending of parents and children is unusual (Reiss & Farrington, 1991; West & Farrington, 1977). Parents also do not seem to openly support their children in being criminal. This, however, does not mean that children will not copy the parents' behaviour; children can still observe and imitate parents, even if their parents disapprove of this imitation.

1.2.3 Genetic or biological transmission

Next to this *nurture* perspective of social learning, Farrington (2011) describes a *nature* perspective: criminal or aggressive behaviour might be transmitted by genetic mechanisms. Several studies have suggested that there are physiological bases of criminal and aggressive behaviour, such as high testosterone levels (Olweus, 1987) and a low resting heart rate (Farrington, 2007; Raine, 2002a,b). These biological bases tend to be (partly) hereditary and as such they could explain intergenerational transmission. The best way to study genetic versus environmental contributions to behaviour is by using twin or adoption designs (DiLalla & Gottesman, 1991).

Although the current study is unable to examine genetic influences, it is important to note that several studies have demonstrated a genetic impact on criminal or antisocial and on aggressive and violent behaviour (P. A. Brennan, Mednick & Mednick, 1993; Grove et al., 1990; Mason & Frick, 1994; Mednick, Moffitt & Stack, 1987; Raine, Brennan, Farrington & Mednick, 1997; Rhee & Waldman, 2002; Waldman & Rhee, 2006; Brendgen et al., 2005; Cadoret, Leve & Devor, 1997; DiLalla & Gottesman, 1991; DiLalla, 2002; Hudziak et al., 2003). The body of research on biological and hereditary bases of criminal and violent behaviour is still growing and recently more attention has focused on the interaction of someone's genetic make-up and the environment. A genetic predisposition for aggressive behaviour does not necessarily mean that someone will actually develop this behaviour; it is not a deterministic process. The environment will influence how the genetic potential develops. The *genotype*, the genetic potential or inherited *instructions*, will interact with the environment to produce the *phenotype*, the observable outcome of the genotype, in this case the violent or criminal behaviour. Furthermore, certain genes might moderate the impact of certain experiences on the risk for developing delinquent behaviour (Caspi et al., 2002; Jaffee et al., 2005; Kim-Cohen et al., 2006; Rutter, 2007). Although it remains outside the scope of the current study to investigate this genetic potential, it is important to acknowledge its possible impact and its interaction with the environment in intergenerational transmission.

1.2.4 Official bias against certain families

The fifth mechanism is that official justice systems, such as the police and the court, are biased against known criminal families. As a result, they pay more attention to these families, which means that family members are more likely to be officially processed (prosecuted, cautioned and convicted) after an offence and thus appear in official statistics more often. West and Farrington (1977) found support for this in the *Cambridge Study of Delinquent Development*. This explanation asserts that there is no real transmission; there only seems to be an association because (after equating for offending) children of convicted parents will be officially processed more frequently than children without convicted parents. It does appear, however, that official bias is not the only explanation for intergenerational continuity in antisocial behaviour. In their research, West and Farrington (1977) demonstrated that sons of antisocial fathers, in addition to having more convictions, also showed a higher level of self-reported antisocial behaviour than sons of non-convicted parents.

1.2.5 Assortative mating

The last mechanism focuses on assortative mating: 'the tendency for people to form unions with similar others' (Moffitt, Caspi, Rutter & Silva, 2001, p. 185). People tend to affiliate with those who are similar to them, and antisocial people tend to marry or cohabit and have children with other antisocial people. Children with two criminal parents have an increased risk of showing antisocial behaviour; they experience a 'double whammy' effect (Moffitt et al., 2001, p. 195; West & Farrington, 1977). They inherit an antisocial phenotype twice and grow up in a criminogenic home environment.

There are several possibilities to explain why this phenomenon happens. First, antisocial people are likely to meet other antisocial people, because they share the same class background and move in the same social and professional circles. They go to the same schools, shops, clubs, pubs, and so on.

This is called '*social homogamy*' (Farrington, 2011, p. 133). In their research on the Dunedin Study, however, Krueger et al. (1998) found no evidence of this. A second possibility is that antisocial people make an active choice to mate with someone who shares the same values and background. Their partners will not disapprove of their delinquent lifestyle. This is termed '*phenotypic assortment*' and is related to the description above about the interaction between genotype and phenotype: people with an antisocial potential will choose to mate with other people with similar behaviour and personality (Farrington, 2011, p. 133). Third, it might be difficult for an antisocial person to find a prosocial person who would welcome a relationship. Prosocial people might avoid social contact with delinquents, which limits the potential *pool* of partners for antisocial people. An investigation into the exact causes of assortative mating is beyond the scope of this study, but it is clear that it seems to lead to crime-prone families (Moffitt et al., 2001). If two antisocial people have children together, we can speak of a kind of 'selective reproduction' (Moffitt et al., 2001, p. 196).

However, I argue that assortative mating is not a mechanism in itself, because other explanations such as genetic, social learning or risk factor mechanisms are needed to explain transmission in the first place. Assortative mating only posits that the intergenerational transmission is stronger with two criminal parents than with one.

1.2.6 Interactional theory of intergenerational transmission

Another theory aiming to explain intergenerational transmission is Thornberry's intergenerational extension to his and Marvin Krohn's Interactional Theory of Offending (Thornberry, 2005; Thornberry & Krohn, 2001, 2005). Central points of the Interactional Theory are that offending can start at any point in someone's life and that someone's (offending) behaviour will interact with other realms of life. Causal influences will be different at various developmental stages and, for example, parents will have more influence on behaviour in childhood, while peers will have more influence during adolescence. The intergenerational extension to this theory posits that people who were involved in delinquent behaviour during adolescence will face problems making successful transitions into adult roles including parenthood. This in turn will impact on their children's development. Thornberry (2005, p. 183) acknowledges a direct influence of antisocial behaviour in one generation to the next - both in the form of social learning as well as genetically - but predominantly explains transmission through an indirect mediation of family processes (or risk factors) such as 'family conflict, hostility, and especially by the quality of parenting'. People involved in antisocial behaviour are more likely to have children at a young age, experience structural adversity, are likely to continue antisocial behaviour and substance use, experience more stress, and have weak prosocial bonds all of which might lead to problems in raising their children. This theory focuses on mediating factors. Parents' delinquency has a strong effect on their own development, transition into adult roles, parenting styles and thereby the effectiveness of their parenting, which in turn will increase the risk that their children will develop criminal behaviour.

I will not test this theory in the current study, but the theory provides an interesting theoretical framework that also includes several of the mechanisms that Farrington discusses. Thornberry's theory could be seen as an extension of the transmission of a criminogenic environment mechanism with a particular focus on the interaction between parents' own delinquency, parenting styles and the extent to which they can provide an environment that encourages prosocial instead of antisocial behaviour.

1.3 Research questions and outline of the dissertation

1.3.1 Outline

Having outlined the theoretical perspective of this research, I will now provide a brief overview of the dissertation. After discussing the research questions, I provide a description of the datasets used to investigate intergenerational transmission and discuss the empirical tools and ways of analysing this information. Subsequently, this dissertation consists of five empirical chapters each shedding light on different aspects of intergenerational transmission. In Chapter 2, I explore whether a specific transmission of violent behaviour exists, or whether this is part of a transmission of general criminal behaviour. In Chapter 3, I examine the impact of timing and frequency of parental criminal behaviour and the impact of risk factors on intergenerational transmission. In Chapter 4, transmission is investigated using so-called developmental trajectories. The last two topics are more related to penal policy and political environment. In Chapter 5, I look at whether official bias exists and also investigate this in combination with labelling effects. In Chapter 6, I examine whether parental imprisonment might add extra risk for children of convicted parents. Finally, in the Discussion (Chapter 7) I give an overview of the findings and discuss strengths and limitations of this study. I also discuss these results in the view of contemporary society and present implications for future research and policy. Below I present the research questions for each of the empirical chapters.

1.3.2 Intergenerational specialisation in violence

Although previous studies have investigated intergenerational transmission of violence and of criminal behaviour, the majority do not compare these two types of transmission. As such, it is unclear whether there is a specific transmission of violent offending from parents to children. The first question of this dissertation is *do parents who have been convicted of a violent offense transmit criminal and violent behaviour more strongly than parents who were convicted, but never for violence?* In order to draw any inferences about violence specialization in intergenerational transmission, it is important to establish what constitutes a violent offender and whether or not such a type of criminal can be distinguished from others (Blumstein, Cohen, Roth & Visher, 1986; Farrington, 2003a). I will therefore first discuss how violent offenders can be defined and will then apply this to the study of intergenerational transmission. Two approaches are combined to study whether specialised violence transmission exists.

1.3.3 Timing and frequency of parental crime in the child's life and risk factors

Because the number of people with violence convictions and the frequency of these convictions was low in the samples used in this study, it was not possible to investigate the remaining research questions focusing on violence only. In the next chapter, I therefore turn to the transmission of general offending (including violence) where I focus on both the *timing* as well as *frequency* of parental offending. Not only the fact that parents have a conviction, but the timing and frequency of parental offending might be important in explaining transmission of criminal behaviour to children. Based on the mechanisms of intergenerational transmission, one would expect more persistent offenders to have more persistently offending children. In the first part of this chapter, I will investigate whether the frequency of parental convictions impacts on offspring offending.

Second, timing of the parent's criminal behaviour in the child's life might impact on transmission. For example, an association between parental offending before a child's birth and that child's later offending militates against transmission through social learning but supports genetic mechanisms or transmission of a criminogenic environment. Furthermore, the impact of a parent's conviction might be different at different ages and developmental stages of the child. Is there something like a sensitive period when children are more vulnerable to adverse influences like parental criminal behaviour?

Third, I will investigate the impact of risk factors on intergenerational transmission. For example, if children whose parents had been convicted after their birth commit more crime than those whose parents had only been convicted before their birth, this would support dynamic theories of transmission such as social learning, because children whose parents had been convicted after the child's birth had a (stronger) criminal and antisocial role model. However, it could also be possible that this group grew up in a more criminogenic environment with more risk factors for crime. Therefore I will also investigate the impact of risk factors in this transmission. The research questions examined are (a) *do offspring have more criminal convictions when parents had more convictions?* and (b) *does the timing of parents' criminal convictions in the offspring's life have an impact on offspring offending?* and (c) *could growing up in a criminogenic environment with risk factors explain intergenerational transmission?*

1.3.4 Intergenerational continuity of conviction trajectories

In the following chapter, I will combine several criminal career parameters including frequency, timing of parental offending, but also the age of onset and peak offending age by investigating conviction trajectories for both parents and children. Where in the previous chapter timing of parental offending in the child's life was investigated, in this chapter timing of parental offending in the parent's own life will be examined. By employing the semi-parametric, group-based trajectories methodology (Nagin, 2005) it is possible to investigate specifically the timing and volume of criminal behaviour in parents and children. Thus, the third question of this dissertation is (a) *do children of more persistent offending parents have more convictions than children of more sporadic offending parents?* and (b) *do specific types of parent offending trajectories predict similar types of offspring offending trajectories?*

1.3.5 Official bias and labelling

In the second chapter I started to include environmental features in the study of intergenerational transmission by examining risk factors or a criminogenic environment. The fourth empirical chapter will focus more specifically on the penal environment by investigating whether official bias exists against children of convicted parents. I will investigate this by comparing offspring's self-reported delinquency and their official convictions. If official bias exists, one would expect a stronger relationship between parental convictions and offspring convictions than between parental convictions and offspring self-reported offending. Furthermore, other variables that might bias the police against certain families will be investigated such as poor housing, low family Socio-Economic Status (SES), low family income, and a father's poor job record. Moreover, I will extend the study of official bias and include examination of labelling effects. Labelling occurs when someone's offending behaviour increases after involvement in the criminal justice system, after an official conviction. Official bias is defined in an intergenerational context; children of convicted parents have a higher risk of conviction because official justice systems pay more attention to these children; these children's self-reported offending may or may not be higher than the behaviour of children of unconvicted parents. I will first investigate whether official bias exists and second, I will examine whether an offspring conviction increased individuals' offending behaviour. Moreover, I will study the interaction between someone's own conviction and a convicted parent. The research questions investigated are (a) *do children of convicted parents have a higher risk of conviction after controlling for their self-reported offending?* and (b) *do other biasing variables such as poor housing, low family SES, low family income or a father's poor job record increase this conviction risk?* and (c) *does a conviction subsequently increase people's self-reported offending behaviour?* and (d) *is this labelling effect stronger for people whose parents had been convicted?*

1.3.6 Parental imprisonment

The final empirical chapter concentrates on the question whether offspring of prisoners display more criminal behaviour than offspring of convicted but not imprisoned parents. This will be investigated in England as well as the Netherlands to enable cross-national comparisons. This comparison is informative, because in the period during which this study's subjects experienced parental imprisonment (1946-81), Dutch prisons and penal policy were much more humane and liberal than in England. It is interesting to see whether the impact of parental imprisonment varies by social and penal context. The research questions addressed in this chapter are (a) *do children of prisoners display more criminal behaviour than children of convicted but not imprisoned parents?* and (b) *are the results different in the Netherlands and England?*

Each chapter will provide a discussion of relevant literature and previous research on the topic addressed. I will present a discussion of findings and answers to these research questions and implications for future research, practice and policy.

1.4 Methodology

1.4.1 Cross-national comparison: England and the Netherlands

A key element of this dissertation is the use of data from England as well as the Netherlands. Two prospective longitudinal datasets were used in the research for this dissertation. By comparing a group of people born in the same period (between 1946-1962) but in different countries, it is possible to replicate findings. Furthermore, differences between the countries may be explained by variations in policies in these countries. As Farrington and Loeber (1999, p. 300) stated: 'Cross-national comparisons of risk factors for delinquency are important for addressing the question of how far the causes of delinquency are similar in different times and places.'

In Chapters 2 and 4, replication of the results is the main motivation to compare the results. One would not expect different results based on different policies. In Chapter 6, where the impact of parental imprisonment will be studied, the comparison is interesting from a policy perspective. As will be described in more detail in Chapter 6, after the Second World War, the Netherlands became known as an extremely tolerant country with humane penal and prison policies (Downes, 1988; Downes & Van Swaaningen, 2007). England, in comparison, developed more repressive and punitive policies. Of course, it is very difficult to disentangle the impact of penal policies from the many other factors that might influence offending, but comparing the impact of imprisonment in these two countries in a period where their policies differed markedly might offer an explanation for any differences in the impact of these policies on offspring of convicted and imprisoned people.

1.4.2 England: The Cambridge Study in Delinquent Development

Cambridge Study in Delinquent Development (CSDD) is a prospective longitudinal study that has followed 411 males from London born around 1953. At the time they were first contacted in 1961-1962, these males were all living in a working-class inner-city area of South London. The sample was chosen by taking all of the boys who were then aged 8-9 and on the registers of six state primary schools within a one-mile radius of a research office that had been established. Hence, the most common year of birth for these males was 1953. In nearly all cases (94 per cent), their family breadwinner in 1961-1962 (usually the father) had a working class occupation (skilled, semi-skilled, or unskilled manual worker). Most of the boys were white and of British origin. Donald J. West originally directed the study and David P. Farrington, who has worked on it since 1969, has directed it since 1982. The males have been studied at frequent intervals between the ages of eight and fifty. Information on criminal convictions and self-reported delinquency was collected over the course of these years. Additionally, police records of offending of the parents and siblings of these 411 males have been collected. For more information and major findings see West (1969, 1982), West and Farrington (1973; 1977), Farrington and West (1990), Farrington (1995, 2003b), and Farrington et al. (2006; 2009).

For the research carried out in this dissertation, the full biological siblings of the original 411 men were included in the analyses. Investigating the siblings increased the sample size and enabled a broadening of the analyses as females were included. Because the data collection started with families that had at least one boy born in 1953-1954, the data set did not contain families with girls only. Therefore the proportion of males versus females in the current sample is around 2:1.

1.4.3 The Netherlands: The NSCR Transfive Study

Data collection in *Transfive* started with a group of 198 high-risk, working-class boys (G2), born around 1899 in the Netherlands. These adolescent males had all been sent to a reform school (Harreveld) between 1911 and 1914. Some were sent because they exhibited problem behaviour or minor delinquency, and others because their parents could not take proper care of them according to guardian organisations. Using genealogical and municipal records, all descendents of these men have been traced, with a retrieval rate of 100%. Dutch municipal records contain personal details for everyone born in the Netherlands and everyone moving into the country. Residents are obliged to notify the municipality of any changes (births, moves, deaths) and thus it was possible to trace every descendent using these records. Conviction data were available for their children (G3), grandchildren (G4) and great-grandchildren (G5). Partners were also included in the dataset, which enabled analysis of transmission from both parents. *Transfive* is directed by Catrien Bijleveld. For more information see Bijleveld and Wijkman (2009) and Bijleveld, Wijkman, and Stuifbergen (2007).

For comparison of these datasets, a comparable sample was taken from both: offspring born between January 1946 and September 1962. Only offspring born after the Second World War was included. In the Netherlands, a famine took place in the winter of 1944-1945. I did not want to include children whose mothers suffered from food shortage when they were pregnant. September 1962 was chosen as the cut-off date, because I wanted conviction data for all subjects until their 40th birthday. The last criminal record search for the *CSDD* siblings took place in September 2002. Criminal behaviour peaks in the teens and twenties and most criminal behaviour will have stopped or stabilised by age forty (Blumstein et al., 1986; Farrington, 1986; Piquero, Farrington & Blumstein, 2007). Taking this age limit provided for a large enough sample with a relatively long measurement period to enable investigation of the criminal career. Taking the birth range 1946-1962 resulted in a sample of 1184 subjects in the *CSDD* (782 males and 402 females) and 804 subjects in *Transfive* (412 males and 392 females). In the *CSDD*, all child subjects came from the same study generation, being the original men born around 1953 and their siblings. In *Transfive*, the original G2 men were born around the same year, but their children and grandchildren were born in a wider range of years. Consequently, offspring in the sample taken for this dissertation came from G3 ($n=48$), G4 ($n=740$) and G5 ($n=16$). The average year of birth for this sample was 1955.

People who died or emigrated before their 19th birthday were excluded from the analyses. When people had emigrated, it was not possible to measure their convictions. I did not want to include people who were not 'at risk' for their parents possible criminal behaviour in this period or for whom it was not possible to measure their behaviour.

1.4.4 Measures

Criminal convictions

For the *CSDD*, convictions and imprisonments were searched in the central Criminal Record Office in London (see Farrington, Barnes & Lambert, 1996). The date when the offence was committed was used to time the delinquent incidents. If no commission date was known, the conviction date was used. Offences were defined as acts leading to convictions, and only one offence per day was counted. This rule was adopted so that each separate behavioural act could yield only one offence; if all offences had been counted, the number of offences would have been greater than the number of criminal behavioural acts, resulting in an overestimation of criminal behavioural acts (Farrington et al., 2006).

For *Transfive*, conviction information was collected using the computerised, paper and microfilmed archives of the Dutch Criminal Records Documentation Service ("judicial documentation"). These are complete conviction data, apart from the filmed archive which may miss some conviction data for those sample members born in the Almelo jurisdiction before 1967; this applies to no more than 3 % of respondents in G3 and G4. Registrations which resulted in a conviction were counted. Acquittals and so-called technical dismissals (dismissals of the case by the public prosecutor because of insufficient evidence and the case being expected to result in acquittal) were not counted. They were left out because it was not certain that the person committed the offence. Cases which were never dispositioned, or which resulted in a policy dismissal (i.e. dismissal of the case because the prosecutor deemed it unfeasible to prosecute, for example because the perpetrator had already paid damages), were counted as they had been registered by the judicial authorities.

Convictions were counted for relatively serious offending ranging from theft, burglary, fraud to robbery, sexual offences and murder. Minor offences such as public drunkenness and traffic offences were excluded. Violent behaviour included sexual offences, insulting or threatening behaviour, robbery, assault, wounding, murder and manslaughter.[2] Convictions for weapon offences were also included in the definition of violence, since Farrington (2001a) previously showed with the *CSDD* that over half of those convicted of possessing an offensive weapon also had a conviction for a violent crime. Furthermore, through the practice of plea-bargaining, people who were originally prosecuted for weapon offences and violence might admit to the weapon offence and as a result the violent offence would be dropped. Consequently, they would only have a weapon conviction while in reality they had committed violence as well. It is important to realise that weapon ownership as a social phenomenon in Europe differs from that in the United

---

[2] This follows the Home Office UK and CBS (Statistics Netherlands) standard offence classification of violence (Kalidien & De Heer-de Lange, 2011; Research Development and Statistics Directorate, 1998).

States. The Netherlands and England have low levels of gun ownership and civilian ownership of firearms is illegitimate without a license and tightly regulated and controlled (Cukier & Chapdelaine, 2001). Hand guns are prohibited, except for the police. People carrying a gun are an exception and a weapon offence is serious. Carrying a weapon is deviant behaviour, usually related to other forms of violent behaviour. This paper investigates a constellation of violent behaviour and being convicted for weapon offence is a vital part of this constellation. Therefore it is important to include these convictions in the operationalization of violent offenders.

For both parents and offspring, convictions for offences committed between the 12th and 40th birthday were counted. In the Netherlands, criminal responsibility starts at age 12, therefore it was chosen to measure criminal convictions from the 12th birthday.[3] There is one exception to this, which will also be highlighted in the respective Chapter 6. In this chapter parental imprisonment will be studied and I wanted to measure the offspring's offending after the parental imprisonment. Therefore convictions between the 19th and 40th birthday were measured in that chapter. A (violent) offender in this dissertation is therefore defined as someone who had been convicted of a (violent) offence between these ages. Using such a comparable measure follows Thornberry's (2009, p. 300) design criteria stating that 'intergenerational studies should have comparable measures of G2 and G3 antisocial behaviour that cover the same ages or the same developmental stages'. Every chapter will give a detailed explanation of the predictor and outcome variables used in the analyses.

1.4.5 Data Analytic Approach

Generalized Estimating Equations (GEE)

Both datasets contained siblings clustered within families. With the clustering of siblings, conventional measures of variance are inappropriate, because those do not take into account the dependencies between cluster members (Ananth, Platt & Savitz, 2005). Therefore the data have been analysed using Generalized Estimating Equations (GEE) in SPSS (For more technical information on GEE see: Lipsitz, Laird & Harrington, 1991; Zeger & Liang, 1992). GEE uses this within-cluster similarity. It weights each cluster of data according to the within-cluster correlation (Hanley, Negassa, Edwardes & Forrester, 2003). When there is no correlation between family members, the cluster receives a weight of 1 and cluster members are treated as if they were independent subjects. Highly correlated siblings receive a lower weight.

---

[3] In England, criminal responsibility starts at age 10. By taking age 12 as the lower age limit, some crimes under the age of 12 have been disregarded. Some people might be erroneously counted as non-offenders while they might have shown criminal behaviour before the age of 12. In the *CSDD*, there were no fathers who were convicted before their 12th birthday and not afterwards, but there was one mother, one sister, two brothers and one original man who had been convicted before their 12th birthday and not afterwards.

Using these weights, GEE then analyses the relationships between the variables considering the dependencies within clusters. GEE can deal with a large number of small clusters and is therefore especially suited for the current data with a large number of families, generally consisting of fewer than 10 members in each(Liang & Zeger, 1993). Within GEE it is possible to choose different analytical models. Depending on the research question and outcome studied, logistic or negative binomial regression analysis was used. I will specify in each chapter which analytical model has been used. In general, logistic regression will be used with dichotomous outcomes and negative binomial regression with continuous count outcomes. Since criminal behaviour is measured, the continuous outcome is likely to be skewed; many people will never have been convicted. With such a skewed distribution it is inappropriate to run an ordinary least squares linear regression analysis. Negative binomial regression analysis suitably deals with skewed distributions.[4]

Other approaches: Latent Class Analysis and Group-Based trajectories modelling

This dissertation employs a variety of quantitative methods, depending on the research question addressed. Techniques such as Latent Class Analysis (McCutcheon, 1987) and the semi-parametric, group-based trajectories methodology (Nagin, 2005) will be explained in more detail in the respective Chapters 2 and 4.

1.5 Summary

In summary, this dissertation employs data from two prospective longitudinal studies to investigate intergenerational transmission of criminal and violent behaviour. This also involves a cross-national comparison and the use of advanced methodological techniques. Several mechanisms that could explain intergenerational transmission will be examined. In the next chapter, I will first investigate whether specific transmission of violence exists.

---

4 One could also decide to use a zero-inflated poission regression analysis with count variables, but it is not possible to use this type of analysis with GEE in SPSS.

Chapter 2

Specialised versus versatile intergenerational transmission of violence*

'I got a whoopin' when I was a kid for not fightin'. I got beat up and every time I ran home, my mama beat my ass. [...] So I learned how to fight and start beatin' everybody's ass that said something to me, and I got suspended from school and I got my ass whooped.'

(Giordano, 2010, p. 71)

2.1 Introduction

The first step in the study of intergenerational transmission is to examine whether transmission might be different for violent versus general criminal behaviour. As outlined in the previous chapter, children whose parents show criminal behaviour have a higher risk of becoming criminal themselves (Farrington, 1997; Thornberry, 2009) and, similarly, children of aggressive parents have a higher risk of becoming aggressive (Avakame, 1998a,b; Conger et al., 2003). It is unclear, however, whether there is transmission specifically of violent offending from parents to children or a transmission of criminal behaviour in general, which might include violent offending. This chapter investigates whether fathers who have been convicted of a violent offence are more likely to transmit criminal and violent behaviour than fathers who were convicted, but never for violence.

---

* An earlier version of this chapter was published as: S. Besemer (2012). Specialised versus versatile intergenerational transmission of violence: A new approach to studying intergenerational transmission from violent versus non–violent fathers: Latent Class Analysis. *Journal of Quantitative Criminology, 28*, 245-263.

In order to enable any inferences on violence specialisation in intergenerational transmission, it is important to establish what constitutes a violent offender and whether or not such a type of criminal can be distinguished from others (Blumstein et al., 1986; Farrington, 2003a). In the past, criminal career researchers (Capaldi & Patterson, 1996; Farrington, 1991, 2003a, 2007; Piquero et al., 2007) concluded that offending is versatile rather than specialised: Violent offenders also tend to commit other types of crime. According to Piquero et al. (2007, p. 80), 'violent offenders are simply frequent offenders who happen to commit a violent offense during their career'. Viewed in this light violent crime is not necessarily a homogeneous subset of behaviour different from other law-breaking behaviour, instead it 'is part of a general tendency to criminal behavior' (Capaldi & Patterson, 1996, p. 208). Recently, however, using different approaches and analytical techniques, studies have demonstrated 'stronger indications of specialization' (Francis, Soothill & Fligelstone, 2004, p. 420; Osgood & Schreck, 2007; Sullivan, McGloin, Pratt & Piquero, 2006; Sullivan, McGloin, Ray & Caudy, 2009). The conclusion that violent offenders are no different from frequent offenders appears to be less supported by recent approaches.

Traditionally, specialisation in an individual's career has been investigated using Farrington, Snyder and Finnegan's (1988, p. 461) 'forward specialization coefficient' (FSC), which assesses the degree of specialisation for subsequent offence types (Sullivan et al., 2009). Subsequently, the 'diversity index' (DI) was introduced, which measures specialisation at the individual rather than the offence level (Agresti & Agresti, 1978, p. 208; Bouffard, Wright, Muftic & Bouffard, 2008; Mazerolle, Brame, Paternoster, Piquero & Dean, 2000; Piquero, Paternoster, Mazerolle, Brame & Dean, 1999; Sullivan et al., 2009; Wright, Pratt & Delisi, 2008). The DI is an estimate of the likelihood that two convictions in a person's offending career will be different (Sullivan, et al., 2006). Studies using the FSC or DI tend to conclude that there is no specialisation within criminal careers. More recent research has used either Latent Class Analysis (LCA) (Francis et al., 2004; McCutcheon, 1987; McGloin, Sullivan & Piquero, 2009; Soothill, Francis & Fligelstone, 2002; Sullivan et al., 2009) or Item Response Theory (IRT) in a multilevel regression framework (Osgood & Schreck, 2007; Sullivan et al., 2009).[5] FSC and DI are relatively basic approaches to analyse the specialisation question. They reduce the data to whether or not someone has a (violent) conviction and study offence to offence transitions. LCA and IRT, in contrast, include information on profiles of convictions and thereby they seem to give a more balanced solution to the question of specialisation in crime (Sullivan et al., 2009). They focus on the total criminal career and appear to be more congruent with reality: There are no offenders who exclusively commit violent offences, but at the same time, it is possible to recognise a group of offend-

---

5 It goes beyond the scope of this chapter to fully discuss IRT in multilevel regression, for more information see Osgood and Schreck (2007) and Sullivan et al. (2009). Latent Class Analysis will be explained in more detail under the method section (2.4) of this chapter.

ers who commit more violence than others and who show a constellation of violent and aggressive behaviour. As Felson (2009, p. 33) stated: 'Clearly, the versatility cup is half empty and half full. There is enough versatility to suggest that a general theory of deviance [...] helps us understand criminal violence. There is enough specialization to suggest that there is a need for explanations of individual differences in violence, independent of the tendency to engage in deviance.' The earlier traditional approaches for investigating specialisation have been unable to demonstrate this.

These issues are relevant for a related topic: specialisation in intergenerational transmission. Having a violent parent increases the risk of violence in children, but it is unclear whether this transmission is violence-specific or whether there is a transmission of general criminal behaviour including violence (Conger et al., 2003; Farrington, 1997). More than thirty years ago, McCord (1977) concluded that intergenerational transmission was not crime-specific but more general. She divided crimes into eleven types: traffic offences, drunkenness, victimless sex crimes, white-collar business crimes, use of illegal drugs, property destruction, larceny, assault, rape, other crimes against order, and murder or attempted murder. She then tested whether there were similarities in the first crime for which father and son were convicted, whether they had committed similar types of crime over the course of their lives and whether there were similarities in the most serious crime they had committed. Her results suggest that intergenerational similarities are due more to transmission of 'general attitudes, rather than crime-specific behaviours' (McCord, 1977, p. 89). McCord (1988) suggests that parental aggressiveness leads to criminal behaviour in general which connects to findings in the Cambridge Study of Delinquent Development (Farrington, Gundry & West, 1975; Osborn & West, 1979). However, these three previous studies on specialisation in intergenerational transmission all used a relatively simplistic form of analysis whereby data is reduced to whether or not fathers and sons were convicted of a violent offence at some point in their career. This approach is comparable to the traditional approaches used in studies into specialisation in an individual's career (FSC and DI). Analogous to research on specialisation in an individual's career, applying one of the more recent techniques to specialisation in intergenerational transmission might lead to different conclusions from those reached thirty years ago.

One might expect violence specialisation in intergenerational transmission for two reasons. First, violence is different from other criminal behaviour since aggressiveness can be regarded as a personality trait. Aggression is not just behaviour, but appears to be a relatively stable trait over someone's life course, similar to the stability typically found for intelligence (Farrington, 2007; Huesmann, Eron, Lefkowitz & Walder, 1984; Kokko & Pulkkinen, 2005; Olweus, 1979). Personality traits are at least partly heritable which supports the idea of violence specialisation in intergenerational transmission (Blonigen, Hicks, Krueger, Patrick & Iacono, 2005; Bouchard,

2004; Bouchard & Loehlin, 2001). Furthermore, since aggression is a trait, it is expected that violent offending parents will also show violent behaviour at home (Capaldi, DeGarmo, Patterson & Forgatch, 2002). Children will be exposed to violent behaviour more than to other types of criminal behaviour, which could increase the odds of imitation of this behaviour by the children. The theoretical background will discuss these explanations in more detail.

2.2 Theories of specialisation in intergenerational transmission

In the Introduction, I discussed mechanisms of intergenerational transmission: social learning, genetic mechanisms, intergenerational exposure to or mediation through multiple risk factors, and official bias. Some of these could be applied to specialisation in intergenerational transmission. Social learning means that parents may teach their children delinquent behaviour or a *criminal* attitude. McCord (1988) and Simons, Wu, Johnson, and Conger (1995) suggest that intergenerational transmission of violence can be explained by the transmission of an antisocial orientation. This relates to ideas about *generalised* and *specific* social learning (Bandura, 1977; Black et al., 2010; Kalmuss, 1984). Specific modelling occurs when people imitate exactly the same behaviour as their model, in this case the violent behaviour. Generalised modelling has more to do with the idea of an antisocial syndrome; observing violence can lead to other forms of antisocial behaviour. This corresponds to research which demonstrated that children, after watching violence in experiments, tend to not only display aggressive behaviour, but also general anti-social behaviour (Hearold, 1986). Generalised social learning supports the idea of versatile transmission of aggressive behaviour. This also relates to Gottfredson & Hirschi's general theory of crime (1990) which posits that low self-control, developed and influenced by upbringing, leads to criminal behaviour. They stress the generality of their theory and its applicability to all kinds of criminal behaviour. According to Gottfredson and Hirschi (1990, Hirschi & Gottfredson, 1993) offenders do not specialise and hence, there would be no specialisation in intergenerational transmission either.

Conversely, one would expect social learning to be stronger for aggressive or violent acts than for other criminal behaviours such as fraud or burglary (Bijleveld & Wijkman, 2009). Most parents' convictions happened before the child was old enough to be aware of them.[6] As mentioned previously, violent behaviour can be seen as a stable personality trait (Farrington, 2007; Huesmann et al., 1984; Kokko & Pulkkinen, 2005; Olweus, 1979). Parents

---

[6] In the *CSDD*, 59 per cent of fathers' convictions happened before the child's birth, 64 per cent before the child's 5th birthday, 72 per cent before the child's 10th birthday. In *Transfive*, 56 per cent of fathers' convictions happened before the offspring's birth, 59 per cent before the 5th birthday and 65 per cent before the 10th birthday.

convicted of a violent offence are likely to continue showing aggressive behaviour throughout their offspring's life. Children who experience aggression in the family learn that aggression is legitimate behaviour to solve problems. They acquire aggression-prone models of social information processing (SIP) and an aggressive-impulsive behaviour repertoire (Lösel, Bliesener & Bender, 2007).[7] Moreover, children could see the parent's violence being reinforced and parents might reinforce their children for showing violence themselves (Bandura, 1971; Black et al., 2010). It is less likely that children would observe their parents committing fraud or a burglary. Violence, in contrast, is much more visible and therefore more prone to be observed and imitated. Consequently, intergenerational transmission through social learning is expected to be stronger for violence and aggression than for other less visible types of criminal behaviour. This supports the idea of specialised intergenerational transmission.

Second, criminal behaviour might be transmitted by genetic or biological mechanisms. Violence might have a stronger or different biological basis to other types of criminal behaviour, such as fraud or burglary (P. A. Brennan & Raine, 1997). For instance, impulsiveness is more strongly related to violent crime than to non–violent crime (Farrington, 2007; Felson, 2009), and impulsiveness also seems to be related to neurological processes (DiLalla & Gottesman, 1991; Mednick & Kandel, 1988). Since these biological bases are often inherited, violence might have a stronger intergenerational transmission than other types of criminal behaviour (DiLalla, 2002). In his research on twins, Christiansen (1974) demonstrated a stronger relationship between identical twins for more serious crimes such as violence, suggesting a hereditary component. This also suggests specialised intergenerational transmission.

Third, criminal behaviour could be transmitted through the transferral of risk factors. Crime is then not directly transmitted from parents to children but through a continuity or constellation of antisocial features or a 'larger cycle of deprivation and antisocial behaviour' (Farrington, 2011, p. 133). Studies have concluded that violent offenders are indistinguishable from frequent offenders in terms of risk factors (Capaldi & Patterson, 1996; Farrington, 1991; Piquero, 2000). In line with this, one would expect transmission through risk factors to be similar for violent and non–violent parents, and this would suggest no specific violent intergenerational transmission.

Fourth, criminal justice systems might be biased against known criminal families. As a result, they pay more attention to these families, which means that family members are more likely to be arrested and thus appear in official statistics more often. It is expected that this bias is similar for children of violent and non–violent (but equally frequent) criminal parents. The police and courts will know criminal families when family members have been arrested

---

7 Social information processing refers to the way people perceive and evaluate social situations and initiate a reaction to these situations (Crick & Dodge, 1994; Lösel et al., 2007)

and/or convicted frequently. Hence, they will be biased against families of frequent offenders, and this includes violent offenders.

Testing these different mechanisms remains outside the scope of this chapter. They do illustrate, though, how specialised or versatile intergenerational transmission might be explained.

2.3 Hypotheses

This chapter aims to connect the research in specialisation in individuals' careers to the study of specialisation in intergenerational transmission. *Are sons of violent fathers more likely to display violence and/or criminal behaviour than sons of fathers who have been convicted, but not of a violent offence?* This question is answered in two ways. First, a more traditional approach is used where people are defined as violent offenders when they have been convicted of a violent offence at least once. Violent offenders tend to commit more offences than non–violent offenders (Capaldi & Patterson, 1996; Cohen, 1986; Farrington, 1991; Loeber, 1988; Loeber, Farrington, Stouthamer-Loeber & Van Kammen, 1998; Piquero, 2000). Hence one cannot simply compare violent fathers with non–violent fathers, because the latter will commit fewer crimes. Therefore sons born to violent offenders will be compared with sons born to non–violent but equally frequent offenders. Second, Latent Class Analysis will be used to examine whether a violent offender group is distinguishable among convicted fathers and whether sons of fathers in this group are more likely to offend (violently) than sons of fathers in the other group(s).

For each of the two approaches, the following three hypotheses will be tested:

1. Sons born to violent fathers have a greater risk of being convicted than sons born to convicted, but non–violent fathers (violence in fathers increases son's prevalence of general convictions).

2. Sons born to violent fathers exhibit more criminal behaviour than sons born to convicted, but non–violent fathers (violence in fathers increases son's frequency of general convictions).

3. Sons born to violent fathers have a greater chance of being convicted of violence than sons born to convicted, but non–violent fathers (violence in fathers increases son's prevalence of violent convictions).[8]

The first two hypotheses test whether violent fathers are more likely to transmit offending behaviour than non–violent fathers. Perhaps there is no clear specialised violent intergenerational transmission, but violent fathers

---
[8] Offspring's frequency of violent offending was not studied, since the number of violence convictions was sparse.

might transmit more criminal behaviour than non–violent fathers. Hypothesis 3 tests whether intergenerational transmission is specialised rather than versatile.

2.4 Method

2.4.1 Sample

These hypotheses were tested using data from both *the Cambridge Study in Delinquent Development* (CSDD) and *the NSCR-Transfive Study* (Transfive). These were described in more detail in the Introduction (see page 13). The current investigation examined the males and their fathers. Initially, the intention was to also study daughters and mothers who had been convicted of a violent offence. However, there were only two mothers in the *CSDD*, eight mothers in *Transfive* and few daughters convicted of violence. Furthermore, females tend to have fewer convictions than males. Since these numbers for females were so low, it was decided to focus on males only.

2.4.2 Measures

Outcome Variables

The outcome variable for hypothesis 1 was whether sons had been convicted between the 12th and 40th birthdays. For hypothesis 2 the outcome variable was the number of convictions in this period for sons who were convicted. For hypothesis 3 the outcome variable was whether sons had been convicted of a violent offence between the 12th and 40th birthdays. Violent sons were compared with sons who had been convicted, but not of a violent offence.

Predictor Variable

The predictor variable in both approaches was whether sons had a violent versus a non–violent father.[9] In the traditional approach this was defined as whether fathers had convictions for violence. Violent offenders tend to have more convictions than non–violent offenders (Capaldi & Patterson, 1996; Farrington, 1991; Piquero, 2000). Therefore sons of violent offenders could not be simply compared with sons of non–violent offenders. To disentangle violence and offending frequency, it was important to test whether there was a difference in offending frequency between violent and non–violent fathers.

---

[9] As explained in the Introduction (see page 15), in *Transfive* policy dismissals were included in the count of convictions. They were included in offspring offending behaviour and in the analysis to identify the latent classes among fathers. However, fathers were only included in the analysis to investigate the strength of intergenerational specialisation when they had official convictions, but not if they only had dismissals. So: fathers with dismissals only were excluded, but dismissals were included. This was done to make the analyses with *Transfive* comparable to the analyses with the *CSDD*, because dismissals were never counted in the *CSDD*.

In the *CSDD*, violent fathers ($n = 21$) had on average 3.62 convictions (SD=3.41), while non–violent but convicted fathers (n=71) had on average 2.08 convictions (SD=1.93). This is just not significantly different $t(24)=1.97$, $p=.061$; however, it did represent a medium-sized effect $r=.37$. Since this difference was almost significant and it represented a medium-sized effect, violent fathers were also compared with fathers who were never convicted of a violent offence, but had at least two convictions (n=32). These non–violent fathers had on average 3.41 convictions (SD=2.26), which was not significantly different from the average of violent fathers $t(31)=0.252$, $p=.803$. Since the difference between violent and non–violent fathers was not significant, but had a medium effect size, sons of violent fathers were compared with non-violent fathers as well as with non–violent fathers who had been convicted at least twice.

In *Transfive*, violent fathers (n=30) had on average 4.10 convictions (SD=3.16), while non–violent but convicted fathers (n=56) had on average 1.82 convictions (SD=1.89). This is significantly different $t(40)=3.62$, $p=.001$; and it represented a large effect $r=0.50$. Since this difference is significant, violent fathers were then compared with fathers who were never convicted of a violent offence, but had at least two convictions (n=19). These non–violent fathers had on average 3.42 convictions (SD=2.61), which is not significantly different from that of violent fathers $t(47)=0.817$, $p=.438$. In the analyses with *Transfive*, sons of violent fathers were thus compared with sons of non-violent fathers who had been convicted at least twice.

Subsequently, the predictor variable of having a violent versus non–violent father was defined using LCA.

2.4.3 Analytic Approach

Analytic Approach: Latent Class Analysis (LCA)

LCA was performed using the Mplus statistical package (Version 5.21; Muthén & Muthén, 1998-2009). LCA empirically identifies latent classes among a group of subjects using two or more observed, manifest variables (McCutcheon, 1987). The latent class variable is hypothetical or theoretical and it is not possible to directly observe this variable. LCA is analogous to factor analysis (FA), but in LCA categorical or discrete variables are analysed, while FA analyses continuous variables. LCA assumes that covariation among the observed variables results from each observed variable's relationship to the latent variable. Given the latent classes, these observed variables are independent and unrelated, which is called 'local independence' (McCutcheon, 1987, p. 14).

This study tried to identify an unobserved, latent variable of type of offenders. The observed, manifest variables were types of offences. To summarise these types of offences, the Home Office Offenders Index Codebook was used (Research Development and Statistics Directorate, 1998). This Codebook groups offences among the following ten categories: Violence against the person, Sexual offences, Burglary, Robbery, Theft and handling stolen goods, Fraud and forgery, Criminal damage, Drug offences, Other (excluding motoring offences), and Motoring offences. In the *CSDD* data threats and weapon offences were also recorded. In the Home Office Codebook threats are categorized depending on the kind of offence. In the *CSDD* data, however, the kind of offences to which these threats related were not always recorded. Therefore two extra categories were created: Threats and Weapon offences. The category Motoring offences was not used, because minor offences such as traffic offences were not included in the operationalisation of criminal behaviour in this dissertation (see the Introduction, page 15). For each offender, an indicator (0,1) variable was formed for each of these offence categories according to whether or not the offender had been convicted of any of the offences forming that group when aged 12-39. The number of times that a conviction for a category appeared was not recorded. For LCA it was decided to focus on breadth of offending instead of volume. This allows the investigation of offender types without the confounding factor of frequency of offending.

LCA identifies groups of offenders with a similar pattern of offending behaviour. Consequently, it might be possible to identify a group of offenders who commit more violence than others, though not every person in this group necessarily has a conviction for a violent offence. A high probability of membership to this class could be an indicator of a certain lifestyle that includes violence and aggression (Francis et al., 2004). It is important to realise that LCA does not create a clear dichotomy based on whether people have a conviction for a certain type of offence, but looks at the total picture of offending behaviour.

LCA investigates how these offence types cluster together among the group of offenders and tries to identify clusters or classes. The goal is to find the optimal solution, where 'there will be some number of classes where all classes are distinct, but where adding an additional class to the model provides no extra explanatory power' (Francis et al., 2004, p. 57). To do this, LCA uses maximum likelihood estimation. Several criteria can be used to determine the optimal number of classes. These criteria give an indication of model fit based on differences between the estimated model and the observations. The Bayesian Information Criterion (BIC) is often used. The BIC is based on likelihood, but also corrects for the number of parameters fitted and for the number of observations. Therefore, BIC estimates model fit, but also looks at parsimony of the model. For deciding on the number of classes, one chooses the model with the minimum BIC value, since this number is an indicator of the difference between the model and the observed data and one wants that difference to be as small as possible (D'Unger, Land, McCall & Nagin, 1998). However, with a small (or large) sample size, the sample size adjusted BIC (SABIC) might be more appropriate (Tofighi & Enders, 2008; Yang, 2006). Furthermore, Nylund, Asparouhov, and Muthén (2007) compared criteria for LCA and illustrated that the Bootstrap Likelihood Ratio Test (BLRT) also proved to be a consistent indicator of deciding on the number of classes in a study population, especially with a small sample. When looking at the BLRT output, one should look at the model that has a significance that is lower than .05, since that means that the model gives a significantly better fit than the model with one class less. In the current study, BIC, SABIC as well as BLRT were used to decide which model fitted best.

Furthermore, the content of the classes is important. A model with classes that have no reasonable interpretation is of little use. Hence, after inspecting the model criteria, it is important to look at the content of the classes. These can be defined on the basis of the conditional item probabilities,[10] which represent the chance that someone in that class will score 1 on that specific item. After deciding which model fits the data best, it is possible to assign subjects to the latent classes.

Analytic Approach: Generalized Estimating Equations (GEE)

As described in the Introduction (page 16), the hypotheses were analysed using Generalized Estimating Equations (GEE) whenever siblings were included in the sample. For the present analyses, logistic regression was used for the prevalence outcome and negative binomial regression for the frequency outcome. Negative binomial regression was used because the outcome variable frequency of son's offending (hypothesis 2) was highly skewed; many people had never been convicted. With such a skewed distribution it was inappropriate to run a linear regression analysis. Negative binomial regression analysis suitably deals with skewed distributions.

2.5 Results

2.5.1 Traditional approach

For each of the analyses, I will first discuss results for the *CSDD* and then for *Transfive*. The results for the traditional approach are presented in table 2.1.[11] In the *CSDD*, there appeared to be no difference in the prevalence of general offending between sons with a violent and non–violent father (53.7 versus 59.7 and 57.0%). Similarly, there was hardly any difference in the frequency of general offending (7.62 versus 5.60 and 5.53 convictions). When looking at son's violent offending there seemed to be a difference between the

---

[10] The conditional item probability is comparable to the factor loading in factor analysis.
[11] The N in table 2.1 and table 2.6 represent the number of sons in each group. Since the sample also included siblings from the same fathers, the number of fathers was lower than the N of sons. The OR and B values were corrected for this using GEE.

Table 2.1: Sons' general and violent offending for violent and non-violent fathers

	A		B		C		A versus B	A versus C
	Father offended violently		Father offended, not violently		Father offended > 2, not violently		OR (95 % CI)	OR (95 % CI)
Son convictions	N		N		N		B (p)	B (p)
England								
Prevalence general convictions	54	53.7 %	176	59.7 %	93	57.0 %	0.76 (0.38-1.52)	0.85 (0.40-1.78)
Frequency	29	7.62	105	5.60	53	5.53	0.21 (.397)	0.18 (.522)
Prevalence violence convictions	29	62.1 %	105	42.9 %	53	50.9 %	2.05 (0.91-4.60)	1.60 (0.69-3.74)
The Netherlands								
Prevalence general convictions	26	50.0 %			28	46.4 %		1.04 (0.40-2.72)
Frequency	12	5.33			13	2.77		0.65 (.076)
Prevalence violence convictions	13	53.8 %			13	46.2 %		1.83 (0.35-9.70)

Frequency is number of convictions for sons between age 12 and 40, only sons who were convicted for at least one offense were included in this average value; 95 % CI, 95 % confidence interval; FO, father offended; * p < .05

groups: 62.1 % of convicted sons of violent fathers had convictions for violence, compared with 42.9 % of sons of fathers convicted of offences not including violence, and 50.9 % of sons of fathers who had been convicted at least twice but never for violence. However, none of these differences was significant.

In *Transfive*, there is little difference in the prevalence of general offending between sons with a violent and non–violent father (46.4 versus 50.0 %). Sons of violent fathers seem to have more convictions than sons of non–violent fathers (5.33 versus 2.77 convictions), but this difference is not significant.[12] The difference in violent offending is slightly larger than for general offending (46.2 versus 53.8 %), but far from significant (OR = 1.8, 95 % CI 0.35-9.70).

The results from the traditional approach do not support hypothesis 1. Furthermore, the results with the *CSDD* do not support hypothesis 2, although the results with *Transfive* tend to support the hypothesis that sons of violent fathers commit more general crime. However, this difference is not significant and the numbers involved in the analyses with *Transfive* are low. The results from the traditional approach tend to support hypothesis 3 that sons of violent fathers have a higher risk of displaying violence, but (in the analyses with the *CSDD*) only when sons of violent fathers are compared with the first comparison group of sons of non–violent fathers. It is preferable to compare sons of violent fathers with sons of non–violent fathers who were convicted at least twice as not to confound with the frequency of father's offending and these results do not support hypothesis 3.

2.5.2 Latent Class Analysis

For each of the offence categories, it was recorded whether or not the father had been convicted of any of the offences forming that group when aged 12-39. In the *CSDD*, no fathers were convicted of weapon offences or drugs during that period, and hence these categories were excluded from the LCA. Table 2.2 presents an overview of the models with increasing number of classes, and the values for the Bayesian Information Criterion (BIC), the sample size adjusted BIC (SABIC) and the Bootstrap Likelihood Ratio Test (BLRT). As mentioned in the Method section, these criteria were used to decide on the number of classes that described the data best.

First, one looks at the lowest value of BIC in the table, which turned out to be the model with just one class. Second, the SABIC was lowest for the model with three classes. Third, the BLRT was only significant for the model with two classes. The criteria did not lead to one conclusion on which model fitted the data best; BIC pointed to one class, SABIC to three and BLRT to two classes. It was therefore important to look at the content

---

12 In the group of sons of violent fathers, one outlier with 25 convictions was excluded. Including this outlier yielded a signifcant difference in frequency of convictions between sons of violent and non–violent fathers (B = 0.901, $p = .025$).

Results

Table 2.2: Overview of results and criteria for the LCA models - fathers - England

Number of classes	1	2	3	4
BIC	**614.870**	635.173	665.548	702.826
SABIC	583.305	568.886	**564.538**	567.094
BLRT		0.0000	0.1304	0.6667

The bold values are the optimal values for each of the criteria

Table 2.3: Overview of results and criteria for the LCA models - fathers - the Netherlands

Number of classes	1	2	3	4
BIC	521.940	**519.046**	541.051	571.010
SABIC	496.689	465.388	**458.987**	460.539
BLRT		0.0000	0.0952	0.5000

The bold values are the optimal values for each of the criteria

of these classes. Table 2.4 describes the content of the two-class model. First, it gives the proportion of fathers that could be identified as a member of the classes; 66.33% of fathers fell in class 1, 33.67% fell in class 2. Then, for each of the two classes, table 2.4 gives probabilities that a father has a conviction for each of the offence types. For instance, a father in class 1 has a probability of 1 to be convicted of theft. In class 2, fathers have a chance of 0.452 of being convicted of violence against the person, and a chance of 0.367 of having a conviction for an offence in the category "other".[13] Class 1 was therefore labelled as a property (offence) class, and class 2 was labelled as a violent–other class. Fathers in class 2 also have a probability of 0.354 of being convicted of theft. This shows that although all people in class 1 had a conviction for theft, this does not mean that every person with a theft conviction automatically falls into class 1. LCA looks at the combination of offence types; fathers with a theft conviction in class 1 will have a different combination of theft with other types of offences than fathers in class 2 with a theft conviction.

Since the SABIC was lowest for the three-class model, the content of the classes in this model was also studied. Classes 1 and 2 in this model were similar to the ones in the two-class model. The third class, however, was difficult to interpret, because it only contained three people and the probabilities for theft, violence and other offences were similar to either class 1 or class 2. Based on the interpretability and the BLRT, the two-class model for fathers was chosen.

In *Transfive*, no fathers were convicted of robbery or drugs between their 12th and 40th birthdays and therefore these categories were excluded from

---

[13] The "other" category consists of a range of convictions, such as going equipped for stealing, being a suspected person, loitering, tampering with a motor vehicle, and cruelty to animals. For detailed information see the Home Office Offenders Index Codebook (Research Development and Statistics Directorate, 1998).

Table 2.4: Describing the two-class model for fathers - conditional item probabilities - England

	Class proportions	
	Class 1	Class 2
Item	66.33 %	33.67 %
Violence	0.000	0.452
Sex	0.030	0.103
Burglary	0.147	0.194
Robbery	0.033	0.000
Theft	1.000	0.354
Fraud	0.160	0.201
Damage	0.027	0.141
Other	0.092	0.367
Threats	0.013	0.071

Table 2.5: Describing the two-class model for fathers - conditional item probabilities - the Netherlands

	Class proportions	
	Class 1	Class 2
Item	61.12 %	38.88 %
Violence	0.089	0.623
Sex	0.005	0.219
Burglary	0.037	0.140
Theft	1.000	0.519
Fraud	0.039	0.080
Damage	0.000	0.283
Other	0.000	0.283
Weapon	0.036	0.000

the LCA. Table 2.3 presents an overview of the models with increasing number of classes, and the values for the Bayesian Information Criterion (BIC), the sample size adjusted BIC (SABIC) and the Bootstrap Likelihood Ratio Test (BLRT). The BIC value was lowest for the model with two classes; the SABIC was lowest for the model with three classes; and the BLRT was only significant for the model with two classes. Based on the majority of two out of three criteria, the two class model was chosen as the optimal solution. Table 2.5 describes the content of the two classes. The proportions in this table show that 61.12 % of fathers were identified as members of class 1, 38.88 % fell in class 2. Furthermore, it shows that a father in class 1 has a probability of 1 to be convicted of theft. In class 2, fathers have a chance of 0.623 of being convicted of violence against the person, and a chance of 0.283 of having a conviction for an offence in the category damage or other. Class 2 was therefore labeled as a violent–other class and class 1 was labeled as a property (offence) class.

It is interesting to note that the LCA solutions for both samples are quite similar. In both samples, a model with two classes was the optimal solution. Furthermore, in both samples these classes could be described as a theft and a violence–other class.

Offspring offending per father LCA class

The two classes of fathers identified with LCA divided the sons into two groups: sons with fathers in the property class (1) and sons with fathers in the violent–other class (2). These two groups were then compared on the three outcome variables: prevalence and frequency of general offending and prevalence of violent offending. Table 2.6 demonstrates that there are no significant differences for the *CSDD* for general offending between these groups. Looking at sons' violent offending, a significant difference is visible (OR = 2.129, 95 % CI 1.007, 4.585). 62.2 % of convicted sons of violent fathers had been convicted of violence, compared with 41.2 % of convicted sons of fathers in the property class.

Table 2.6: Sons' offending for the two latent classes for fathers: violence/other versus theft

Son convictions	Father violence / other class N	Father theft class N	OR (95 % CI) B (p)
England			
Prevalence general convictions	66 56.1 %	164 59.1 %	0.86 (0.44-1.69)
Frequency	37 7.65	97 5.42	0.28 (.221)
Prevalence violence convictions	37 62.2 %	97 41.2 %	2.13 * (1.01-4.59)
The Netherlands			
Prevalence general convictions	24 37.5 %	71 40.8 %	0.85 (0.36-2.01)
Frequency	9 4.56	29 4.31	0.03 (.936)
Prevalence violence convictions	9 55.6 %	29 44.8 %	1.86 (0.40-8.61)

Frequency is number of convictions for sons between age 12 and 40, only sons who were convicted for at least one offense were included in this average value; 95 % CI, 95 % confidence interval; * p < .05

For *Transfive*, a similar pattern is visible, although none of the differences is significant and the strength of the difference for violent offending is weaker (OR = 1.86 compared with OR = 2.13). The (non-significant) difference found for frequency of offending in the traditional approach is not visible in the LCA analyses for *Transfive*.

As mentioned previously, frequency of offending can confound the analyses since violent offenders tend to have more convictions than non–violent offenders. Therefore, offending frequency was compared for fathers in the two latent classes. In the *CSDD*, fathers in the violent–other class (n = 26) had on average 2.46 convictions (SD = 2.93), fathers in the property class (n = 66) had on average 2.42 convictions (SD = 2.21). This is not significantly different t(90) = -.07, p = .947. Offending frequency did not confound the LCA analyses. In *Transfive*, fathers in the violent–other class (n = 26) had on average 3.85 convictions (SD = 3.22), fathers in the property class (n = 60) had on average 2.22 convictions (SD = 2.33). This is signifcantly different t(37) = -2.33, p = 0.025. However, interestingly enough, children of these more frequent offender group do not show more criminal behaviour and there are no other significant differences between children of these groups. The difference between the number of convictions of fathers in the two classes remains when only fathers with at least two convictions or a violence conviction are included.

The results emerging from the LCA do not support hypotheses 1 and 2, but do support hypothesis 3.

2.6 Discussion

This study investigated whether intergenerational transmission is violence–specific. First, a more traditional approach was taken whereby fathers were divided into two groups based on whether they had been convicted of a violent offence. Second, Latent Class Analysis (LCA) was performed to identify two classes of offending fathers, of which one was defined as a violent–other class while the other could be characterised as a property (offence) class. This was investigated using data from the *CSDD* as well as *Transfive*. The traditional approach demonstrated a higher risk of offending violently for sons of violent fathers compared with sons of non–violent fathers, but this difference was not significant. Furthermore, when these sons were compared with sons of non–violent fathers who were convicted at least twice, the difference was much less substantial. Subsequently, sons of the latent class of violent fathers were compared with sons of the latent class of property fathers. These sons did not differ in their general offending. However, in the *CSDD*, sons whose fathers were in the violent class had a significantly higher risk of violent offending than sons of fathers who were in the property class. A similar pattern was visible for *Transfive*, but the difference between these groups of sons was smaller and non-significant. These results support the hypothesis that intergenerational transmission of offending from fathers to sons is violence–specific.

The difference between the two approaches is how the violent father was defined. The traditional method defines this a priori based on convictions for violence, whereas LCA identifies groups of offenders with a similar profile of offending. LCA 'identifies clusters that group together items that share similar characteristics' (Francis et al., 2004, p. 50). The traditional method can be viewed as a theoretical approach: the theory imposes a structure to the data a priori: by dichotomizing offending in violent versus non–violent. LCA is essentially an inductive approach: the data and 'statistical analysis produce[s] the structure rather than the analyst imposing the structure a priori' (Francis et al., 2004, p. 79). An advantage of LCA here is that all fathers and sons with convictions were included in the comparison. In the traditional method, sons of violent fathers were preferably compared with sons of fathers with at least two convictions, which excluded 39 fathers and their 83 sons from the *CSDD* analyses and 37 fathers and 41 sons in *Transfive*. Using LCA thus increased the N and therefore statistical power. A disadvantage of LCA is that the classes might not be as clear as the theoretically imposed dichotomy in the traditional method, or that the classes might not be the groups you are looking for. For example, not every father in the violent–other class had a conviction for violence.[14] One could say, however, that

---

[14] Following the definition used in the traditional method, in the *CSDD* 65% of fathers in the violence class were originally in the violent father group. The other 35% came from the non–violent father group in the traditional method. In *Transfive*, 92% of fathers in the violence class were originally in the violent father group. The other 8% came from the non–violent

a high probability of membership for this class could be an indicator for 'a style of life' (Francis et al., 2004, p. 79). The patterning of convictions is such that they resemble the violent fathers most. Convictions that make people part of the violent–other class may indicate a life style that includes violent and aggressive behaviour. Offenders in the violent class without an actual violent conviction might be expected to have shown violent behaviour, but this could have gone undetected by the police. Or, they could have exhibited forms of aggressive behaviour that would not necessarily lead to a conviction, such as destroying things or being verbally aggressive. Linking to the earlier mentioned social information processing (SIP), people in this class could have an aggressive-impulsive response repertoire (Crick & Dodge, 1994; Lösel et al., 2007). As mentioned previously, there are no offenders who exclusively commit violent offences, but at the same time there seems to be a group of offenders who commit more violence than others, showing a constellation of behaviour in which violence is prominent.

The current results contradict previous studies that showed no specialisation in violence in intergenerational transmission (Farrington et al., 1975; McCord, 1977; Osborn & West, 1979). Furthermore, analogous to research into specialisation in an individual's career, traditional approaches were unable to detect specialisation while LCA has demonstrated some specialisation in intergenerational transmission.

This study did not directly test theories or mechanisms, but the finding that intergenerational transmission seems to be violence-specific is relevant to some theories. The results show a difference between sons of violent and non–violent offenders and therefore support typological theories that state that different types of offenders exist. LCA shows how a certain group of offenders can be identified based on their conviction pattern. One could say that this group is diverse and not necessarily specialised, since the categorization is not just based on whether fathers have a conviction for violence or not. The LCA group is indeed more diverse than the clear theoretical dichotomy, but that does not mean that it is an incoherent group; they show a similar pattern of convictions over their criminal career. This conviction pattern is notably different from the other group. Furthermore, sons of fathers in this group are significantly more likely to be convicted of violence. The current results show that sons of a certain class of offenders show more violent behaviour than sons of another class of offenders and thereby these results refute the idea that offending or intergenerational transmission of offending is not specialised. Furthermore, the results would support the idea of specific social learning which might be relevant for developmental theories such as Farrington's ICAP theory (2003a) that stress the influence of social

---

father group in the traditional method (including offenders with at least two convictions only). Taking into account all fathers (including the ones with just one conviction who were excluded in the traditional approach), 85 % of fathers in the violence class were originally in the violent father group. The other 15 % were defined as non–violent fathers in the traditional method. The resemblance between the traditional method and LCA is higher in *Transfive* than in the *CSDD*, in terms of groupings of fathers as well as offspring behaviour outcomes.

models such as parents and Catalano and Hawkins' (1996) social development model that combines social learning and social bonding. It has to be noted, however, that the specific intergenerational transmission could also be explained by a possible stronger biological basis for violence compared with other types of criminal behaviour.

This research undoubtedly has limitations and several other interpretations of the results should be considered. One limitation of this study is the absence of females. It was not possible to investigate the transmission from mothers due to a low number of mothers who had been convicted of violence. Similarly, the sample of daughters was too small and their frequency of offending too low to generate reliable conclusions. It is important to study women because intergenerational mechanisms might be different for males and females. Behaviour could be more strongly transmitted in same-gender parent-child relationships (Farrington, Barnes & Lambert, 1996). Most children are more exposed to their mother's behaviour. Furthermore, women convicted of violence are unusual. Being such an exception might lead to more stigma in society and official bodies such as the police might pay more attention to these women and their families. They may also be labelled as disturbed rather than criminal (Hedderman & Gelsthorpe, 1997). According to labelling theory, people will behave according to the label society attaches to them (Lemert, 1967). Additionally, Sherman (1993, p. 459) hypothesized that persistent police action might lead to 'defiance', a 'proud and angry emotion' that can result in antisocial behaviour. In line with this, one might expect intergenerational transmission from violent mothers to be stronger than from fathers. It would be desirable to replicate this research with a dataset that includes more females. This would enable one to test whether specialisation in intergenerational transmission is violence-specific for females as well and whether this specialisation is visible in same-gender as well as opposite-gender parent-child relationships. Furthermore, the number of people involved in the analyses with *Transfive* is relatively low and thus it is hard to generalise these results. However, they do confirm the tendency found in the results with the *CSDD* which strengthens these findings.

In addition, this study only used official data on offending and violent behaviour. Official data always suffer from a *dark number*: part of offending that is not measured by official statistics (Bijleveld, 2007; Fisher & Ross, 2006; Maguire, 2007). This means that we only see part of people's total offending behaviour, we see the 'tip of the iceberg'. People are likely to exhibit more offending behaviour that is invisible to the police, and many people will never appear in official statistics even though they exhibited offending and/or violent behaviour. Official convictions are only indicators of the real offending and violent behaviour. It would be interesting to study specialisation in intergenerational transmission with self-reported data on offending and violent behaviour for both generations. Self-reported data will give a more complete picture of people's actual behaviour and might show a stronger intergenerational relationship. However, longitudinal studies with self-reported data on antisocial behaviour for two generations are rare and may suffer from social desirability bias and memory loss when reports are retrospectively collected.

Despite these limitations, this is the first study in over thirty years that investigates specialisation in intergenerational transmission, and it is the first to connect research into specialisation in an individual's career to specialisation in intergenerational transmission. In line with this, it would be interesting to apply another recent approach, item response theory (IRT) in a multilevel regression framework (Osgood & Schreck, 2007; Sullivan et al., 2009) to specialisation in intergenerational transmission. Furthermore, it would be good to replicate this study with a larger sample to increase the statistical power in both the traditional method and LCA.

Since children of violent offenders have a higher risk of committing future violent crime, it would be desirable to target interventions particularly for these children. For instance, family-based prevention programs, such as parent education and parent management training, have shown to be effective in reducing offspring offending (Farrington & Welsh, 2007). Parent education often involves educating parents about the health of their children, but also serves to improve parents' and children's well being. Parent management training involves training parents to alter their child's behaviour (Kazdin, 1997). Such programs could be offered to parents who have offended violently to prevent their children to exhibit violent behaviour.

2.7 Summary

This chapter investigated whether fathers who have been convicted of a violent offence are more likely to transmit criminal and violent behaviour than fathers who were convicted, but never for violence. First, a more traditional approach was taken where offending fathers were divided into two groups based on whether they had a violence conviction. Second, Latent Class Analysis (LCA) was performed to identify two classes of fathers, one of which was characterised as violent. Sons of fathers in this class had a higher risk of violent convictions compared with sons whose fathers were in the other class.

Chapter 3

The impact of timing and frequency of parental criminal behaviour and risk factors on offspring offending*

'And this is the life we live because we have to live it because I can't get out of it. I don't have the money to get out of this. [...] If I wasn't faced with it everyday when I walk out my door, like the dope man living around the corner and the weed man living right there; my sister smokes, you know what I'm saying? If I wasn't living with all these people all the time, I wouldn't do it.'

(Giordano, 2010, p. 91)

3.1 Introduction

In the previous chapter, I investigated transmission of violent offending and examined whether this is different from transmission of general offending. In this chapter, I turn to the transmission of general crime - including violence - and focus on both the timing of parental criminality as well as its frequency. Most studies investigating intergenerational transmission simply link any life-time offending of the parent to any life-time offending of the

---

* A revised version of this chapter will be published as: S. Besemer (forthcoming). The impact of timing and frequency of parental criminal behaviour and risk factors on offspring offending. *Psychology, Crime and Law.*

child. In order to investigate what explains intergenerational transmission, however, it is important to examine both the timing of parental criminality as well as the frequency. By *timing* I refer to the age of offspring when the parent committed criminal acts leading to conviction, and by *frequency* I refer to the number of parental criminal convictions. This chapter aims to explore intergenerational transmission of criminal behaviour by investigating specifically the impact of the timing and frequency of the parents' criminal behaviour. Furthermore, risk factors will be incorporated in the analyses to examine the impact of a criminogenic environment. This chapter seeks an answer to the following questions: *Do offspring have more criminal convictions when parents had more convictions?* And: *Does the timing of parents' criminal convictions in the offspring's life have an impact on offspring offending?* And: *Could growing up in a criminogenic environment with risk factors explain intergenerational transmission?*

3.2 Theoretical Background

Several theoretical frameworks are relevant to these research questions. First, I will briefly discuss the previously described mechanisms of transmission (see Introduction) as proposed by Farrington (2011). Second, I will connect these questions to static versus dynamic theories or a *population heterogeneity* versus *state dependence* viewpoint. Third, the idea of a *critical* or *sensitive period*, a developmental psychological concept, will be explained and a connection will be made to the current research. Fourth, this will be linked to the concepts of a cumulative developmental versus life-course perspective (Ireland, Smith & Thornberry, 2002) or whether experiences early in life versus more proximal events will have a stronger impact. This will be followed by a discussion of previous research on timing and frequency.

In the Introduction I discussed Farrington's (2011) six explanations for intergenerational transmission: intergenerational exposure to multiple risk factors, mediation through environmental risk factors, teaching and co-offending, genetic mechanisms, assortative mating, and official (police and justice) bias. By investigating the timing and frequency of parental criminality in the child's life it is possible to examine some of these mechanisms. For example, an association between parental offending only before a child's birth and that child's later offending militates against transmission through social learning but supports genetic mechanisms or transmission of a criminogenic environment. Similarly, one would expect that, if social learning were the mechanism responsible for transmission, children whose parents are more frequent offenders would have an increased risk of offending themselves. The social learning mechanism explains transmission through direct and mutual influences of family members on each other; the parent is a social role model for the children (Bandura, 1973, 1977). Moreover, according to Sutherland's Differential Association Theory people will commit delinquent acts when they have learned more motivations to break rather than to follow the law (Sutherland & Cressey, 1955). When parents are more frequent offenders, children have more opportunities to observe and imitate their parents' delinquent behaviour and motivations and thus one would expect more offspring crime. Similarly, one would expect more official bias, a stronger biological basis and more risk factors when parents are more persistent offenders. Thornberry (2005) also hypothesizes that more frequent and persistent offenders will transmit criminal behaviour to their children more strongly. Parents' delinquency has a strong effect on their own development, transition into adult roles, parenting styles and thereby the effectiveness of their parenting. The more persistent their offending, the stronger the impact on their parenting and the higher the risk that their children will develop criminal behaviour.

By investigating risk factors it is possible to examine whether a criminogenic environment could explain intergenerational transmission. Children whose parents have been convicted might grow up in a more criminogenic environment characterised by risk factors such as low family Socio-Economic Status (SES), low family income, poor housing, large family size, teen mother at birth of first child, parental conflict, parents' low interest in education, and poor job record of the father. These risk factors might explain why these children have a higher conviction rate.

Investigating timing and frequency of criminal behaviour also relates to theories on *population heterogeneity* versus *state dependence*; or whether the development of criminal behaviour is static versus dynamic (Nagin & Paternoster, 1991, 2000). Population heterogeneity assumes that people differ in their propensity to exhibit criminal behaviour. This can be seen as a static theory of crime; people are born in a certain way or behaviour patterns are developed early in life, but later experiences do not influence people's behaviour. An example of a static theory is Gottfredson & Hirschi's general theory of crime (1990). According to Gottfredson and Hirschi children develop self-control early in life and this will determine whether they commit crime. If criminal behaviour is transmitted from parents to children this is due to transmission of self-control, and parental convictions after childhood should not influence offspring's criminal behaviour (Van de Rakt, Ruiter, de Graaf & Nieuwbeerta, 2010). State dependence theorists, in contrast, believe that experiences later in life may influence people's behaviour (Nagin & Paternoster, 1991, 2000). Such theories are dynamic, because the tendency for a certain individual to commit crime can change over the life-course. While criminal behaviour has a causal effect on subsequent criminality, other experiences also influence the tendency to commit crime. If parents are convicted this might influence the child's behaviour at that moment. This could influence the child early in childhood, but also in adolescence. Intergenerational transmission through genetic mechanisms and intergenerational exposure to multiple risk factors would fall under the static explanations, while mediation through environmental risk factors, teaching and co-offending, assortative mating, and official (police and justice) bias could be seen as dynamic theories of intergenerational transmission.

Something that Farrington does not discuss in his mechanisms is whether it matters when the child has been exposed to the parent's criminal behaviour. Is there something that resembles a critical or sensitive period when children are more vulnerable to adverse influences like parental criminal behaviour? The idea of a *critical period* was first proposed for language development (Lenneberg, 1967; Penfield & Roberts, 1959). The critical period hypothesis states that human beings develop language in a specific period of their life. There is an increased sensitivity in this period and if the child is not being stimulated during this critical phase, it is much harder or even impossible to acquire language. The term *sensitive* period appears to apply better to the development of behaviour, because it is less strict; during an optimal period the person is especially responsive to certain stimuli (Berk, 2009; Bukatko & Daehler, 2001). The boundaries of this phase are more loosely defined than those of a critical period (Bornstein, 1989). Stimulation during this sensitive period can exert a long-lasting impact on the development of behaviour, and emotional deprivation or trauma in specific periods might prevent children from developing social skills and appropriate behaviour (Knudsen, 2004; Scott, 1962). Most research on the sensitive period focuses on the development of desired behaviour (Berk, 2009; Bukatko & Daehler, 2001; Harley & Wang, 1997). Hardly any research has been carried out on the existence of a sensitive period for the development of undesirable behaviour such as delinquency.

Applying the idea of a sensitive period to the development of delinquent behaviour, the impact of parents' criminal behaviour might be different at different ages and developmental stages of the child. For example, an advantage for younger children (pre-school age, 0-6 years) might be that they are not aware of their parents' criminal behaviour. A disadvantage is that they have not fully developed their behavioural repertoire and might be more vulnerable to imitating their parents' delinquent behaviour. Furthermore, they might not have developed coping strategies to handle the stressful situation of a parent's conviction and they cannot just run away to their friends to escape a stressful situation. They are also more likely to be present when their parents are arrested.

In contrast, school-age children (7-12 years) are more likely to be at school when their parents are arrested. However, they might be more aware of their parents' illegitimate behaviour and may experience greater stigma from society than younger children. According to Labelling Theory, people behave according to the label society attaches to them (Lemert, 1967). Stigma might cause children to develop delinquent behaviour. These children are also still developing their behavioural repertoire and coping strategies. They are still loyal to their parents, and might therefore be more likely to imitate their parent's delinquent behaviour than older teenagers. Furthermore, they are not yet independent enough to go away and escape a problematic home situation with delinquent parents.

Older children (13-18) do have this advantage of becoming independent. They spend more time without their parents and have more options to escape a possibly detrimental home situation. They might have developed more coping strategies to deal with such a situation (Compas, 1987; Compas, Connor-Smith, Saltzman, Thomsen & Wadsworth, 2001; S. H. Goodman & Gotlib, 1999; Sroufe & Rutter, 1984). However, adolescence is also the period in which delinquent behaviour increases and peer influence becomes more important (Warr, 2002). When adolescents do not want to associate with their parents, they could resist by exhibiting no delinquent behaviour as a reaction. What appears more likely, however, is that they might associate with children from other problem families, which might lead to delinquent behaviour as well (Garbarino, 1989; Myers, Smarsh, Amlund-Hagen & Kennon, 1999). Furthermore, these children are rapidly developing their own personal and social identity, which often involves a lot of insecurity and turbulence. They might experience more stigma and/or stress of having a criminal parent and may be more likely to react to this by engaging in offensive behaviour (Agnew, 1992, 1997; Besemer, Van der Geest, Murray, Bijleveld & Farrington, 2011; Larson & Asmussen, 1991; Larson & Ham, 1993).

Timing of parental criminal behaviour also relates to a cumulative developmental versus life-course perspective (Ireland et al., 2002). The cumulative developmental perspective, based on developmental psychology and psychopathology, assumes that experiences early in life have a long-lasting impact. These experiences will influence children's development, behaviour, and coping skills. According to this perspective, detrimental experiences will have a stronger impact in early childhood than in adolescence. Moffitt's (1993) theory for life-course persistent offenders is a good example; she describes how delinquent behaviour starts in early childhood and develops cumulatively for life-course persistent offenders. The life-course perspective, in contrast, does not deny the impact of experiences early in life, but states that more proximal events have a stronger impact. The life-course perspective assumes a more dynamic development of behaviour, where experiences can always impact on children's development. Sampson and Laub's (1993) age-graded theory of crime is an example of this perspective: it assumes that certain experiences will impact on people's criminal behaviour all through their lives. The cumulative developmental perspective would predict a stronger impact of parental convictions in early childhood, whereas the life-course perspective predicts a stronger impact of parental convictions in later childhood or adolescence.

Few previous studies have focused on the timing of parents' crime in the child's life. Van de Rakt et al. (2010) studied the impact of the timing of parental criminal convictions on offspring offending and found that the risk of conviction for offspring in a certain year increased when the father had been convicted in that year. They also found that this effect was stronger during adolescence. Besemer et al. (2011 and Chapter 6 of this dissertation) examined the timing of parental imprisonment and found that parental incarceration was only related to offspring criminal behaviour when it occurred after the child's seventh birthday. West and Farrington (1977) found that sons whose fathers had been convicted after the son's 10th birthday had only a marginally greater chance of conviction than sons whose fathers' last conviction occurred before the son's birth. Related research has examined the impact of child maltreatment on children's delinquent behaviour and demonstrated that, contrary to most developmental theories of adverse influences that suggest that younger children are more vulnerable (Putnam, 1997), adolescent maltreatment is significantly related to offspring's problem and delinquent behaviour as well as other negative consequences later in life, while childhood maltreatment is not (Eckenrode et al., 2001; Ireland et al., 2002; Smith, Ireland & Thornberry, 2005; Thornberry, Ireland & Smith, 2001).[15]

Similarly, few studies have investigated the frequency of parents' criminal behaviour. West and Farrington (1977) found that fathers with one conviction only and fathers with two or more convictions had the same proportion of convicted sons, which does not necessarily support a social learning mechanism. Van de Rakt et al. (2008) investigated conviction trajectories of both parents and children. They found that children whose fathers belong to a more persistent trajectory group were more likely to also be in such a trajectory group, but Besemer and Farrington (2012 and Chapter 4 of this dissertation) did not find a significant relationship between trajectory groups in the *CSDD* or *Transfive*.

3.3 Hypotheses

This chapter attempts to fill this gap in knowledge by specifically investigating the impact of timing and frequency of parents' criminal behaviour on offspring criminal behaviour. The following hypotheses will be tested in this chapter:

1. The number of offspring convictions increases when a parent has been convicted for more offences.

   If the data support this hypothesis, this supports several of Farrington's proposed mechanisms. When a parent offends more often, stronger social learning is expected, but one might also expect a stronger biological basis, more risk factors, and stronger official bias. This hypothesis is therefore not necessarily to contrast the differ-

---

[15] Parental criminal behaviour and maltreatment are obviously different phenomena, but this research into maltreatment is the closest to what is being studied in the current chapter.

ent mechanisms, but more a first test to see how intergenerational transmission might work and whether one can differentiate between children whose parents are more or less persistent offenders.

2. Offspring of parents who have only been convicted before the child's birth have more criminal convictions than offspring of parents who have never been convicted up to the child's 19th birthday.

3. Having a convicted parent before birth (versus an unconvicted parent) still predicts a higher conviction rate after controlling for risk factors for crime.

Both these groups did not experience parental conviction during their childhood. Even though the first group's parents had been convicted previously, assuming that these parents desisted from crime, these parents were not criminal role models for their children during childhood. We obviously do not know whether these parents really desisted and to what extent they might still have been criminal role models, but for the purpose of this chapter, it is assumed that they indeed desisted from crime. If these parents still transmit criminal behaviour more strongly than parents who have never been convicted, this could be explained by either genetic mechanisms or because these parents continue to live in a criminogenic environment, thereby transmitting certain risk factors to their children.

To investigate whether a more criminogenic environment can explain a higher conviction rate for the first group, several variables known to be risk factors for criminal behaviour will be included in a multivariate regression analysis. The Method section will describe these risk factors in more detail.

4. Intergenerational transmission is stronger when parents have been convicted after the child's birth compared with before the child's birth only.

5. Having a parent convicted after the child's birth (versus before birth) still predicts a higher conviction rate after controlling for risk factors for crime.

As with hypothesis 2, it is assumed that parents who had been convicted only before their child's birth desisted from crime. Thus, these parents were a less criminal role model than parents who had been convicted after the child's birth. When the data confirm this hypothesis, it demonstrates that the experience of a parental conviction makes a difference. This would support dynamic theories of transmission such as the social learning mechanism, because children whose parents had been convicted after the child's birth had (stronger) criminal role models. Conviction after the child's birth could also be an indicator that the often protective function of marriage and parenthood - a *turning point* towards a non-criminal life style - did not work (Sampson & Laub, 2005; Theobald & Farrington, 2009). It could also be possible that this group grew up in a more criminogenic environment with more risk factors for crime. To investigate this last option, again risk factors for criminal behaviour will be included in a multivariate regression analysis.

6. Intergenerational transmission is stronger when parents have been convicted when the child was older.

The theories discussed above suggest that parental crime and convictions can have an impact for specific reasons at different ages and do not clearly point to one age group that might be more vulnerable than others. Previous research, however, tends to conclude that older children are more strongly impacted by parental conviction, imprisonment, and maltreatment (Van de Rakt et al., 2010; Besemer et al., 2011; Eckenrode et al., 2001; Ireland et al., 2002; Smith et al., 2005; Thornberry et al., 2001). Therefore it is expected that intergenerational transmission is stronger when children were older at the time of parental conviction. When the data confirm this hypothesis, this also supports dynamic theories of crime and a life-course perspective. It would strengthen the idea that stigma and identification with the criminal parent might be important in intergenerational transmission.

3.4 Method

3.4.1 Sample

These hypotheses were tested using data from the *Cambridge Study in Delinquent Development* (CSDD) (see page 13 for more information). The current investigation studied the original men, their parents and their full biological siblings. It was not possible to do the analyses with the *NSCR-Transfive Study* (Transfive), because comparable risk factors were never collected in *Transfive*.

3.4.2 Measures

Outcome Variables

The outcome variable for all hypotheses was the offspring's conviction rate, defined as the number of convictions for crimes committed between the 12th

and 40th birthdays. In this variable, non-offenders are also included. Thus, an offender in this chapter is defined as someone who had been convicted of an offence between these ages. The hypotheses were studied separately for all children, and for sons and daughters separately. Separating the analyses by offspring gender was done, because boys and girls might react differently to stressful life events such as parental convictions (Farrington, Barnes & Lambert, 1996). In general, boys exhibit more externalizing problem behaviour such as delinquency, while girls have more internalizing problems such as anxiety and depression (Capaldi et al., 2002; Robins, 1966, 1986). Investigating differences between the two genders remains outside the scope of this chapter, but results are mentioned for each gender separately, precisely because girls tend to show less criminal behaviour.

Predictor Variables

Hypothesis 1 posits that the frequency of parents' crime will influence offspring's criminal behaviour: the more convictions the parent had, the more convictions the child will have. Before investigating whether the frequency of parents' offending was related to offspring offending, it was investigated whether the fact that the parent had a conviction was significantly related to offspring offending. The reason this variable was used is because the aim of this hypothesis was to find out whether the frequency of parents' crime had a separate impact on offspring offending behaviour over and above the fact that parents had a conviction. Therefore, two predictor variables were used: a dichotomous variable indicating whether parents had a conviction between their 12th and 40th birthdays, and a continuous variable with the number of convictions in this period. The dichotomous predictor variable was coded 1 if either the father or the mother had a conviction between their 12th and 40th birthdays. Initially, the intention was to study mothers and fathers separately as well. However, mothers had few convictions. Since the prevalence and frequency of mother's offending was so low, it was decided not to examine the impact of timing and frequency of mother's offending separately. Instead, information on both parents was taken together.

For hypotheses 2 to 6 several predictor variables with groups of children were computed. For hypotheses 2 and 3, two groups were created: one with children whose parents had only been convicted before the child's birth and not up until the child's 19th birthday versus those whose parents had never been convicted up until the child's 19th birthday.[16] For hypotheses 4 and 5, the first group from hypotheses 2 and 3, children whose parents had only been convicted before the child's birth, was compared with children whose parents had been convicted at some point between the child's birth and 19th birthday (without looking at what occurred before or after this period). For hypothesis 6, three groups were compared: children whose parents had been

---

16 Convictions after the child's 19th birthday were not taken into account. This study investigated parental convictions in the offspring's childhood or before the child's birth.

convicted when the children were between 0-6, 7-12, versus 13-18 years old. These groups are not mutually exclusive: children whose parents had been convicted in more than one period, have been included in every period in which their parents had been convicted.[17]

Furthermore, for hypotheses 3 and 5, risk factors were added to the analysis. First, it was investigated which risk factors were significantly related to the outcome variable: the offspring's conviction rate between the 12th and 40th birthdays. The following eight variables were significantly related to the offspring's conviction rate: low family Socio-Economic Status (SES), low family income, poor housing, large family size, teen mother at birth of first child, parental conflict, parents' interest in education, and poor job record of the father. These are all dichotomous variables measured at either age eight or ten, coded 1 if the child had the risk factor, coded 0 if the factor was absent (for more details on how these were measured, see Farrington & Painter, 2004). Multiple risk factors have a cumulative effect: the more risk factors, the more problem behaviour (Farrington et al., 2009; Loeber et al., 1998; Thornberry et al., 2003). The eight risk factors also correlated with each other. Therefore, these risk factors were summarised by taking their mean value. The risk factor mean was included in a multivariate regression analysis together with the variable indicating whether parents had been convicted only before birth versus never (hypothesis 3), respectively with the variable indicating whether parents had been convicted only before birth versus afterwards (hypothesis 5).

3.4.3 Analytic Approach

Analytic Approach: Generalised Estimating Equations (GEE)

Negative binomial regression analysis was used in Generalized Estimating Equations (GEE) (see the Introduction, page 16 for more information). Furthermore, the predictor variable number of parental convictions (hypothesis 1) was positively skewed and therefore log-transformed in the analysis. A value of one has been added to all scores before performing the log natural transformation.[18]

---

[17] Analyses with mutually exclusive groups led to similar conclusions. Furthermore, analyses where groups were combined (0-6 and 7-12, 7-12 and 13-18, 0-6 and 13-18) and compared with each other and with the groups studied in this chapter did not lead to significant results. The age cut-off points were chosen to create groups with a similar age interval. Furthermore, 0-6 years of age represents a pre-school age, 7-12 represents primary school, while 13-18 year olds are likely to be in secondary school, further education or working.

[18] Log natural transformation of a count variable with a skewed distribution is recommended (Tabachnick & Fidell, 2007) and used widely in criminological research (e.g. Krahn, Hartnagel & Gartrell, 1986; Messner, 1989; Neapolitan, 1994, 1995, 1997). The following formula was used for the log natural transformation: $Log(x) = Ln(x+1)$.

Table 3.1: Impact of parental conviction (when parent aged 12-39) on offspring's conviction rate 12-39

Offspring convictions	Parents no conviction		Parent conviction		CR ratio PC / PN	B	95 % CI	p
	N	CR (SD)	N	CR (SD)				
All children	790	0.82 (2.46)	394	2.43 (4.75)	3.0	1.12	0.77-1.47	.001
Sons	521	1.15 (2.90)	261	3.35 (5.51)	2.9	1.12	0.75-1.48	.001
Daughters	269	0.18 (0.93)	133	0.64 (1.58)	3.6	1.26	0.47-2.06	.002

95 % CI B, 95 % Confidence interval B; CR, conviction rate; N, number of children; PC, parent conviction; PN, parent no conviction; SD, standard deviation.

Table 3.2: Impact of *number of* parental convictions (when parent aged 12-39) on offspring's conviction rate 12-39

Offspring convictions	N	B	95 % CI	p
All	1184/397	0.78	0.57-1.00	.001
Sons	782/397	0.82	0.59-1.04	.001
Daughters	402/242	0.77	0.39-1.16	.001

95 % CI B, 95 % Confidence interval B; N, number of children / number of parents.

3.5 Results

3.5.1 Parents' frequency of convictions

First, offspring offending was regressed on whether parents had a conviction or not. This proved to be a significant predictor of offspring's conviction rate (see table 3.1). The conviction rate ratio - calculated as the mean conviction rate for children with a convicted parent (CR PC) divided by the mean conviction rate for children whose parents have no convictions (CR PN) - is 3; children whose parents had been convicted had three times more convictions than children whose parents had not been convicted. This applied to sons as well as daughters. Second, parents' frequency of offending was used as a predictor variable. The continuous variable was a sum of the number of convictions the father and mother each had between their 12th and 40th birthdays. This also proved to be a significant predictor of offspring conviction rate (see table 3.2). The more convictions parents had, the more convictions children had. Again, this applied to sons as well as daughters.

Our third step combined the dichotomous and continuous variable, because the aim was to investigate whether the frequency of parents' crime had a separate impact on offspring offending behaviour over and above the fact that the parent had a conviction. Only children whose parents had at least one conviction were included, and the number of parental convictions was used as the predictor variable. The results demonstrate that the number of parental convictions was a significant predictor of offspring's conviction

Table 3.3: Impact of the number of parental convictions (when parent aged 12-39) on offspring's conviction rate for parents who had at least one conviction

Offspring convictions	N	B	95 % CI	p
All	394/103	0.47	0.09-0.85	.015
Sons	261/103	0.59	0.20-0.97	.003
Daughters	133/68	0.28	-0.36-0.91	.395

95 % CI B, 95 % Confidence interval B; N, number of children / number of parents.

Table 3.4: The impact of timing of parents' convictions on offspring's conviction rate

Parental conviction:	All offspring N CR (SD)	Sons only N CR (SD)	Daughters only N CR (SD)
Never until offspring's 19th birthday	733 0.62 (1.83)	479 0.88 (2.19)	254 0.11 (0.46)
Before offspring's birth only	110 1.62 (3.13)	76 2.20 (3.56)	34 0.32 (1.04)
When offspring 0-18	332 2.76 (5.23)	220 3.74 (6.03)	113 0.82 (2.01)
When offspring 0-6	192 2.73 (5.19)	128 3.59 (5.95)	64 1.02 (2.40)
When offspring 7-12	138 3.70 (6.38)	89 5.06 (7.39)	49 1.24 (2.56)
When offspring 13-18	134 3.09 (5.67)	83 4.42 (6.63)	51 0.92 (2.41)

CR, conviction rate; N, number of children; SD, standard deviation.

rate, over and above the parents having a conviction (table 3.3). To give an indication of the magnitude of the number of parental convictions: children whose parents had one parental conviction had on average 1.64 convictions (SD=3.33), children whose parents had 2-3 convictions had 2.23 convictions (SD=4.20), while children whose parents had 4 or more convictions had on average 3.51 convictions (SD=6.19). There was no significant relationship when daughters were analysed separately. The results support hypothesis 1 that the number of offspring convictions increases when parents have been convicted more often.

3.5.2 Timing of parents' crime in the child's life

After examining the frequency of parental criminal behaviour, timing was investigated. Descriptive results are presented in table 3.4, which presents the average conviction rates and standard deviations for each of the groups compared and the number of offspring involved. These results will be described more fully in each of the following sections.

Parent convicted before the child's birth versus never

Hypothesis 2 posits that children whose parents had been convicted only before the child's birth would have a higher conviction rate than children whose parents had never been convicted either before or during the offspring's childhood. The results for comparing these two groups are presented

Table 3.5: Comparing offspring's conviction rate for children whose parents had only been convicted before the child's birth versus those whose parents had never been convicted up until the child's 19th birthday and the impact of risk factors

		CR ratio	B	95 % CI B	p
All children	step 1–PCB vs. PN	2.6	0.96	0.52- 1.39	.001
	step 2–PCB vs. PN		0.82	0.40- 1.25	.001
	Risk factors		1.13	0.26- 1.99	.011
Sons	step 1–PCB vs. PN	2.5	0.88	0.44- 1.31	.001
	step 2–PCB vs. PN		0.72	0.30- 1.14	.001
	Risk factors		1.33	0.42- 2.24	.004
Daughters	step 1–PCB vs. PN	2.9	1.10	-0.12- 2.32	.076

95 % CI B, 95 % Confidence interval B; CR, conviction rate; PCB, parental conviction before birth child only; PN, parent never convicted up until child's 19th birthday.

in table 3.5 (step 1). Children whose parents had only been convicted before the child's birth had significantly more convictions than children whose parents had never been convicted (1.62 versus 0.62, B=0.96, p<.001). Even though parents had only been convicted before the child's birth, their children still committed more crime than children whose parents had never been convicted.[19]

To investigate whether the difference between these groups could be explained by the transmission of a criminogenic environment, the risk factor mean was included in the regression analysis. Children whose parents had never been convicted have a lower risk factor mean compared with children whose parents had been convicted before birth. These two groups differ significantly on four of the risk factors: children whose parents had never been convicted have a lower chance to come from a large family, to live in poor housing, to have a mother who was a teenager when her first child was born and to have a father with a poor job record. The risk factor mean was included in a multivariate regression analysis together with the variable indicating whether parents had been convicted only before birth versus never. This was only done where the groups were significantly different in the previous analysis (step 1, all children and sons only). The results presented in table 3.5 (step 2) demonstrate that the significant relationship for group membership (parent never convicted versus convicted before the child's birth) remained when controlling for risk factors. When risk factors were added to

---

[19] One could hypothesize that parents who have been convicted before the child's birth might have been imprisoned during the offspring's childhood. Nine out of the 110 children (8.2 %) whose parents had only been convicted before the child's birth experienced parental imprisonment during their childhood. Previous research (see Murray & Farrington, 2008b; Murray et al., 2009; Besemer et al., 2011, and Chapter 6 of this dissertation) has shown that parental imprisonment increases the risk of offspring offending. Therefore, a variable for parental imprisonment was added to the analyses comparing children whose parents had been convicted before the child's birth versus children whose parents had never been convicted. Although parental imprisonment was a significant predictor of offspring conviction rate, having a convicted parent remained an independent significant predictor as well. In the interest of space, the models are not included; they are available upon request.

Table 3.6: Comparing offspring's conviction rate for children whose parents had only been convicted before the child's birth versus those whose parents had been convicted between the child's birth and 19th birthday and the impact of risk factors

		CR ratio	B	95% CI B	p
All children	step 1 –PCB vs. PC 0-18	1.7	0.55	0.10-1.00	.017
	step 2 –PCB vs. PC 0-18		0.36	-0.09-0.81	.120
	Risk factors		1.27	0.54-2.00	.001
Sons	step 1 –PCB vs. PC 0-18	1.7	0.64	0.19-1.10	.006
	step 2 –PCB vs. PC 0-18		0.43	-0.01-0.87	.057
	Risk factors		1.47	0.77-2.17	.001
Daughters	step 1 –PCB vs. PC 0-18	2.6	0.80	-0.34-1.94	.167

95% CI B, 95% Confidence interval B; CR, conviction rate; PCB, parental conviction before birth child only; PC 0-18, parent convicted between child's birth and 19th birthday.

the analysis, the impact of the parent's conviction became slightly smaller in every analysis (the Bs are smaller). Apparently, risk factors explain part of the difference in conviction rate between children whose parents had been convicted only before birth versus never. However, the conviction itself also has an impact. Apparently, parents who had been convicted before their child was born transmit a propensity to their children to commit crime, even though these children did not actually experience parental conviction. It appears that both the fact that parents had been convicted and the presence of risk factors explains the difference between these two groups. The results support hypothesis 2 as well as hypothesis 3. The next step in the analyses compared children whose parents had only been convicted before birth with children whose parents had been convicted during the offspring's childhood.

Parent convicted before versus after the child's birth

Hypothesis 4 posits that children whose parents had been convicted after the child's birth exhibit more criminal behaviour than children whose parents had been convicted only before their birth. The results for comparing these two groups are presented in table 3.6 (step 1). Children whose parents had been convicted only before the child's birth had on average 1.62 convictions, compared with 2.76 convictions for children whose parents had been convicted after the child's birth (table 3.4). This was significantly different (CR ratio = 1.7, B = 0.55, p = .017). When sons and daughters were analysed separately, the strength of the difference between the two groups appeared to be stronger for daughters (CR ratio = 2.6 versus 1.7), but the difference was not significant (p = .167).

The difference between children whose parents had been convicted before birth versus afterwards could be explained by the observation that the latter group experienced parental conviction and had a stronger criminal role model, but similarly, there could be a difference in risk factors between these groups. Children whose parents had been convicted only before the child's

Table 3.7: The impact of the timing of parents' convictions in the child's life on offspring's conviction rate

		CR ratio	B	95 % CI B	p
All children	PCB vs. PC 0-6	1.7	0.55	0.07-1.03	.025
	PCB vs. PC 7-12	2.3	0.81	0.31-1.30	.001
	PCB vs. PC 13-18	1.9	0.64	0.14-1.14	.011
	PC 0-6 vs. 7-12	1.4	0.20	-0.07-0.48	.143
	PC 0-6 vs. 13-18	1.1	0.10	-0.17-0.37	.471
	PC 7-12 vs. 13-18	0.8	-0.10	-0.46-0.25	.572
Sons	PCB vs. PC 0-6	1.6	0.57	0.09-1.06	.021
	PCB vs. PC 7-12	2.3	0.85	0.35-1.35	.001
	PCB vs. PC 13-18	2.0	0.71	0.21-1.21	.005
	PC 0-6 vs. 7-12	1.4	0.16	-0.09-0.41	.217
	PC 0-6 vs. 13-18	1.2	0.09	-0.13-0.32	.417
	PC 7-12 vs. 13-18	0.9	-0.09	-0.38-0.21	.565
Daughters	PCB vs. PC 0-6	3.2	1.07	-0.14-2.29	.084
	PCB vs. PC 7-12	3.9	1.27	0.04-2.49	.044
	PCB vs. PC 13-18	2.9	0.96	-0.33-2.25	.144
	PC 0-6 vs. 7-12	1.2	0.08	-0.32-0.49	.688
	PC 0-6 vs. 13-18	0.9	0.07	-0.31-0.44	.731
	PC 7-12 vs. 13-18	0.7	-0.18	-0.50-0.13	.254

95 % CI B, 95 % Confidence interval B; CR, conviction rate; PCB, parental conviction before birth child only; PC 0-6, parent convicted at some point between child's birth and 7th birthday; PC 7-12, parent convicted at some point between the child's 7th and 13th birthday; PC 13-18, parent convicted at some point between the child's 13th and 19th birthday.

birth had a lower risk factor mean compared with children whose parents had been convicted after their birth. The latter group was more likely to come from a background with low family income, large family size, poor job record of father and less interest in education by parents. Again, where the groups were significantly different in the previous analysis (step 1, all children and sons only), the risk factor variable was included in a multivariate regression analysis together with the variable indicating whether parents had been convicted only before birth versus afterwards. The results presented in table 3.6 (step 2) demonstrate that the impact of the parental conviction decreased and was just not significant anymore when risk factors were taken into account. Whether parents had been convicted before birth or afterwards was not a significant predictor anymore, but the risk factor variable was. Apparently, the difference between children who experienced parental conviction before birth versus afterwards can be largely explained by the observation that these children differ in the number of risk factors for crime.

These results support hypothesis 4 that intergenerational transmission is stronger when parents have been convicted after the child's birth. However, the results do not support hypothesis 5 strongly; rather they show that this transmission can be largely explained by the observation that children whose parents were convicted after the child's birth had more risk factors for crime; that is, they grew up in a more criminogenic environment.

Offspring age at parent's convictions

For hypothesis 6 three groups were compared: children whose parents had been convicted when the children were between 0-6, 7-12, versus 13-18 years old. Results from the analyses comparing the three groups with each other and with the group of children whose parents had been convicted only before the child's birth are presented in table 3.7. All groups have a higher average number of convictions than children whose parents had only been convicted before the child's birth (CR ratio between 1.6 to 3.9). Children whose parents had been convicted when the children were between ages 7 and 12 had the highest number of convictions (3.70), followed by the 13-18 group (3.09) and the 0-6 group (2.73) (table 3.4). However, the differences between these groups were not statistically significant. When observing sons and daughters separately, a similar pattern is visible: children whose parents had been convicted when they were between ages 7-12 exhibit the highest number of convictions. Again, none of the differences was statistically significant. Even though analyses all showed a tendency for the 7-12 group to have the highest average number of convictions, none of the differences was statistically significant and the effect sizes for the differences were small. The results do not support the hypothesis (6) that intergenerational transmission is stronger when parents have been convicted when the child was older. Further, there does not appear to be a sensitive period for the impact of parental crime. Experiencing a parental conviction in all periods after birth increases offspring's criminal behaviour.

3.6 Discussion

This study investigated whether the frequency of parents' criminal behaviour and timing of parent's criminal behaviour in the child's life has an impact on offspring's criminal behaviour. Furthermore, risk factors were included in the analyses to investigate timing of parental crime. Six hypotheses were tested. First, the results demonstrated that parents' frequency of criminal behaviour was significantly related to offspring offending. Second, examining the timing of parents' convictions, the results demonstrated that even when parents had only been convicted before birth, their children had more convictions than children whose parents had never been convicted before or during the offspring's childhood. Third, this difference remained significant when risk factors were taken into account, even though the risk factors explained part of the difference. These results support static theories of transmission such as genetic mechanisms and/or transmission of the criminogenic environment. Fourth, children whose parents had been convicted after the child's birth had more convictions than those whose parents had only been convicted before the child's birth. Fifth, however, the impact of a parental conviction after birth decreased and became insignificant when risk factors

Discussion

were taken into account. Sixth, children whose parents had been convicted when the children were between age 7 and 12 had the highest conviction rate, but none of the differences comparing the impact of parental conviction at different ages was significant.

There are some interesting patterns in these results worth discussing. First, although the age group 7-12 had the highest conviction rate, none of the differences between the age groups was significant. The results demonstrate an impact of parental conviction in each age group and do not support the idea of a sensitive period for the impact of parental criminal behaviour. The results could not differentiate between the cumulative developmental and life-course perspective; parental conviction in all age periods had an impact on offspring offending. This study did not find such strong results as found in an earlier study of the impact of timing of maltreatment with the Rochester Youth Development Study (Ireland et al., 2002; Smith et al., 2005; Thornberry et al., 2001). It would be valuable to replicate the current study using different samples of people to investigate the impact of timing of parental convictions on offspring offending behaviour.

Second, when comparing children whose parents had been convicted before versus after the child's birth, risk factors were more important than the parental conviction itself. This supports the transmission of a criminogenic environment more than the social learning perspective. After taking into account this criminogenic environment it does not matter whether children actually experienced the parental conviction; they exhibit similar levels of criminal behaviour. Unfortunately, this study does not have information on risk factors for the parents nor information on the temporal sequence of risk factors and parent and offspring. Thus, it was not possible to differentiate between the risk factor mechanisms discussed in the Introduction (see page 4). This study is unable to make statements about what is actually causing the behaviour. The risk factors could be causing the offspring's offending separately from the parents' offending; the risk factors could be causing the parents' as well as the offspring crime; or the parent's offending could be causing the risk factors and the risk factors could then cause the offspring offending. It would obviously be interesting to investigate whether these risk factors are part of a larger syndrome of antisocial behaviour or whether these are mediating factors in intergenerational transmission.

Even though this study could not differentiate between the risk factor mechanisms, it does demonstrate that it is important to include risk factors for crime when investigating the timing of parents' criminal behaviour. The results demonstrate that part of the difference between children whose parents had been convicted before versus after the child's birth and between this latter group and children whose parents had never been convicted could be explained by the presence of risk factors in the offspring's life. Children whose parents had been convicted grow up in a more criminogenic environment characterised by low family SES, low family income, poor housing, large family size, teen mother at birth of first child, parental conflict, parents' low interest in education, and poor job record of father. This criminogenic environment is even stronger when parents had been convicted after the child's birth. Farrington's (2011) postulation that intergenerational transmission can be explained by transmission of a cycle of deprivation and antisocial behaviour is thus supported.

Third, even though studying gender differences remained outside the scope of this chapter, it is interesting to compare the results for males and females. In the frequency analyses, the number of parental convictions over and above the fact that parents have a conviction is only a significant predictor for sons, but not for daughters. This insignificance might be due to the lower number of girls in the sample, but the magnitude of the impact also appears to be smaller for girls than for boys (the B is smaller). An explanation for this difference might be that boys and girls react differently to stressful life events such as parental convictions. In general, boys exhibit more externalizing problem behaviour such as delinquency, while girls have more internalizing problems such as anxiety and depression (Capaldi et al., 2002; Robins, 1966, 1986). Examining family life transitions in a sample born between 1920-40, Huschek and Bijleveld (2011) found that a convicted but not imprisoned father increased the odds for girls but not for boys to have a non-standard marriage pattern. This involved, for example, a turbulent marriage pattern including several divorces and children born out of wedlock and late childless marriages. A standard pattern, in contrast, consisted of a marriage followed by the birth of one or more children and a low prevalence of divorce. The increased prevalence of a non-standard marriage life for daughters might be a sign of a different reaction pattern following a parent's conviction. However, the difference between girls who experienced parental conviction before versus after birth is larger than the difference for boys, although the difference is not significant for girls (CR ratio 2.6 versus 1.7 for boys). This does not support this explanation. Moffitt et al. (2001) studied boys' and girls' different reactions to several risk factors such as parental criminality. Yet, they found few differences between the sexes in the effect of these risk factors, so this explanation of different reaction patterns appears not universal.

What do these results mean to policy makers who want to break the cycle and reduce intergenerational transmission of criminal behaviour? It appears that parents' criminal behaviour, but also risk factors for crime, are related to more offspring crime. Some of these risk factors are static and hard to change such as a large family size or having a mother who was a teenager when her first child was born. Other risk factors are slightly more open to change such as low family income, poor housing, poor job record of father and low interest in education by parents. The current study was unable to investigate whether there is a causal relationship between these risk factors and offspring criminal behaviour, but if they are mediators and if there is a causal relationship this might be an opportunity to prevent or reduce intergenerational transmission of criminal behaviour. Apart from family-based prevention programs that focus on parents' child rearing techniques (for more information see for example Farrington & Welsh, 2007; Kazdin, 1997), it might be fruitful to target these dynamic risk factors. For example, improving someone's employability might not only decrease that person's criminal behaviour (as demonstrated by Van der Geest, Bijleveld & Blokland, 2011; Verbruggen, Blokland & Van der Geest, 2011), but also their offspring's future criminal behaviour. Even the more static factors, such as teenage motherhood, are open to intervention.

It must be recognised that the results from this study might not be easily generalisable to today's situation or to other countries. This sample of boys and girls was born in England in the 1940-60s when family structures were different from today. Genetic mechanisms of transmission might stay the same, but the influence of other social role models apart from the parents might be larger nowadays. Nowadays and in other societies it might be easier to escape a criminogenic environment. In England, geographical and cultural class boundaries were strong, and birth class had a strong forecasting effect on children's life-path (Blanden, Gregg & Machin, 2005; Breen, 2004; Musterd, 2005). In other societies it might be easier to escape a criminogenic environment, while in England parental conviction and associated factors may have sustained risk factors for crime further in life because they are much more connected to social and cultural class factors.

As with every other study, this study has its limitations. As in the previous chapter, only official data for criminal behaviour have been used, and these suffer from a dark number (for more information, see page 36). Official convictions are only indicators of offending behaviour. It would be interesting to investigate the impact of timing and frequency of parental crime using self-reported data on offending behaviour for both generations.

Second, there are obviously many more factors involved in intergenerational transmission besides the timing and frequency of parental behaviour and the risk factors that were included in the multivariate analyses. Official bias or assortative mating was not investigated specifically and the mechanisms discussed could also be examined in other ways (official bias will be studied in Chapter 5). It is vital that more studies are carried out to increase knowledge on intergenerational transmission of criminal behaviour.

Despite these limitations, this study has contributed to our understanding of intergenerational transmission on several points. As far as known to the author, no other study previously investigated the presence of a sensitive period and the impact of timing of parental crime in the child's life on offspring offending into adulthood. Only one study (West & Farrington, 1977) previously investigated the number of fathers' convictions specifically and two others used the conviction trajectory method (see Chapter 4 of this Dissertation and Besemer & Farrington, 2012; Van de Rakt et al., 2008) but none included mothers' convictions. By using a large prospective sample with information on convictions of both parents, this study demonstrated support for static as well as dynamic explanations of intergenerational transmission such as genetic mechanisms, the transmission of a criminogenic environment and/or mediation through risk factors.

3.7 Summary

This chapter explored mechanisms of intergenerational transmission of criminal behaviour by investigating timing and frequency of parents' criminal behaviour and the impact of risk factors. Parents' number of criminal convictions was positively related to offspring convictions. Furthermore, children whose parents had only been convicted before the child's birth had more convictions than those whose parents had never been convicted. Children whose parents had been convicted after their birth had even more convictions, but risk factors explained part of this difference. When parental convictions at different ages were examined, children whose parents had been convicted between their 7th and 13th birthdays exhibited more criminal behaviour than children whose parents were convicted in other periods, but none of the differences was significant. The results do not show proof for a sensitive period for the impact of parental criminal behaviour. The results demonstrate support for static as well as dynamic explanations of intergenerational transmission such as genetic mechanisms, the impact of a criminogenic environment and/or mediation through risk factors.

Chapter 4

Intergenerational transmission of criminal behaviour: conviction trajectories of fathers and their offspring*

> *'It's like, dang, I'm following in my mom's footsteps.'*
> (Giordano, 2010, p. 116)

4.1 Introduction

In the previous chapter criminal career parameters such as timing and frequency were investigated in relation to intergenerational transmission. This chapter aims to explore the intergenerational transmission of criminal behaviour by employing the semi-parametric, group-based trajectories methodology (Nagin, 2005). Trajectories encompass frequency as well as other criminal career parameters such as the age of onset and peak offending age. Instead of timing in the child's life, this chapter investigates timing of criminal behaviour in the parent's own life. Based on the mechanisms described in the Introduction and as discussed in the previous chapter (see page 41), one would expect intergenerational transmission to be stronger for more persistent offenders.

---

* An earlier version of this chapter was published as S. Besemer and D.P. Farrington (2012). Intergenerational transmission of criminal behaviour: conviction trajectories of fathers and their offspring. *European Journal of Criminology, 9*, 120-141.

Apart from studying the frequency of parent's offending and timing in the child's life, it is important to consider timing in the parent's life. Deviant behaviour peaks in adolescence (Blumstein et al., 1986; Farrington, 1986; Piquero et al., 2007) and it is quite common to display some antisocial behaviour during this period. It is, however, a sign of greater deviance if such behaviour continues after adolescence. Moffitt (1993) describes this as adolescence-limited versus life-course persistent offending. According to Moffitt (1993, p. 674), many adolescents display antisocial behaviour to bridge a temporary 'maturity gap'. They actually mimic the behaviour of life-course-persistent offenders, who have been displaying antisocial behaviour since they were much younger. Moffitt (1993) states that life-course-persistents' antisocial behaviour has an early onset and will continue until much later in life due to biological and neuropsychological problems. Her theory is linked to ideas of grouping offenders according to different life-course trajectories (Nagin, Farrington & Moffitt, 1995; Nagin & Land, 1993). Depending on the population studied, three to six groups of offenders have been identified: one group will never be convicted; one or more groups will only display antisocial behaviour during adolescence (the earlier mentioned adolescence-limiteds); one or more groups will exhibit delinquent behaviour throughout their lives (either low- or high-level chronics); and there might be a late-onset group of offenders (Blokland, Nagin & Nieuwbeerta, 2005; Fergusson, Horwood & Nagin, 2000; Nagin et al., 1995; Nagin & Land, 1993; Piquero, 2008; Van der Geest, Blokland & Bijleveld, 2009; Wiesner & Windle, 2004).

It is important to deal with behavioural heterogeneity that might exist in a population (Piquero et al., 2001). Different groups of people might follow different patterns of criminal behaviour. These various developmental pathways might require different etiological explanations. Farrington (1999, p. 156) states that:

> most prior criminal career research treats offenders as homogeneous, but different types of people may have different types of careers [...]. Research is needed on what are the most useful typologies of offenders, and on their different developmental pathways to criminal careers.

Similarly, intergenerational transmission might be different for parents with different criminal behaviour trajectories. For example, based on Moffitt's theory (1993) one would expect intergenerational transmission to be stronger for life-course-persistent than for adolescence-limited parents for three reasons. First, her theory explains life-course-persistents' antisocial behaviour as having a biological origin, and this hereditary basis could be passed on to children. Some studies (Waldman, Levy & Hay, 1995) indeed found that antisocial behaviour that is earlier in onset is more heritable, although others did not (Slutske et al., July 1997). Second, a life-course-persistent parent will display more delinquent behaviour and will therefore be a stronger criminal role model for children according to social learning theories. Third, police and justice bodies might be more strongly biased against families with life-course-persistent offenders. With life-course-persistent parents one would thus expect a stronger nurture as well as nature base for this behaviour and therefore a stronger transmission.

By investigating whether intergenerational transmission is different for people whose parents have different conviction trajectories, this chapter aims to link research into criminal careers and life-course trajectories with the study of intergenerational transmission. West and Farrington (1977) previously studied the impact of the number of parental convictions in the *Cambridge Study in Delinquent Development* (CSDD). They found that fathers with one conviction only and fathers with two or more convictions had the same proportion of convicted sons. However, they did not examine the trajectory of these convictions. Previous research in intergenerational transmission often relates any life-time offending by the parent to any life-time offending by the child (e.g. Farrington et al., 2001; Rowe & Farrington, 1997; Thornberry, 2005; Thornberry et al., 2003). An exception is the study by Van de Rakt et al. (2008) that investigated the trajectories of both parents and children. They found that children whose fathers belong to a more persistent trajectory group are more likely to also be in such a trajectory group. Slutske et al. (July 1997) also found that persistent antisocial behaviour is more heritable than antisocial behaviour that is limited to either childhood or adulthood. Van de Rakt et al. (2008), however, do not test whether the relationship between trajectories of fathers and children is significant, nor do they give an effect size for this relationship. These authors observe that more research on this topic is needed; replication of the results would be desirable. Furthermore, Van de Rakt et al. (2008) describe several disadvantages of previous studies in intergenerational transmission, such as small samples and retrospective designs, no measures of parental influence on their children after adolescence, lack of females in the sample, lack of a control group, and an abundance of descriptive tests without any theory testing. In line with this, the current chapter will investigate intergenerational transmission in trajectories using the *CSDD* in an attempt to overcome some of these disadvantages.

Previous studies linking any lifetime offending of the parents and children or using a summary variable for offending by parents and children make inefficient use of longitudinal data. By employing trajectory analysis (Nagin, 2005) to link parents' and children's criminal behaviour, better use is made of longitudinal data. This approach is an important advance because it captures the dynamic dimension of offending behaviour by summarising its developmental course in the form of trajectory groups (Nagin, 2005). As Nagin (2005, p. 146) argues, the 'result is a far richer summary of the pattern of interconnection' in the developmental course of parents' and children's behaviour.

4.2 Hypotheses

Using this method, the following hypotheses will be tested in this chapter:

1. Children of more persistent offending fathers will have more convictions than children of more sporadic offending fathers.

2. Father and offspring trajectories are similar.

3. *Non-offending* father trajectories tend to predict *non-offending* child trajectories.

4. Fathers and offspring will have similar *offending* trajectories (as opposed to *non-offending* trajectories).

Initially, the intention was to estimate trajectory models for mothers as well. However, model estimation did not yield reliable results, because mothers had few convictions. Therefore, I chose to focus on fathers only.

4.3 Method

4.3.1 Sample

These hypotheses were tested using data from both the *Cambridge Study in Delinquent Development* (CSDD) and the *NSCR-Transfive Study* (Transfive). These were described in more detail in the Introduction (see page 13). The current investigation examined fathers, sons and daughters from the *CSDD* and fathers and sons from *Transfive*. It was not possible to reliably estimate models for mothers in either data set or for daughters in *Transfive*. In *Transfive*, there were 37 daughters with convictions, of which three were outliers with respectively 36, 62, and 89 convictions between the 12th and 40th birthdays. There were another two outliers with 7 convictions when they were aged 39 that significantly disturbed the model as well. This led to 32 remaining daughters, of whom the majority had just one (20 women) or two (9 women) convictions. This sample was not diverse and large enough to reliably estimate trajectory models and therefore it was decided to not use trajectories for daughters in *Transfive*.

4.3.2 Measures

Outcome Variables

The outcome variable for hypothesis 1 was the offspring's conviction rate, defined as the number of convictions for crimes committed between the 12th and 40th birthdays. The outcome variable for hypotheses 2, 3, and 4 is the offspring's trajectory, defined by Group-Based Trajectory Modelling.

Method 63

Predictor Variable

The predictor variable was the father's offending trajectory, defined by Group-Based Trajectory Modelling.[20]

4.3.3 Analytic Approach

Analytic Approach: Semi-Parametric Group-Based Trajectory Modelling

Group-based modelling was performed using the SAS macro *proc traj* (Jones & Nagin, 2007; Jones, Nagin & Roeder, 2001). Separate trajectories were estimated for fathers, sons and daughters. Rather than assuming an average age-crime curve for every individual, Nagin and Land's (1993) semi-parametric group-based modelling approach identifies a number of different groups of individuals who display similar behavioural trajectories. This technique allows variation between groups of individuals and allows for different age-crime curves. See Nagin (2004b) for a non-technical overview of the group-based modelling technique.

A zero-inflated Poisson model was used. The distribution of the number of convictions is skewed since convictions are relatively rare events; i.e. there are many people with zero convictions or a low number of convictions. Using an inflation parameter allows subjects to have '"temporary" spells of non-offending without recording a change in their overall rate of offending' (Bushway, Thornberry & Krohn, 2003, p. 138).

If people died or were in prison for a whole year during the observation period, i.e. before the age of 40, this was controlled for; unobserved years were coded as missing and did not contribute to estimating the trajectories.[21]

---

[20] Similar to the analyses in Chapter 2 and as explained in the Introduction, in *Transfive* policy dismissals were included in the count of convictions as they were registered by the judicial authorities. They were included in offspring offending behaviour and in the analysis to indentify trajectory groups among fathers. However, when investigating intergenerational transmission, fathers with only dismissals were categorised as non-offending fathers to make the Dutch analyses comparable to the English analyses, because dismissals were never counted in the *CSDD*. Analyses for *Transfive* were also run including the dismissals and results were comparable. When results differed, this is indicated under the Results section.

[21] The trajectories were also estimated while correcting for time spent imprisoned if this was less than a year. The time spent imprisoned was accounted for and the corrected rate of offending was calculated with the following formula (Van der Geest et al., 2009):

$$\text{Corrected rate of offending} = \frac{\textit{off}_{tj}}{\textit{Exposure}_{tj}}$$

$$\textit{Exposure}_{tj} = 1 - \frac{\textit{Number of days incarcerated}}{365}$$

And

$$\textit{Exposure}_{tj} = 1 - \frac{\textit{Number of days incarcerated}}{730}$$

It was decided, however, to use the models without this correction. Models estimated with a corrected rate of offending gave roughly the same results, which confirms previous trajectory

It is important to control for mortality to prevent the problem of 'false desistance', where it would look as though someone had desisted whereas in fact the person had passed away (Eggleston et al., 2004, p. 23).

The goal of trajectory analysis is to find the optimal solution where groups of individuals with distinctive individual-level trajectories can be identified, but where adding an additional group to the model offers no extra explanatory power (Nagin, 2005). Selection of models is based on formal statistical criteria and on interpretability of the models. The test used to determine the optimal number of groups is the Bayesian Information Criterion (BIC). BIC gives an indication of model fit based on differences between the estimated model and the observations, but also corrects for the number of parameters fitted and for the number of observations. BIC estimates model fit, but also looks at how parsimonious the model is; the lower the number of trajectory groups, the better. For deciding on the number of classes, one chooses the model that maximises BIC, and since BIC is always negative, this will be the value closest to zero. This number is an indicator of the difference between the model and the observed data, and that difference should be as small as possible (D'Unger et al., 1998). *Proc traj* produces two BIC values: one for a smaller sample size, one for a larger sample size. The smaller sample size reflects the number of people in the sample, while the larger sample size pertains to the total number of assessments used in the model estimation across individuals and time (Nagin, 2005). So, in this case, the larger sample size will be the number of people multiplied by the number of years for which we know their number of convictions (every year from age 12 to 39). Neither BIC value is better than the other, it is important to take both into account. If the BIC values pointed to different models as the optimal solution, I chose the model that was most parsimonious: the model with the lowest number of trajectory groups. Furthermore, the content and shape of the trajectories is important in choice and interpretation of the models. Models with trajectories that have no reasonable interpretation or with trajectories that are not distinctive are of little use. Hence, after inspecting the BIC, it is important to inspect the content and shape of the trajectories.

After estimating which model describes the sample best, it is possible to use the posterior probability of group membership to measure the probability that an individual might belong to a specific trajectory group (Nagin, 2005). Using the highest probability, *proc traj* will assign every individual to a specific group.[22]

---

analyses with the original men of the *CSDD* (Piquero, et al. 2010). Correcting for incarceration is most common with offender samples, where everyone offended (Piquero, 2008). It is less common with a (high risk) population sample, such as the *CSDD*. On the one hand, it is important to correct for time spent imprisoned because people are less likely to offend while imprisoned (Eggleston, Laub & Sampson, 2004; Piquero et al., 2001). On the other hand, people can and do still offend while they are in prison. Neither solution, correcting versus not correcting, is optimal and entirely reflects the *true* situation.

22 This is one way of assigning individuals to groups, which L. A. Goodman (2007) calls modal assignment. L. A. Goodman also demonstrates an approach (for Latent Class Analysis) in

Analytic Approach: Generalised Estimating Equations (GEE)

After assigning people to classes, the hypotheses were analysed using Generalized Estimating Equations (GEE) (see the Introduction, page 16 for more information). For hypothesis 1 negative binomial regression was used because the outcome variable frequency of offspring offending was highly skewed; many people had never been convicted. To compare fathers' and offspring's trajectories (hypothesis 2) ordinal probit regression was used, which gives a χ^2. Pearson's χ^2 test examines whether two categorical variables, in this case the fathers' and offspring's trajectory memberships, are related to each other (Field, 2005). Adjusted Standardised Residuals (ASRs) were calculated to identify which groups were responsible for significant differences.[23] A residual greater than 2.0 was considered to indicate a significantly higher proportion than expected, and a residual less than -2.0 was taken to indicate a significantly lower proportion than expected if there was no relationship between fathers' and offspring's trajectory groups (Bursik, 1980; Haberman, 1973). Furthermore, odds ratios were calculated to test whether different types of father offending trajectories predict different types of offspring offending trajectories (hypothesis 4).

4.4 Results

In this section, I first present the model estimation for fathers, after which offspring of the different groups of fathers are compared. After estimating models for sons and daughters, the resemblance between trajectories of fathers and sons and of fathers and daughters is presented. For each section, I will first discuss results for the *CSDD* and then for *Transfive*.

4.4.1 Fathers' conviction trajectories - England

In the *CSDD* sample of 397 fathers, 92 (23.2%) had a conviction between their 12th and 40th birthdays. Of the convicted fathers, 53.2% had one con-

---

which people with a similar response pattern are *randomly* assigned to a class to get the proportions of the probabilities of group membership. For example, if individuals with a certain response pattern have a probability of .8 to be in a certain class A and .2 to be in a certain class B, following the modal assignment, all these individuals would be classified as class A. Following the random assignment, 80% of these people will be classified as A, 20% as B. Modal assignment minimizes incorrect classifications, while random assignment approximates the proportion of individuals in each group to be the posterior probability of group membership. Random assignment takes the uncertainty of group classification into account. When we assign people to classes in *proc traj* to be able to calculate with them, modal assignment is used and the group uncertainty is ignored. Currently, however, this is the only way in *proc traj* to assign people to classes.

23 It was not possible to calculate ASRs using GEE. To account for the fact that the sample consisted of fathers with multiple children, ASRs were calculated for samples where one child was randomly chosen for every father. The ASR values reported are the mean value of fifty randomly taken samples.

Figure 4.1: Age-crime curves for fathers' convictions - England

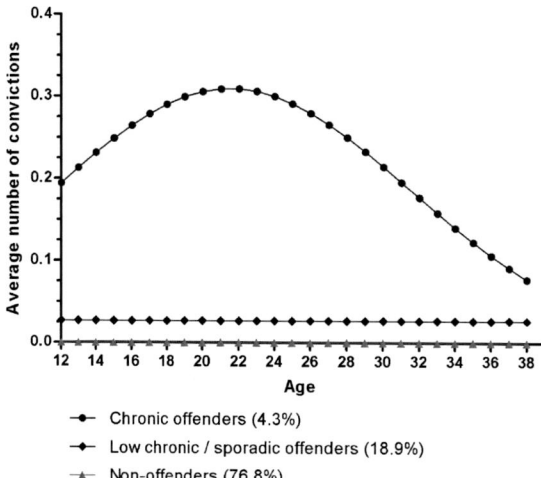

viction, 19.6 % had two convictions, 15.2 % had three to five convictions and 12.0 % had six convictions or more.

First, trajectories for fathers were estimated. Following Nagin (2005), model selection consisted of two steps. Model estimation began with models comprising three groups or more. In the first step a decision was made about the number of groups in the model. The second step concerned the shape of each group's trajectory within the chosen model. A trajectory shape can be zero (non-offending), flat, linear, quadratic or cubic (for more technical information see Nagin, 2005). In the first step, the model search began with models composed of quadratic trajectories. The low BIC pointed towards a four-group model, the high BIC to a three-group model (see Appendix). In the second step, three-group models with different kinds of trajectories were estimated. A three-group model with one non-offending (with an actual and predicted delinquency of 0), one intercept-only and one quadratic trajectory appeared to be the best estimation for this sample of fathers.

The resulting model is presented in figure 4.1. For ease of reporting, the three groups are labelled as follows: non-offending fathers (NO), low chronic or sporadic offenders (LC), and chronic offenders (CO). Non-offending fathers (76.8 %) had no convictions. Sporadic offenders (18.9 %) had on average 1.5 convictions. Chronic offenders (4.3 %) had relatively many convictions (on average 6.5) over the whole observation period with a peak during the late teens and early twenties.

4.4.2 Fathers' conviction trajectories - the Netherlands

In the *Transfive* sample of 351 fathers, 91 (25.9 %) had a conviction between their 12th and 40th birthdays. Of these fathers, 50.5 % had one conviction,

Results

Figure 4.2: Age-crime curves for fathers' convictions - the Netherlands

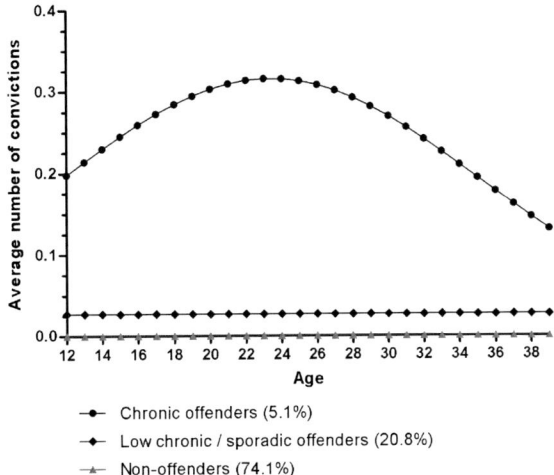

24.2 % had two convictions, 9.9 % had three to five convictions and 15.4 % had six convictions or more.[24]

Model estimation for *Transfive* fathers also began with models comprising three groups or more. In the first step, the model search began with models composed of quadratic trajectories. Both BIC values pointed towards a three-group model (see Appendix). In the second step, three-group models with different kinds of trajectories were estimated. The low BIC value pointed towards a model with one non-offending (with an actual and predicted delinquency of 0) and two quadratic trajectories. The high BIC value pointed towards a model with one non-offending, one intercept-only and one quadratic trajectory. Since this last model is similar to the model found with the CSDD, this model was chosen to continue doing analyses with.

The resulting model is presented in figure 4.2. The three groups are labelled as follows: non-offending fathers (NO), low chronic or sporadic offenders (LC), and chronic offenders (CO). Non-offending fathers (74.1 %) had no convictions. Sporadic offenders (20.8 %) had on average 1.4 convictions. Chronic offenders (5.1 %) had relatively many convictions (on average 7.4) over the whole observation period, showing a declining trend.[25]

---

24 These numbers include dismissals. When excluding dismissals, 86 fathers (24.5 %) had a conviction between their 12th and 40th birthdays. Of the convicted fathers, 52.3 % had one conviction, 20.9 % had two convictions, 10.5 % had three to five convictions and 16.3 % had six convictions or more.

25 Again, these numbers include dismissals. Furthermore, five fathers who, based on the estimation including dismissals, were included in the low/sporadic offending group, are included in the non-offending group for the following analyses. Including these five fathers in the non-offending trajectory group and excluding dismissals, non-offending fathers (75.5 %) had no convictions, while sporadic offenders (19.4 %) had on average 1.4 convictions and chronic offenders (5.1 %) had on average 7.2 convictions.

4.4.3 Offspring offending behaviour per father trajectory group

In the *CSDD*, offspring of sporadic (LC) and chronic (CO) fathers have a higher conviction rate than offspring of non-offenders (table 4.1). However, the difference in conviction rates between offspring of LC and CO fathers is not significant.[26] In *Transfive*, offspring of sporadic (LC) and chronic (CO) fathers also have a higher conviction rate than offspring of non-offenders, but none of the differences between the groups is significant.[27] Hypothesis 1 stated that offspring of more persistent offenders will have more convictions than offspring of more sporadic offending fathers. The groups found in this sample cannot necessarily be described as the adolescent-limited and life-course persistent groups described by Moffitt (1993), because the sporadic offender group tends to offend during the whole lifetime as well. One could say, however, that the sporadic offender group is a less serious group than the chronic offender group and hence, one could expect stronger intergenerational transmission. However, the current results do not provide convincing evidence for this hypothesis, because there is no significant difference between offspring of sporadic and chronic offenders.

4.4.4 Sons' conviction trajectories - England

To test the other hypotheses, conviction trajectories were estimated for sons in both samples and for daughters in the *CSDD*. In the *CSDD*, the sample contained 782 sons, of whom 323 (41.3%) had a conviction between their 12th and 40th birthdays.[28] Of the convicted sons, 35.6% had one conviction, 18.3% had two convictions, 21.0% had three to five convictions and 25.1% had six convictions or more.

In the first step of model estimation for *CSDD* sons, a five-group model resulted in the best BIC value (see Appendix). In the second step, several five-group models were compared and a model with two flat and three quadratic lines gave the best BIC value for this sample of sons. The resulting model is presented in figure 4.3. The five groups are labelled as follows: non-offenders

---

[26] The *p*-value signifies an almost significant difference for all offspring and for males ($p=.061$ and .052), but closer inspection of the data revealed that this is due to an outlier with 38 convictions. Removing this outlier from the analyses results in a B-value of 0.43 (95% CI -0.13-1.00, $p=.135$) for all children and a B-value of 0.51 (95% CI -0.11-1.13, $p=.108$) for males only. Furthermore, inspection of the prevalence and frequency of offspring offending separately revealed even smaller differences between the two groups of offspring.

[27] Using the trajectory groups without excluding the fathers with dismissals only, there was a significant difference between offspring of non-offending fathers (CR=0.56, SD=1.90) and offspring of low/sporadic fathers (CR=1.01, SD=2.64), B=0.60, 95%CI 0.05-1.15, $p=.033$.

[28] The prevalence of convictions is higher among sons than among fathers. As West and Farrington (1977) note, this can be explained by two things. First, when fathers were in their peak age of offending, the rate of convictions in the general population was lower; fewer people were convicted than when sons were in their peak age of offending. This pattern is visible in both studies. Second, fathers were all family men at some point. Therefore they are less likely to have a conviction than the sample of sons which would also include males with no family ties (Sampson & Laub, 2005; Theobald & Farrington, 2009).

Table 4.1: Offspring conviction rate between 12th and 40th birthdays per father trajectory group

	Trajectory group fathers																	
	Non-offending			Low / sporadic			Chronic			NO-LC			NO-CO			LC-CO		
	N	CR	(SD)	N	CR	(SD)	N	CR	(SD)	B	95 % CI	Sig.	B	95 % CI	Sig.	B	95 % CI	Sig.
England																		
All offspring	833	0.86	(2.53)	273	2.14	(4.10)	78	3.86	(6.81)	0.95 *	0.59- 1.30	.001	1.51 *	0.91- 2.11	.001	0.57	-0.03- 1.16	.061
Males	552	1.20	(2.97)	178	2.98	(4.74)	52	5.35	(7.89)	0.93 *	0.56- 1.30	.001	1.57 *	0.95- 2.20	.001	0.63	-0.01- 1.27	.052
Females	281	0.20	(0.98)	95	0.57	(1.60)	26	0.88	(1.45)	1.04 *	0.18- 1.91	.019	1.41 *	0.46- 2.37	.004	0.33	-0.63- 1.28	.505
The Netherlands																		
All offspring	601	0.59	(1.93)	149	0.91	(2.61)	43	0.79	(2.11)	0.46	-0.13- 1.05	.125	0.24	-0.53- 1.00	.546	-0.19	-.106- 0.68	.667
Males	312	0.96	(2.42)	79	1.42	(2.94)	15	1.93	(3.28)	0.38	-0.22- 0.98	.211	0.67	-0.12- 1.46	.094	0.29	-0.60- 1.18	.520
Females	289	0.19	(1.09)	70	0.34	(2.05)	28	0.18	(0.48)	0.57	-0.95- 2.09	.462	-0.08	-1.16- 0.99	.879	-0.64	-2.25- 0.98	.442

* p<.05; 95 % CI, 95 % Confidence interval; CO, chronic offending fathers; CR, conviction rate; N, number of offspring; NO, non-offending fathers; LC, low or sporadic offending fathers; PC, parental conviction; SD, standard deviation.

Figure 4.3: Age-crime curves for sons' convictions - England

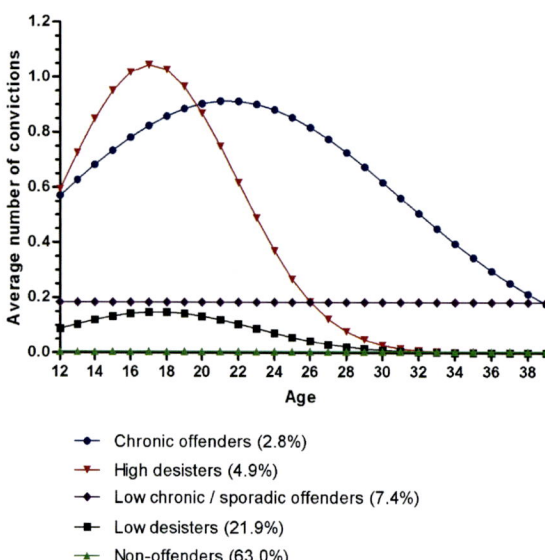

- Chronic offenders (2.8%)
- High desisters (4.9%)
- Low chronic / sporadic offenders (7.4%)
- Low desisters (21.9%)
- Non-offenders (63.0%)

(NO - 63.0%) who had no or a single conviction; low desisters (LD - 21.9%) who had on average 2 convictions during their teens and early twenties and then desisted from committing crime; low chronic offenders (LC - 7.4%) who continued to have convictions (on average 5) over the whole life-course; high desisters (HD - 4.9%) who had relatively many convictions (on average 11) during their teens and early twenties and then desisted; and chronic offenders (CO - 2.8%) who had relatively many convictions (on average 18) over the whole observation period with a peak during the late teens and early twenties. These five groups are similar to the ones found previously for the original men in the *CSDD* (Piquero et al., 2007).

4.4.5 Sons' conviction trajectories - the Netherlands

The *Transfive* sample consisted of 409 sons, of whom 138 (33.7%) had a conviction between their 12th and 40th birthdays.[29] Of the convicted sons, 50.0% had one conviction, 15.2% had two convictions, 14.5% had three to five convictions and 20.3% had six convictions or more.[30]

In the first step, models were estimated in which all groups were quadratic. The high BIC value pointed to a three-group model, the low BIC value

---

29 Three outliers were excluded from the analyses, because they had 25, 60 and 67 convictions between their 12th and 40th birthdays. This meant that there were years in which someone had 24 convictions. The mean number of convictions per year was around 1-3, and averages around 3 always included such an outlier. I estimated models with and without outliers, but including these outliers disturbed model estimation. Therefore these three people were excluded from the analyses.
30 All numbers for sons include policy dismissals.

Results   71

Figure 4.4: Age-crime curves for sons' convictions - the Netherlands

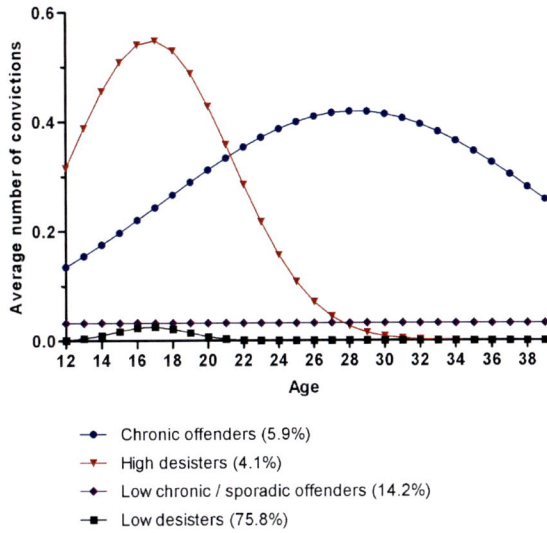

pointed to a five-group model. Since these values reached such different conclusions, models were subsequently estimated with at least one intercept-only group. The high BIC value pointed to a four-group model, the low BIC value to a five-group model. In the second step, three-group as well as four-group models were estimated, and a four-group model with one intercept-only and three quadratic groups appeared to have the best BIC value for this sample of sons. The resulting model is presented in figure 4.4. The four groups are labelled as follows: low desisters (LD - 75.8%) who had no convictions or a single conviction during their teens and early twenties and then desisted from committing crime; low chronic offenders (LC - 14.2%) who continued to have convictions (on average 1.6) over the whole life course; high desisters (HD - 4.1%) who had relatively many convictions (on average 5.7) during their teens and early twenties and then desisted; and chronic offenders (CO - 5.9%) who had relatively many convictions (on average 9) over the whole observation period with a peak during the late teens and early twenties. The shapes of these four groups are similar to the groups found with the *CSDD*, though the average number of convictions per year is lower than in the *CSDD* model. The model for *CSDD* sons also included a clear non-offending trajectory. This trajectory seems to be combined with the low desisting group in *Transfive*. Furthermore, the frequency of offending in the chronic offender group in *Transfive* appears to increase until the late twenties (peak around 28-29 years old), while offending in the chronic group in the *CSDD* starts declining from the early twenties (peak around 21-22 years old). Models with a specific non-offender group in *Transfive* were estimated, but this did not lead to a better model fit.

Figure 4.5: Age-crime curves for daughters' convictions - England

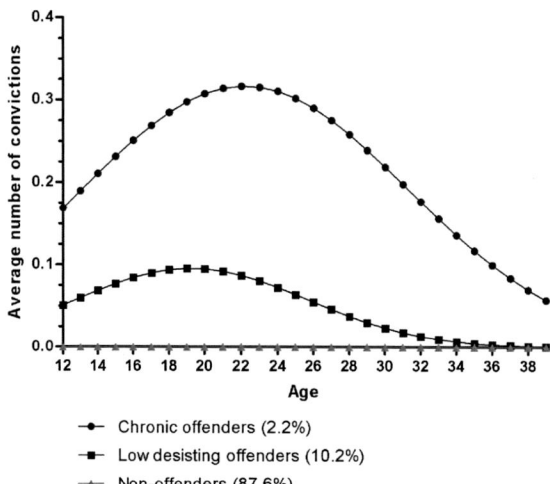

4.4.6 Daughters' conviction trajectories - England

The sample contained 402 daughters, of whom 50 (12.4%) had a conviction between their 12th and 40th birthdays. Of the convicted daughters, 42.0% had one conviction, 22.0% had two convictions, 26.0% had three to five convictions and 10.0% had six convictions or more.

Similar to fathers and sons, the model search for daughters began with models composed of quadratic trajectories. This pointed towards a model with three groups (see Appendix). A three-group model with one non-offending group and two quadratic curves gave the best BIC value for three-group models. The resulting model is presented in figure 4.5. The three groups are labelled as follows: non-offenders (NO - 87.6%) who had no convictions; low desisting offenders (LD - 10.2%) who had on average 2 convictions and desisted in their twenties; and chronic offenders (CO - 2.2%) who had relatively many convictions (on average 7) over the whole observation period with a peak during the late teens and early twenties.

4.4.7 Intergenerational resemblance of conviction trajectories

After modelling offspring trajectories, these were compared with fathers' trajectories. For the *CSDD*, proportions of sons for every combination of father and son trajectory group are presented in table 4.2. The proportions of sons per group of fathers and the ASRs are presented in table 4.3. The overall association between fathers' and sons' trajectories was significant ($\chi^2(1) = 29.31, p < .001$).

Table 4.2: Resemblance between fathers and sons: percentages of group membership for fathers and sons - England

	Father's trajectory						
	Non-offenders		Low offenders		Chronic offenders		
Son's trajectory	N	%	N	%	N	%	Total %
Non-offenders	387	49.5	85	10.9	21	2.7	63.0
Low desisting	112	14.3	49	6.3	21	1.3	21.9
Low chronic	29	3.7	21	2.7	8	1.0	7.4
High desisting	17	2.2	14	1.8	7	0.9	4.9
High chronic	7	0.9	9	1.2	6	0.8	2.8
		70.6		22.8		6.6	100

Table 4.3: Resemblance between fathers' and sons' groups: proportion of sons per father group and Adjusted Standardised Residuals - England

		Father's trajectory			
Son's trajectory		Non-offenders	Low offenders	Chronic offenders	Total
Non-offenders	%	70.1	47.8	40.4	63.0
	ASR	4.8*	-3.6*	-2.6*	
Low desisting	%	20.3	27.5	19.2	21.9
	ASR	-1.9	1.9	0.3	
Low chronic	%	5.3	11.8	15.4	7.4
	ASR	-1.9	1.3	1.4	
High desisting	%	3.1	7.9	13.5	4.9
	ASR	-2.2*	1.3	2.1*	
High chronic	%	1.3	5.1	11.5	2.8
	ASR	-3.3*	2.3*	2.4*	
Total		100.0%	100.0%	100.0%	

% = percentage of column, per father group; ASR = Adjusted Standardised Residual; * p<.05

This value gives an indication for the whole table, but does not say much about the specific relationships. The ASRs demonstrate that non-offending (NO) fathers have a significantly higher proportion of non-offending (NO) sons and a significantly lower proportion of high desisting (HD) and chronic offending (CO) sons. This pattern is reversed for chronic offending (CO) fathers; they have a significantly higher proportion of HD and CO sons, but a significantly lower proportion of NO sons. Low chronic offending (LC) fathers have a significantly lower proportion of NO sons and a significantly higher proportion of CO sons. LC fathers appear to have a higher proportion of LC and HD sons than expected, but this is not significant. Moreover, the proportion of LC or HD sons among LC fathers and CO fathers does not differ significantly from each other (7.9% versus 13.5% and 5.1% versus 11.5%, OR=1.91, 95% CI: 0.60-6.10 and OR=2.43, 95% CI: 0.70-8.48). These results suggest that chronic offending fathers are no better than low chronic offending fathers at predicting chronic offending sons.

For *Transfive*, proportions of sons for every combination of father and son trajectory group are presented in table 4.4. The proportions of sons per group of fathers and the ASRs are presented in table 4.5. The over-

Table 4.4: Resemblance between fathers and sons: percentages of group membership for fathers and sons - the Netherlands

	Father's trajectory						
	Non-offenders		Low offenders		Chronic offenders		
Son's trajectory	N	%	N	%	N	%	Total %
Low desisting	243	59.9	56	13.8	10	2.5	76.1
Low chronic	42	10.3	13	3.2	2	0.5	14.0
High desisting	15	3.7	1	0.2	1	0.2	4.2
High chronic	3.0	12	9	2.2	2	0.5	5.7
		76.8		19.5		3.7	100

Table 4.5: Resemblance between fathers' and sons' groups: proportion of sons per father group and Adjusted Standardised Residuals - the Netherlands

		Father's trajectory			
Son's trajectory		Non-offenders	Low offenders	Chronic offenders	Total
Low desisting	%	77.9	70.9	66.7	76.1
	ASR	2.0*	-1.4	-0.7	
Low chronic	%	13.5	16.5	13.3	14.0
	ASR	-0.8	0.9	-0.1	
High desisting	%	4.8	1.3	6.7	4.2
	ASR	0.4	-0.6	0.2	
High chronic	%	3.8	11.4	13.3	5.7
	ASR	-2.1*	1.7	1.2	
Total		100.0%	100.0%	100.0%	

% = percentage of column, per father group; ASR = Adjusted Standardised Residual; * p < .05

all association between fathers' and sons' trajectories was just significant (χ^2 (1) = 3.965, p = .046). The ASRs demonstrate that non-offending (NO) fathers have a significantly higher proportion of non-offending (LD) sons and a significantly lower proportion of chronic offending (CO) sons. None of the other ASRs is significant. Furthermore, the proportion of LC or HD sons among LC fathers and CO fathers does not differ significantly from each other (1.3% versus 6.7% and 11.4% versus 13.3%, OR = 5.64, 95% CI: 0.36-89.10 and OR = 1.22, 95% CI: 0.24-6.10). These results suggest that chronic offending fathers do not predict chronic offending sons better than low chronic offending fathers.

For both data sets, the significant χ^2 confirms hypothesis 2 that father and son trajectories are similar in some respects. Furthermore, the ASRs show that non-offending fathers tend to predict non-offending sons (although in *Transfive* this group is combined into one low desisting group), which confirms hypothesis 3. However, the odds ratios do not support hypothesis 4, that different types of father offending trajectories predict different types of offspring offending trajectories. Associations for the *CSDD* appear stronger than for *Transfive*.

A similar pattern was visible for fathers and daughters (table 4.6 and 4.7). The association between fathers and daughters' trajectories is signifi-

Table 4.6: Resemblance between fathers and daughters: percentages of group membership for fathers and daughters

	Father's trajectory						
	Non-offenders		Low offenders		Chronic offenders		
Daughter's trajectory	N	%	N	%	N	%	Total %
Non-offenders	257	63.9	78	19.4	17	4.2	87.6
Low desisting	21	5.2	12	3.0	8	2.0	10.2
Chronic offenders	3	0.7	5	1.2	1	0.2	2.2
		69.9		23.6		6.5	100

Table 4.7: Resemblance between fathers' and daughters' groups: proportion of daughters per father group and Adjusted Standardised Residuals

		Father's trajectory			
Daughter's trajectory		Non-offenders	Low offenders	Chronic offenders	Total
Non-offenders	%	91.5	82.1	65.4	87.6
	ASR	2.3*	-1.5	-1.8	
Low desisting	%	7.5	12.6	30.8	10.2
	ASR	-1.8	0.7	2.0*	
Chronic offenders	%	1.1	5.3	3.8	2.2
	ASR	-1.3	1.6	-0.1	
Total		100.0 %	100.0 %	100.0 %	

% = percentage of column, per father group; ASR = Adjusted Standardised Residual; * p < .05

cant ($\chi^2(1) = 13.76, p < .001$). The ASRs demonstrate that non-offending (NO) fathers have a significantly higher proportion of non-offending (NO) daughters than expected by chance. Chronic offending (CO) fathers have a significantly higher proportion of low desisting (LD) daughters. This proportion of LD daughters is also significantly higher than the proportion of LD daughters among low chronic offending (LC) fathers (30.8% versus 12.6%, OR = 2.99, 95% CI: 1.03, 8.68). Again, similar to the case of fathers' and sons' trajectories, CO fathers do not predict chronic offending (CO) daughters better than LC fathers. The significant relationship can be attributed mostly to the fact that non-offending fathers have non-offending daughters, while offending fathers (LC and CO) have offending daughters. The results for daughters also confirm hypotheses 2 and 3, but not hypothesis 4. The odds ratios actually show a counter-intuitive result: chronic offending fathers predict low desisting daughters.

Even though the GEE analyses demonstrate a significant relationship between fathers' and offspring's offending trajectories, more detailed analysis of the separate cells does not support hypothesis 4, that specific father offending trajectories predict similar specific offspring offending trajectories. They confirm the previous results for hypothesis 1, that offspring of fathers who have a more chronic conviction trajectory do not show more criminal behaviour than offspring of sporadically offending fathers.

4.5 Discussion

This study investigated intergenerational transmission by employing the group-based trajectories methodology. Three types of trajectories for fathers were found in the *Cambridge Study in Delinquent Development* as well as in the *NSCR Transfive Study*: non-offenders (NO), low chronic or sporadic offenders (LC), and chronic offenders (CO). Among daughters in the *CSDD*, three types were identified: non-offenders (NO), low desisters (LD), and chronic offenders (CO), and two additional groups were identified among *CSDD* sons: low chronic offenders (LC) and high desisters (HD). Among *Transfive* sons, offending groups were identified that were similar to those found among *CSDD* sons, although there was no clear non-offending group identified among *Transfive*. The main conclusions of this chapter are:

- Offspring of more persistent offending fathers do not have more convictions than offspring of sporadic offending fathers. In the *CSDD*, offspring of LC and CO fathers have significantly more convictions than offspring of NO fathers, but offspring of LC fathers do not differ significantly from offspring of CO fathers.

- Although father and offspring trajectories look similar, the significant relationship can be explained by the observation that non-offending father trajectories tend to predict non-offending child trajectories.

- Chronic offending (CO) fathers do not predict chronic offending (CO) or high desisting (HD) sons better than sporadic (LC) fathers.

- Surprisingly, chronic offending (CO) fathers predict low desisting (LD) daughters better than sporadic fathers. This is a result not expected based on the intergenerational theories.

The general conclusion from this study is that, surprisingly, the intensity of the father's career does not predict the intensity of the child's career. The results demonstrate a strong intergenerational transmission of criminal behaviour, but it is the fact that fathers have a conviction rather than what their conviction trajectory looks like that is related to offspring convictions. This confirms previous analyses with the *CSDD* original men, in which fathers with one conviction in adulthood or convictions as a juvenile only were compared with fathers with two convictions or more (West & Farrington, 1977).[31]

However, the results from this chapter do not confirm analyses from the previous chapter which showed that the frequency of parental convictions is significantly related to offspring conviction rate. Two reasons could explain

---

[31] The current study also checked whether results were different for the original *CSDD* men versus their brothers. Analyses run separately for the original men and for their brothers lead to the same conclusion; that there is no convincing support for the hypothesis that more persistent offenders have more persistent offending children.

this difference. First, in the trajectory analyses a dichotomy was created by comparing two groups of children from two *types* of fathers, whereas a continuous measure (number of convictions) was used in Chapter 3. When using a dichotomous measure, some subtlety in the variable is lost, and this could explain why no significant differences were found in this chapter. Second, in this chapter trajectories of *fathers only* were studied, while the frequency variable in Chapter 3 included convictions by mothers as well as fathers. Taking both parents into account is important, since they will both impact on their offspring's development (see for example Thornberry et al.'s (2009, Thornberry, 2009) research on the impact of fathers and mothers and ongoing contact with their offspring). The assortative mating concept (see Introduction, page 7) becomes relevant here, since transmission will be stronger when two parents have shown criminal behaviour. If one parent is criminal, but the other is not, this non-criminal parent could act as a protective factor in the offspring's development. Unfortunately it was not possible to examine the impact of fathers' and mothers' convictions separately in Chapter 3, because the number of mothers with a conviction was too low. It would be interesting to investigate the possibility of the different impact of fathers' versus mothers' convictions. As already discussed in Chapter 2 (see page 36), there is less criminal activity among women and intergenerational transmission and social learning may be stronger in same-gender relationships (Farrington, Barnes & Lambert, 1996).

What do these results mean for theories of intergenerational transmission? They confirm previous findings (see for example Bijleveld & Wijkman, 2009; Farrington et al., 2001; Ferguson, 1952; Gorman-Smith et al., 1998; Rowe & Farrington, 1997; Thornberry, 2005; H. Wilson, 1975) that demonstrate that having a convicted father increases the chance and the number of offspring convictions. However, contrary to what was expected based on taxonomic theories and theories on intergenerational transmission, there is no difference between offspring of sporadic and more persistent offenders. The trajectories found for fathers did not resemble the adolescent-limited versus life-course persistent offender groups as described by Moffitt (1993). However, the results did show two distinct offending trajectories, one of which displayed more chronic and frequent offending, but offspring of these chronic offenders did not exhibit significantly more criminal behaviour than offspring of sporadic offenders. This study was not able to test theories directly, but the results do not support the stronger biological, social learning and official bias influence as hypothesized in the Introduction of this chapter.

This study undoubtedly has limitations. As in the previous chapters, only official data have been used, and these suffer from a dark number: the part of offending that is not measured by official statistics (Bijleveld, 2007; Fisher & Ross, 2006; Maguire, 2007). The difference between official convictions and self-reported offending might be different for people with different conviction trajectories. Perhaps persistent offenders commit relatively more unseen offences compared with sporadic offenders. Or, seemingly adolescent limited-offenders might learn how to avoid getting caught as they get older. People who are included in the offending trajectories all have at least one conviction and thereby they are more homogeneous than the whole sample of fathers. It was not possible to discriminate or measure the offending of fathers without a conviction. It is likely that there are fathers without a conviction who have actually shown some kind of delinquent behaviour. If one would use self-reported data on offending, this would lead to a finer gradation of volume and timing of offending, and it is possible that this would lead to different results. Therefore, it would be interesting to investigate trajectories of offending with self-reported data on offending behaviour for both generations.

Second, the samples were relatively small, especially for females. More trajectory groups tend to be found when a sample consists of a greater number of convicted individuals and more measurements per individual (D'Unger et al., 1998; Eggleston et al., 2004; Nagin & Tremblay, 2005a). Generally, the number of groups identified is stable with a sample of over 300-500 individuals, so this study's sample sizes should be large enough (Nagin & Tremblay, 2005a). The difference in number of trajectory groups between (*CSDD*) sons versus fathers and daughters, however, could possibly be explained by the fact that the sample of sons is twice as large and that sons have more convictions than daughters or fathers. It would be interesting to amalgamate the sample of fathers and sons and estimate trajectory models for this combined group. This would facilitate comparison of father and son trajectories. I did try this alternative way of analysis using the *CSDD* and the resulting model was comparable to the model with five groups for sons. However, the number of fathers in some groups was extremely low. As a result it was not possible to compare the father and son models reliably. It would be interesting to estimate models for an amalgamated sample of parents and offspring in a larger data set with enough convictions for both generations. The number of mothers with convictions was even smaller: too small to identify a reliable model. It is unfortunate that it was not possible to examine mothers' trajectories, because intergenerational mechanisms might be different for males and females (see also page 36). Accordingly, it would be interesting to see whether investigating intergenerational resemblance of conviction trajectories from mothers to children would yield the same conclusion as for fathers. It would be desirable to replicate this research with a dataset that includes more females.

Third, it is important to realise that describing groups of people in terms of their trajectories does not mean that these categories are a perfect reflection of reality. Categorising people using the semi-parametric, group-based trajectory methodology is a way of describing the data. It is certainly no proof of the existence of clearly distinguishable groups that follow exactly the trajectory of the group they have been assigned to. Offenders are not species that exclusively belong to a certain type. The technique of trajectory modelling should be used as a heuristic tool and the results should not be perceived as the truth (Nagin, 2004a, 2005; Nagin & Land, 1993; Nagin & Tremblay, 2005a,b; Piquero, 2008; Skardhamar, 2010). An example is the finding that a model with four groups for the *Transfive* sons was the best estimation, which forced the 66.3 % of sons without a conviction in a group with another 9.5 % of sons with one conviction in adolescence. It would be more intuitive to have a clear non-offending group, but the technique decided that a model with a combined group described the data better. It is possible that a larger sample would have led to five trajectory groups (the sample of *Transfive* sons consisted of 409 males compared with 782 sons in the *CSDD*).

Despite these limitations, this study increased our knowledge on several points. Referring back to Van de Rakt et al.'s (2008) identification of the limitations of previous studies on intergenerational transmission, the current study improved on existing work by using large prospective samples including a control group with non-offending parents. Furthermore, fathers' and offspring's criminal behaviour was measured up until age forty. Additionally, this study improved on van de Rakt et al. by investigating the relationship between parent and offspring trajectories more closely by calculating ASRs for each combination and ORs comparing proportions of offspring in trajectory groups for different father trajectories. Thereby it demonstrated that, although there appears to be a relationship between father and offspring trajectories, this can be attributed to the finding that non-offending fathers have non-offending offspring, while fathers in conviction trajectories have more offspring in conviction trajectories. As mentioned previously, this has been known for decades. The current results contradict Van de Rakt et al. (2008), who concluded that offspring of fathers in a more persistent trajectory group have a higher chance of belonging to a similar trajectory group.

As far as is known to me, this and Van de Rakt et al.'s study are the only ones so far that have investigated intergenerational transmission by employing the semi-parametric, group-based trajectories methodology. Since these studies reach different conclusions, it is vital that this research is replicated, preferably with large samples including many females. This and Van de Rakt et al.'s study are the first step in unravelling intergenerational transmission using trajectories. These studies raise new questions and thus it is essential to investigate trajectories and intergenerational transmission in relationship to other factors such as types of offending, ongoing contact between parents and children and generalisability of the results to other circumstances.

4.6 Summary

This chapter investigated father and offspring criminal careers by employing the semi-parametric, group-based trajectories methodology. The findings demonstrate that offspring of sporadic and chronic offenders had significantly more convictions than offspring of non-offenders. However, contrary to expectations based on taxonomic and intergenerational theories, chronic offending fathers did not have more chronic offending offspring than sporadically offending fathers. The results demonstrate strong intergenerational transmission of criminal behaviour, but it is the fathers having a conviction rather than their conviction trajectory that was related to offspring convictions.

Chapter 5

Official bias in intergenerational transmission and the impact of labelling on criminal behaviour*

'Seeing dad get arrested... it's really hard. [...] Right when my bus pulled up they were bringing him out in handcuffs. It kind of embarrassed me, but I was just like, "You know, whatever." My dad didn't say nothing. He just got in the car. And I hate cops to this day. Because I seen them take my dad away. [...] but the way they arrested them was.. it wasn't right. They didn't have to stun him with the stun gun... not like that. That was not right.'

(Giordano, 2010, p. 99)

5.1 Introduction

In the preceding chapters of this dissertation I focused on characteristics of the offending behaviour and their relation to intergenerational transmission. In this chapter, I will shift the focus to the reaction of the police and justice agencies towards this offending behaviour and the impact of these reactions on offspring offending. One of the explanations Farrington (2011) proposes

---

* An edited version of this chapter was submitted as: S. Besemer, D.P. Farrington, and C.C.J.H. Bijleveld (submitted). Official bias in intergenerational transmission of criminal behaviour.

for intergenerational continuity of criminal behaviour is official bias. According to this mechanism official justice systems are biased against known criminal families. As a result, they pay more attention to these families, which means that family members are more likely to be caught and thus appear in official statistics more often. This explanation asserts that there is not necessarily a real transmission of behaviour; there only seems to be an association because children of convicted parents will be caught more frequently than children without convicted parents.

An important concept related to official bias in intergenerational transmission is labelling. Classic Labelling Theory proposes that people will act in accordance with the label attached to them by society (Becker, 1963; Lemert, 1967). This label might be a crucial event leading to a more persistent delinquent life course. Revised versions of Labelling Theory recognise two major theoretical perspectives of how an official label as delinquent might increase someone's criminal behaviour (Bernburg, 2009; Paternoster & Iovanni, 1989; Sampson & Laub, 1997). First, the label or stigma might influence someone's self-perception. Amplification of the deviant behaviour occurs as a result of conforming to the criminal stereotype. Sherman (1993, p. 459) proposed the concept of 'defiance'. He described how fairness and legitimacy (or procedural justice) of an imposed sentence are vital for the effectiveness of it. When individuals perceive a punishment as unfair, they can develop a certain pride that results in an increase of their criminal behaviour. Farrington (1977) and Murray, Blokland, Farrington & Theobald (forthcoming) indeed found an increase in hostility towards the police after a conviction.

Second, the criminal label might block conventional and non-criminal pathways and thereby pushes people into a criminal lifestyle. For example, people might have trouble finding a stable job when they have a criminal record (see for example Murray et al., forthcoming and Van der Geest, 2011). Bernburg and Krohn (2003) revealed that a conviction had a negative impact on educational attainment which in turn increased offending. This supports the idea of blocked conventional opportunities following a criminal label. Also, people might identify more with deviant social groups after receiving a criminal label (Bernburg, Krohn & Rivera, 2006). Previous studies on labelling effects have shown a considerable impact of convictions on subsequent criminal behaviour (Bernburg & Krohn, 2003; Farrington, 1977; Farrington, Osborn & West, 1978; Murray et al., forthcoming; West & Farrington, 1977).

This chapter aims to combine these two perspectives on official bias in intergenerational transmission and labelling effects. By doing this, it is important to distinguish these two concepts clearly. Official bias is defined in an intergenerational context; children of convicted parents have a higher risk of conviction because official justice systems pay more attention to these children. However, the number of self-reported offences of these children is not necessarily higher than of offspring of unconvicted parents. Labelling occurs when someone's offending behaviour increases after involvement in the criminal justice system, such as after an official conviction. I will first investigate whether official bias increases the risk of conviction for offspring with convicted parents and second, I will examine whether an offspring conviction increases individuals' offending behaviour. Moreover, the interaction between someone's own conviction and a convicted parent will be investigated. Below I will first discuss previous research on official bias and labelling.

5.2 Previous research on official bias and labelling

West and Farrington (1977) found support for official bias in the *Cambridge Study in Delinquent Development* (CSDD). They grouped sons according to four different levels of self-reported offending and then split these into two groups: parent convicted versus parent not convicted. At all levels of self-reported offending, boys with convicted fathers were more likely to be convicted themselves than were boys with unconvicted fathers. It does appear, however, that official bias is not the only explanation for intergenerational continuity in antisocial behaviour. West and Farrington (1977) also found that sons of convicted fathers, in addition to having more convictions, also showed a higher level of self-reported antisocial behaviour than sons of non-convicted parents. Additionally, Farrington (1979) investigated the relationship between self-reported offending and convictions and the influence of risk factors on this relationship. Most of these risk factors such as an erratic parental employment record, poor housing conditions and poor parental child- rearing were related to official convictions, but not to self-reported offending. More recently, Farrington (2001a) examined childhood predictors of adult violence measured by self-reports and official convictions. Having a convicted parent and coming from a low income family were more strongly related to convictions for violence than to self-reports, which supports the idea of official bias. However, low social class was related to self-reported violence, but not to convictions for violence. As far as I know, no other studies on official bias in intergenerational transmission of crime have been carried out.

That does not mean that bias in the justice system has not been studied. Several studies have been carried out on whether differential treatment exists in the justice system depending on race, gender, or social background (Daly, 1994; Hagan, 1974; Mitchell, 2005; Pratt, 1998; Pruitt & Wilson, 1983). The results are not always consistent, often depending on the research design, although some tendencies have been found. Females are less likely to be arrested than males and are at an advantage in several stages of delinquency case processing in the court (Bishop & Frazier, 1991; Sealock & Simpson, 1998; Spohn & Beichner, 2000). However, Daly (1989, 1994) has argued that this can be explained by defendants' familial relations. Numerous studies have shown that Black or Hispanic offenders are more likely to be arrested, convicted, and imprisoned (Bishop, 2005; Bishop & Frazier, 1996; P. K. Brennan & Spohn, 2008; Bridges & Crutchfield, 1988; Leiber & Johnson, 2008; Mitchell, 2005; Nelson, 1994; Petersilia, 1983, 1985; Sealock & Simpson, 1998; Wu & Fuentes, 1998). Though some studies did not find this bias (Huizinga et al., 2007; Jolliffe et al., 2003). Most relevant to bias in intergenerational transmission is that people from a low socio-economic background seem to be arrested disproportionately often (Sealock & Simpson, 1998; Wu & Fuentes, 1998). Farrington et al. (2003) also showed that courts might be biased against known offenders: continuity of offending was greater for court referrals than for self-reports. It seems surprising with the wealth of research into bias in the justice system, that there is such a paucity of research on bias against criminal families.

This study attempts to fill this gap by combining the approaches used previously to investigate official bias and by combining the two perspectives of official bias in intergenerational transmission and labelling effects. Hagan and Palloni (1990) attempted to link these two processes with their paper on the reproduction of a social class, but they focused on the latter of these two processes and did not examine whether the concept of official bias exists. Using data from the *Cambridge Study in Delinquent Development*, they investigated the impact of a conviction (son's labelling) and a parental conviction (parents' labelling: official bias). They found support for the idea of the 'social reproduction of a criminal class', a process in which the criminal justice system is responsible for the reproduction of criminal behaviour of offenders' children through their treatment of these children (Hagan & Palloni, 1990, p. 265). They demonstrated that the labelling effect was stronger for people with a convicted father compared with people whose fathers had not been convicted. Unfortunately, their design suffered from methodological flaws. They treated several measures of self-reported offending as independent, when this was not actually the case. For example, they treated self-reported offending at ages 16-17 as independent of self-reported offending at ages 14-15 and used self-reported offending at ages 16-17 to predict self-reported offending at ages 18-19. This is problematic, because self-reported offending at ages 16-17 is measured up to that age and therefore includes offences at ages 14-15. Similarly, self-reported offending at ages 16-17 overlaps with self-reported offending at ages 18-19 (which referred to the previous three years) and therefore it is not possible to treat them as independent variables. Because of these flaws, it is important to replicate this study using independent measures to investigate whether the effect found by Hagan and Palloni (1990) is valid.

Most studies examining labelling effects have investigated this only up to the age of 22, whereas this study will look at offending behaviour until age 32. An exception is the study by Murray et al. (forthcoming), who demonstrated robust relationships between juvenile conviction and adult criminal behaviour, antisocial personality and multiple life outcomes such as employment, relationships, and mental health up to age 48. It is important to look at offending behaviour into adulthood since offending after the early twenties might indicate a more serious offending pattern. Deviant behaviour peaks in adolescence (Blumstein et al., 1986; Farrington, 1986; Piquero et al., 2007) and it is quite common to display some antisocial behaviour during this period. It is, however, a sign of greater deviance if such behaviour continues after adolescence or starts in adulthood. It is vital to examine how labelling impacts offending in the long run.

More importantly, when studying labelling effects, it is crucial to observe the temporal sequence of the labelling event and subsequent deviant behaviour, while controlling for differences in deviant behaviour before the labelling event occurred. The majority of previous studies investigating labelling effects (Bernburg & Krohn, 2003; Bernburg et al., 2006; De Li, 1999; Farrington, 1977; Farrington et al., 1978; Stewart, Simons, Conger & Scaramella, 2002; West & Farrington, 1977) have failed to clearly distinguish these periods.[32] Bernburg and Krohn (2003), for example, measured official intervention at ages 13.5-16.5 while controlling for self-reported offending at ages 14-16. Another example is West and Farrington (1977, Farrington, 1977) who compared people with and without a conviction between ages 14-18 on their self-reported offending between these same ages (while controlling for self-reported offending before the age of 14).[33] By not separating these periods in time, it is unknown whether the self-reported offending behaviour measured has not already increased because of a conviction during this period. It is crucial to know people's self-reported offending behaviour before they were first convicted and compare the level of self-reported offending after the conviction. This study improves on previous research into labelling by clearly separating these periods in time.

Further, this study builds upon earlier research of official bias by looking at different variables that could bias police and other justice agencies against certain families. Besides parental convictions, other factors are also considered including poor housing conditions, low family income, low family socio-economic status (SES) and a father's poor employment record. People from lower class backgrounds, who live in poor housing, or whose fathers are unemployed might attract more attention from the police and justice agencies. These features may make children easily targetable and recognizable for the police (McAra & McVie, 2005). Furthermore, where previously official bias was investigated until age 21 (Farrington, 1979; West & Farrington,

---

[32] Kaplan and Johnson (1991) and Johnson et al. (2004) separated these periods clearly by investigating delinquency at time 1, justice system involvement at time 2 and delinquency at time 3. Murray et al. (forthcoming) also separate these periods well.

[33] West & Farrington (1977, Farrington, 1977) attempted to more clearly separate these periods by examining a small subset of people who were first convicted after age sixteen. They show some evidence of worsening behaviour after a conviction; their self-reported offending only started to deteriorate after age sixteen and not between fourteen and sixteen.

1977), this study will extend this into adulthood until age 32. After examining whether official bias exists and whether children of convicted parents have a higher risk of conviction, this study investigates whether a conviction subsequently increased these individuals' offending behaviour. Furthermore, the interaction between official bias and labelling will be investigated. Using data from the *Cambridge Study in Delinquent Development* (CSDD) the following hypotheses will be studied:

5.3 Hypotheses

1. The relationship between biasing variables (factors that could bias official justice agencies against certain families such as parental convictions, low family income, low family SES, poor housing conditions and a father's poor employment record) and offspring convictions is stronger than the relationship between biasing variables and offspring self-reported offending.

2. There is a significant relationship between biasing variables and offspring convictions, when controlling for self-reported offending.

3. A conviction subsequently increases the number of an individual's self-reported offences: there is a significant relationship between having a conviction between ages 19 and 26 and self-reported offending between ages 27 and 32, after controlling for the level of self-reported offending between ages 15 and 18.

4. This labelling effect is stronger for people whose parents have been convicted.

First, it is important to establish that parental convictions are more strongly related to offspring convictions than to offspring self-reported offending. When police and justice agencies are biased against certain families, one would expect the chance of offspring being caught and convicted to increase, but not necessarily the actual behaviour to increase (unless labelling effects occur, see hypothesis 3). It is important to distinguish between self-reported offending and official convictions. Measures of self-reported offending depend on the accuracy of memory, the willingness to admit, and the true extent of delinquent involvement, which is a hypothetical construct that cannot be measured directly. Self-reported offending is perceived as a reflection of the committed criminal behaviour, while convictions are a combination of the committed behaviour and the reactions of police and justice agencies. This distinction is important for the analyses in this chapter.

Several tests have been carried out in the *CSDD* to examine the validity of self-reports (Farrington, 1979, 1989; Farrington et al., 2006). Self-reported delinquency significantly predicts future criminal records of convictions. Furthermore, 91 % of delinquent acts leading to convictions were admitted in self-reports at age 14 and at age 18, 94% of convicted boys admitted that they had been convicted (Gibson, Morrison & West, 1970; West & Farrington, 1977). It appeared that participants responded truthfully and there were no signs of serious problems of deliberate concealment or distortion. Numerous other studies also showed that the validity of self-reports is generally acceptable according to traditional psychometric criteria (Jolliffe et al., 2003). This chapter investigates a sample of young white males, a category in which validity is generally highest (Farrington, 2001b; Jolliffe et al., 2003).[34] Throughout this chapter, self-reported offending is assumed to be a reflection of the actual committed criminal behaviour.

After examining whether biasing variables are more strongly related to offspring convictions than to self-reported behaviour, it is important to check that these variables significantly predict a conviction over and above the observation that people commit a certain amount of crime (hypothesis 2). To investigate this, self-reported offending needs to be held constant. In other words, the impact of a parent's conviction should be examined for people with comparable levels of self-reported offending. As discussed above, for this study it is assumed that self-reported offending can be perceived as a reflection of the committed criminal behaviour while convictions are a combination of this behaviour and the response of official agencies such as the police and courts. The discrepancy between these two measures thus reflects this official response. If there were no bias in the justice system, there should be no variation in the discrepancy between these measures. The risk of a conviction given a certain level of self-reported offending should be the same if there were no bias. By testing whether this discrepancy between self-reported offending and official convictions varies depending on variables such as having a convicted parent, low family income, low family SES, poor housing conditions or poor job record, one can investigate whether these variables indeed bias official agencies against offenders with these characteristics.

One could object by saying that these same variables also predict criminal behaviour themselves and might be aetiological variables of criminal behaviour, however this is exactly why these variables could bias official agencies against offenders. Official agencies know that people with these characteristics are more likely to commit criminal behaviour, and thus these features help focus the attention of official agencies. Precisely for that reason, it is important to investigate the discrepancy between self-reported offending and official convictions to enable examining the response of official agencies.

Hypotheses 3 and 4 focus on the labelling process. As explained previously, it is important to observe the temporal sequence of convictions and self-reported behaviour when investigating the impact of convictions. Two

---

34 In general, validity is lower for females and for older respondents (Farrington, 2001b; Maxfield, Weiler & Widom, 2000). Also, some studies show lower validity for blacks (Hindelang, Hirschi & Weiss, 1981; Huizinga & Elliott, 1986) or ethnic minorities (Junger, 1990), but others did not find a difference between white and black respondents (Farrington, Loeber, Stouthamer-Loeber, Van Kammen & Schmidt, 1996; Jolliffe et al., 2003; Maxfield et al., 2000). Jolliffe et al. (2003) demonstrated an exceptionally low validity for Asian females.

groups of people will be compared, all of whom were not convicted before age 18; none of these people could have experienced labelling up to age 18. Part of this group was convicted during the following years (age 19-26), while the remaining were not convicted. Subsequently, the level of self-reported offending in the following period (age 27-32) will be compared for these two groups. I will examine whether this level of self-reported offending is significantly related to having a conviction in the previous period (19-26) while controlling for the level of self-reported offending in the first period (15-18). For the purpose of clarity, these periods will be called time 1 (15-18), time 2 (19-26), and time 3 (27-32). If the convicted group has a significantly higher level of self-reported offending in the period following conviction, this supports the idea that a conviction increases offending behaviour.

I will also investigate whether the impact of a conviction is stronger for people whose parents have been convicted than for people whose parents have not been convicted. By doing this I connect the two processes of official bias and labelling.

5.4 Method

5.4.1 Sample

These hypotheses were investigated using data from the *Cambridge Study in Delinquent Development* (CSDD) (see page 13 for more information). The current investigation studied the original men only, because self-reported offending data was necessary to investigate the concept of official bias and no such information was available for *CSDD* siblings nor for *Transfive*.

5.4.2 Measures

Self-Reported Offending

Self-reported offending was measured at ages 18 and 32 and referred to the periods between ages 15-18 and 27-32. At age 18, 389 (95%) of the original males were interviewed, and 378 (94%) at age 32. Males who did not have an interview at both ages were excluded from the current analyses. Eighty-nine per cent of 411 men were interviewed at both ages, which resulted in a sample of 365 males. See Farrington et al. (2006) for more information on data collection of the self-reported data. Ten types of offences were enquired about: burglary, theft of motor vehicles, theft from motor vehicles, shoplifting, theft from machines, theft from work, fraud, assault, drug use and vandalism. For the current analyses, a sum of the number of self-reported offences was used. Drug use and fraud were not included in the sum variable, since drug use had a different scale and distribution up to 1,000 (while the others had a scale up to 100) and previous analyses showed that the ratio between self-reported and official convictions for drug use and fraud is high: the chances of being caught for these offences are low (Farrington et al., 2006). If drug offences were included, they would disproportionately dominate the sum variable for self-reported offending.

Outcome variables

To investigate the relationship between biasing variables and self-reported offending versus official convictions (hypothesis 1), these two outcome variables should be comparable. Self-reported offending was measured between ages 15-18 and 27-32. Hence, convictions were counted for these same age ranges.

Furthermore, a dichotomous variable was used for both outcomes, because the different distribution of the variables makes comparison difficult: the number of self-reported offences was much higher. Using dichotomous variables and logistic regression enables a straightforward comparison of effect sizes for self-reported offending versus official convictions through odds ratios. For official convictions, the dichotomy was based on the distribution of people in the sample with (26.0%) and without an official conviction (74.0%). For comparison, a similar distribution was used for the self-reported offending variable. People with 23 self-reported offences or less got a value of 0 on the dichotomous self-report variable, people with 24 self-reported offences or more got a value of 1, resulting in a similar distribution (73.7% versus 26.3%). Offending was common: 83% of the people reported having committed an offence. Basing the dichotomy on whether people had reported one offence would have resulted in a skewed variable with little sensitivity.

For hypothesis 2, official convictions were the outcome and the same dichotomous variable was used. With hypothesis 3 and 4, labelling effects were examined and thus the level of self-reported offending was measured between ages 27 and 32.

Independent variables

To investigate official bias, several biasing variables were used. Biasing variables are defined as factors that could bias official justice agencies against certain families. The first biasing variable used in this study was whether either parent had a conviction before the offspring's 15th birthday. Since offspring offending was measured after this age, parental convictions were taken into account until this moment. In this way, the parental convictions happened before the offspring's behaviour was measured. The other four variables were low family income, low family socio-economic status (SES), poor housing and father's poor job record (for more details on how these were measured, see Farrington & Painter, 2004). These variables were measured at age 10, apart from low family income which was measured at age 8.

Table 5.1: Overview of variables

Dependent variables
Hypothesis 1: Offspring official conviction (15-18+27-32) (one or more conviction=yes)

Offspring self-reported offence (15-18+27-32) (24 self-reported offences or more=yes)

Hypothesis 2: Offspring official conviction (15-18+27-32) (one or more conviction=yes)
Hypothesis 3, 4: Offspring level of self-reported offending (27-32)

Independent variables
Hypothesis 1: Biasing variable (see below)
Hypothesis 2: Biasing variable and level of self-reported offending (15-18+27-32)
Hypothesis 3: Offspring official conviction (19-26) (one or more conviction=yes) and offspring level of self-reported offending (15-18)
Hypothesis 4: Offspring official conviction (19-26) (one or more conviction=yes), offspring level of self-reported offending (15-18), and parent convicted (before offspring's 15th birthday)

Biasing variables
Hypothesis 1, 2: Parent convicted before offspring's 15th birthday
Low family income
Low family SES
Poor housing
Poor job record father

Ages involved in the variables are denoted between parentheses; offspring official conviction (15-18+27-32) means that convictions when the offspring was aged 15-18 and 27-32 were taken into account. Whenever the level of self-reported offending was used as an independent variable, it was log transformed. All biasing variables are dichotomous.

In the analyses for hypothesis 2, self-reported offending was used as an independent variable. This time a continuous measure of self-reported offending was used, since the impact of biasing variables on the risk of conviction was investigated at different levels of self-reported offending.

The independent variables for hypotheses 3 and 4 were whether people had been convicted during time 2 (19-26 years) and their level of self-reported offending for time 1 (15-18 years). For hypothesis 4, the variable parental conviction until the offspring's 15th birthday was added to the analysis. Table 5.1 gives an overview of the variables used in this study.

5.4.3 Analytic Approach

First, it was important to establish that parental convictions were more strongly related to offspring convictions than to offspring self-reported offending behaviour. When police and justice are biased against certain families, one would expect the chance of offspring being convicted to increase, but not necessarily the actual behaviour to increase (unless labelling effects would occur). To test this hypothesis, logistic regression analyses were run with the biasing variables as predictors and the (dichotomous) variables offspring conviction respectively self-reported offending as outcomes.

Second, I examined whether there was a significant relationship between offspring convictions and biasing variables, while self-reported offending was held constant. First, this was done in a way similar to West and Farrington (1977), although here offspring convictions were included until age 32. Sons were grouped according to four levels of self-reported offending (low to high) and then each level was split into two categories based on whether sons had the biasing variable or not. For each of the four levels of self-reported offending, it was then investigated whether sons with the biasing variable had a higher risk of conviction compared with the sons without the biasing variable. Second, partial odds ratios were calculated for each of the biasing variables, taking into account people's self-reported offending. A partial odds ratio is a reflection of the relationship between two variables, in this case the biasing variable and offspring convictions, in which the impact of a third variable, in this case self-reported offending, is held constant (Field, 2005). Calculating the partial odds ratio gives the unique prediction of the impact of the biasing variables on offspring convictions while controlling for self-reported offending. Partial odds ratios were calculated using logistic regression. A continuous variable was used for the level of self-reported offending: the sum of self-reported offences measured at 18 and 32. This variable was highly skewed: many people reported few offences. This variable was therefore log-transformed in the analysis. A value of one was added to all scores before performing the natural log transformation.

Third, turning to the study of labelling, I examined whether there was a significant relationship between a conviction between ages 19 and 26 (time 2) and the level of self-reported offending between ages 27 and 32 (time 3), while controlling for the level of self-reported offending between ages 15 and 18 (time 1). I chose to control for the self-reported offending during time 1, since the self-reported offending during time 2 might have been impacted already by a conviction during that period. Negative binomial regression was used because the dependent variable (self-reported offending between ages 27 and 32) was highly skewed. With such a skewed distribution it was inappropriate to run a linear regression analysis. Negative binomial regression analysis suitably deals with skewed distributions. Furthermore, the predictor variable (self-reported offending between ages 15 and 18) was similarly skewed and therefore log-transformed in the analysis.

Fourth, to investigate whether the impact of a conviction was stronger for people whose parents have been convicted, the interaction between the variables of having a conviction between ages 19-26 and having a convicted parent was investigated. An interaction term (conviction 19-26 * parental conviction) was added to the negative binomial regression. The predictor variables were centred around the mean before analysing them in the regression analysis. Centering variables around the mean is recommended when investigating interaction effects in multiple regression analysis (Aiken & West, 1991).

5.5 Results

5.5.1 Impact of biasing variables on self-reported offending versus official convictions

The results presented in table 5.2 demonstrate that all biasing variables were more strongly related to offspring convictions than to offspring self-reported offending; the odds ratios (ORs) for official convictions were considerably higher than for self-reported offending. All biasing variables were significantly related to offspring convictions, but not all were significantly related to self-reported offending. The ORs differed significantly for self-reported versus official offending for the biasing variables parental conviction and a father's poor job record.[35] The difference approached significance for low family income. These results support hypothesis 1 that the relationship between parental convictions, a father's poor job record and low family income with offspring convictions is stronger than with offspring self-reported offending. In the next step I will investigate whether the relationship between biasing variables and offspring convictions remained significant while controlling for the level of self-reported offending.

5.5.2 Relationship between biasing variables and offspring convictions while controlling for self-reported offending

The first method to test hypothesis 2 involved creating four categories of self-reported offending. The sample of sons was divided into four approximately equal groups: low (0 self-reported offences - 17.3 %), low average (1-5 offences - 31.0 %), high average (6-25 offences - 27.1 %), high (26-353 offences - 24.7 %). Each of these groups was then separated into two based on whether they had the biasing variable or not. Odds ratios (ORs) were calculated to analyse whether sons with the biasing variable had a higher risk of conviction than sons without the biasing variable. Figure 5.1 graphically presents the proportion of children in each group with a conviction. The results presented in table 5.3 demonstrate that in every category, sons of convicted parents had a higher risk of conviction, with ORs ranging from 3.4 to 5.5 indicating a

---

[35] Odds ratios were compared using the formula:

$$z = \frac{LOR_1 - LOR_2}{s_{pooled}}$$

where $LOR_1 = \text{Ln}(1^{st} \text{ odds ratio})$, $LOR_2 = \text{Ln}(2^{nd} \text{ odds ratio})$, and s_{pooled} = the pooled standard error of LOR_1 and LOR_2. s_{pooled} is derived from the formula:

$$s_{pooled} = \sqrt{\frac{(n_1-1)s_1^2 + (n_2-1)s_2^2}{n_1 + n_2 - 2}}$$

where n_1 = sample size of group 1, n_2 = sample size of group 2, s_1 = standard error for LOR_1, and s_2 = standard error for LOR_2.

Table 5.2: Percentage of offspring with a conviction versus self-reported offending in relation to biasing variables.

Biasing variable	Biasing variable not present			Biasing variable present			OC			SR		
	N	OC	SR	N	OC	SR	OR		95 % CI	OR		95 % CI
Convicted parent	260	16.5 %	21.2 %	105	49.5 %	39.0 %	4.90	*	2.95- 8.12	2.35	*	1.43- 3.87
Low family income	281	21.4 %	24.2 %	84	41.7 %	33.3 %	2.63	*	1.55- 4.45	1.61		0.94- 2.76
Low family SES	291	23.7 %	25.4 %	74	35.1 %	29.7 %	1.85	*	1.06- 3.21	1.34		0.75- 2.37
Poor housing	226	19.5 %	22.1 %	139	36.7 %	33.1 %	2.34	*	1.44- 3.79	1.73	*	1.07- 2.79
Poor job record father[a]	300	23.0 %	25.0 %	42	50.0 %	31.0 %	3.52	*	1.79- 6.90	1.54		0.75- 3.16

* $p < .05$; 95 % CI, 95 % Confidence interval; N, number of offspring; OC, official conviction when offspring between ages 15-18 and/or 27-32; OR, odds ratio; SR, self-reported offending between ages 15-18 and 27-32.

a Information on poor job record father is missing for 23 people, so the sample here consists of 342 people.

Table 5.3: Percentage of offspring with a conviction versus self-reported offending in relation to biasing variables.

Offspring convicted (15-18 + 27-32)	Biasing variable not present		Biasing variable present			
	N	OC	N	OC	OR	95 % CI
Parent convicted before child 15						
SR - Low	50	2.0 %	13	7.7 %	4.08	0.24- 70.08
SR - Low average	91	6.6 %	22	22.7 %	4.17*	1.14- 15.23
SR - High average	67	20.9 %	32	59.4 %	5.53*	2.21- 13.87
SR - High	52	42.3 %	38	71.1 %	3.35*	1.37- 8.16
Low family income						
SR - Low	50	4.0 %	13	0 %	0.96	0.91- 1.02
SR - Low average	93	9.7 %	20	10.0 %	1.04	0.21- 5.21
SR - High average	75	28.0 %	24	50.0 %	2.57*	1.00- 6.62
SR - High	63	44.4 %	27	77.8 %	4.38*	1.56- 12.31
Low family SES						
SR - Low	53	3.8 %	10	0 %	0.96	0.91- 1.02
SR - Low average	87	8.0 %	26	15.4 %	2.08	0.56- 7.75
SR - High average	82	29.3 %	17	52.9 %	2.72	0.94- 7.88
SR - High	69	52.2 %	21	61.9 %	1.49	0.55- 4.05
Poor housing						
SR - Low	43	2.3 %	20	5.0 %	2.21	0.13- 37.25
SR - Low average	75	6.7 %	38	15.8 %	2.63	0.75- 9.24
SR - High average	61	24.6 %	38	47.4 %	2.76*	1.16- 6.54
SR - High	47	48.9 %	43	60.5 %	1.60	0.69- 3.69
Poor job record father						
SR - Low	57	3.5 %	3	0 %	0.97	0.92- 1.01
SR - Low average	92	10.9 %	13	7.7 %	0.68	0.08- 5.83
SR - High average	82	28.0 %	13	69.2 %	5.78*	1.62- 20.60
SR - High	69	49.3 %	16	84.6 %	5.66*	1.17- 27.46

* p < .05; 95 % CI, 95 % Confidence interval; N, number of offspring; OC, official conviction when offspring between ages 15-18 and/or 27-32; OR, odds ratio; SR, self-reported offending between ages 15-18 and 27-32.

strong relationship. The OR for the lowest category of self-reported offending was not significant, but equally large. Low family income, the second biasing variable, only increased conviction risk in the two highest categories. Third, low family SES increased conviction risk in the three highest categories, but the risk increase was not significant. Fourth, when sons lived in poor housing, in every category of self-reported offending they had a higher risk of having a conviction, although the increase was only significant in one of the categories. Finally, having a father with a poor job record increased conviction risk significantly in the high average and high categories. The strongest factor increasing offspring convictions, while holding self-reported offending constant, is a parental criminal record. However, low family income, poor housing and a father's poor job record also significantly increased offspring conviction risk, though not necessarily in every category.

Next to following West & Farrington's (1977) approach, another method was used to investigate the impact of official bias on intergenerational transmission. Results from logistic regression analyses are presented in table 5.4. Having a parental conviction, low family income, poor housing, and the

Results 95

Figure 5.1: Percentages of offspring with a conviction between ages 15-18 and/or 27-32, at different levels of self-reported offending with and without biasing variable.

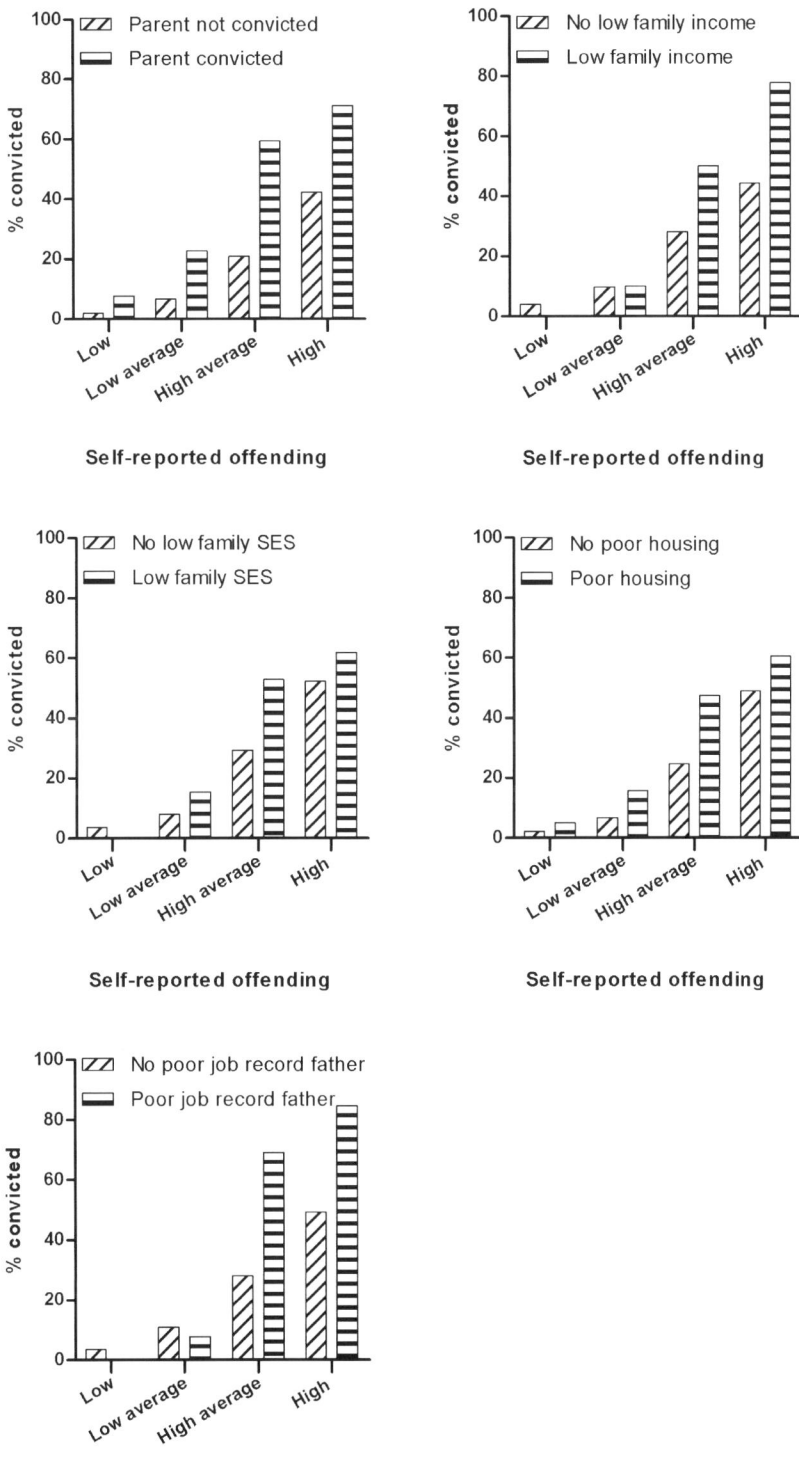

Table 5.4: Partial odds ratios for the relationship between offspring convictions and biasing variables while controlling for self-reported offending.

Offspring convicted (15-18 + 27-32)	OR	95 % CI
Convicted parent	4.14*	2.32-7.38
Low family SES	1.82	0.96-3.44
Low family income	2.51*	1.42-4.45
Poor housing	2.04*	1.17-3.55
Poor job record father	3.22*	1.60-6.51

* $p < .05$; 95 % CI, 95 % Confidence interval; OR, odds ratio.

father having a poor job record all increased conviction risk after controlling for self-reported offending. Parental conviction is the strongest factor (OR 4.1), followed by a father's poor job record (OR 3.2), low family income (OR 2.5), and poor housing (OR 2.0).

Both methods to test hypothesis 2 show that certain factors that might bias official agencies indeed had a significant impact on offspring's conviction risk when self-reported offending was controlled for. It is possible that a parental conviction causes the other biasing variables (low family income, low family SES, a father's poor job record or poor housing). Therefore, I examined whether the biasing variables were independent predictors of official bias when the parental conviction was taken into account. Logistic regression analyses were run where each of the biasing variables was used as a predictor variable together with the parental conviction while at the same time controlling for offspring's level of self-reported offending. Low family income as well as a father's poor job record predicted official bias independently from a parental conviction (OR = 1.97, 95 % CI 1.08-3.59 and OR = 2.06 95 % CI 1.00-4.23). Poor housing was a relatively strong predictor and almost significant (OR = 1.75 95 % CI 0.99-3.10).[36] Two general biasing factors appear from these results. Firstly, a convicted parent increased conviction risk (taking into account someone's self-reported offending). Second, a combination of social circumstances such as low family income, a father's poor job record and living in poor housing appears to bias official agencies against certain offenders.

---

36 I also investigated whether the seriousness of offspring offending might explain a higher risk of conviction. To examine this, a variable for the level of self-reported serious offences was used: the sum of self-reported burglary and violence measured at age 18 and 32. This seriousness variable was added to the multiple logistic regression with the biasing variables and the level of self-reported offending as predictor variables and offspring official conviction between ages 15-18/27-32 as outcome variable. All biasing variables, except for low family SES, remained significant predictors of offspring convictions when controlling for self-reported offending and serious offending. In the interest of space, the models are not included, but they are available upon request.

5.5.3 The impact of a conviction on subsequent offending

After investigating official bias, the analyses will now focus on labelling. Two-hundred and seventy individuals did not have a conviction before their 19th birthday. Thirty-one of these were convicted between their 19th and 27th birthday and these were compared with the 239 people who had not been convicted in either of these periods. The results in table 5.5 (model 1) demonstrate that having a conviction between the 19th and 27th birthday (time 2) and the level of self-reported offending between the 15th and 19th birthday (time 1) were both significant predictors of the level of self-reported offending between the 27th and 32nd birthday (time 3). A conviction predicted someone's later self-reported offending behaviour, even when previous offending behaviour was taken into account.

5.5.4 Interaction between labelling and convicted parent

Model 2 in table 5.5 demonstrates the result of the negative binomial regression analysis where the interaction between having a convicted parent and a conviction on subsequent self-reported offending was added. There is a strong interaction effect of a convicted parent and an offspring conviction on self-reported offending. Furthermore, the impact of a conviction at time 2 becomes an insignificant predictor when the interaction with a convicted parent is taken into account. When the impact of a conviction for the two separate groups was examined, a strong impact of a conviction on someone's offending behaviour was visible for the group whose parents had been convicted ($B=2.04$, 95 % CI = 1.13-2.95, $p=.001$), whereas there was no significant impact of a conviction for the group whose parents had not been convicted ($B=-0.20$, 95 % CI = -0.73-0.34, $p=.473$). This interaction effect is also visible in figure 5.2 and table 5.6, which gives the average number of self-reported offences at the two ages for each of the four groups.[37] The number of self-reported offences decreased between time 1 and time 3 for the first three groups, but the group who had a convicted parent and has been convicted at time 2 shows a sharp increase in self-reported offending between time 1 and time 3. Apparently, there was no labelling effect for the group whose parents have not been convicted, while there was a strong effect for children whose parents have been convicted.[38]

---

[37] Traditionally, when portraying an interaction effect, one would only report the outcome (self-reported offending between ages 27-32) for the four groups. However, since the outcome is heavily influenced by the previous level of self-reported offending, it is more appropriate to show the difference between the current and previous level of offending.

[38] Again, the impact of the seriousness of offspring offending was investigated. The sum of self-reported burglary and violence measured at age 18 was used (self-reported offending measured at age 32 was the outcome variable). This seriousness variable was added to the regression analysis to test the interaction between a parental conviction and offspring conviction on offspring self-reported offending. The interaction remained significant. Furthermore, I examined whether the seriousness of parents' convictions impacted on this relationship. A dichotomous variable was used that was coded 1 when parents had been convicted for burglary, robbery, assault, wounding, insulting or threatening behaviour, sexual offences, murder,

Table 5.5: The impact of a conviction between ages 19-26 (time 2) for offspring with no previous convictions on level of self-reported offending between ages 27-32 (time 3) while controlling for the level of self-reported offending between ages 15-18 (time 1) and the interaction with parental conviction.

Dependent variable: Self-reported offending 27-32	Model 1			Model 2		
	B	95 % CI	p	B	95 % CI	p
Convicted 19-26 or not	0.90	0.51- 1.29	.001	0.38	-0.06- 0.81	.088
Self-reported offending 15-18	0.22	0.11- 0.32	.001	0.36	0.23- 0.48	.001
Convicted parent				-0.41	-0.75- -0.07	.019
Convicted parent*offspring conviction				2.58	1.60- 3.55	.001

Table 5.6: Interaction effect of parental conviction and offspring conviction on self-reported offending.

	Parent not convicted		Parent convicted	
	Offspring not convicted 19-26 (time 2)	Offspring convicted 19-26 (time 2)	Offspring not convicted 19-26 (time 2)	Offspring convicted 19-26 (time 2)
N	196	22	43	9
Mean number of self-reported offences:				
Offspring 15-18 (time 1)	7.05	19.32	9.60	3.56
Offspring 27-32 (time 3)	7.25	13.14	3.91	27.56

Figure 5.2: Interaction effect of parental conviction and offspring conviction on self-reported offending.

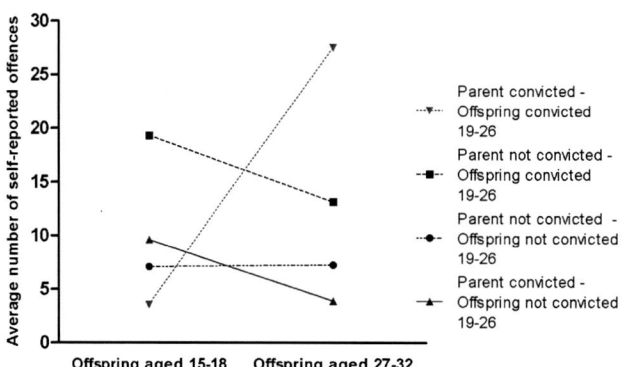

The results support hypothesis 4 and similarly show that hypothesis 3 is only supported for the group whose parents have been convicted and not for people whose parents have not been convicted.

---

manslaughter, drug or weapon offences. This also did not change the results: the interaction effect remained significant. In the interest of space, the models are not included, but they are available upon request.

5.6 Discussion

This chapter investigated official bias in intergenerational transmission as well as the impact of a conviction on subsequent offending behaviour. A convicted parent was the strongest predictor of offspring convictions after controlling for offspring self-reported offending. Low family income, a father's poor employment record and poor housing conditions also predicted offspring convictions independent of having a convicted parent. Thus, next to having a convicted parent, these social circumstances also appear to bias official agencies and increase conviction risk for people with these characteristics. Furthermore, the results show that a conviction subsequently increased an individual's self-reported offending behaviour for the group of people whose parents had been convicted, but not for people whose parents had not been convicted.

West and Farrington (1977) demonstrated support for official bias for offspring with convicted parents. The current study validated these previous results and revealed that certain social circumstances also increase conviction risk for individuals with these factors. It is not surprising that these factors would bias official agencies. For example, police are more likely to patrol large public housing projects or deprived neighbourhoods rather than the suburbs or richer areas, and, consequently, people living in those areas are more likely to be arrested.

Results from this study support the idea that the biasing variables actually cause the offending behaviour, because a convicted parent and poor housing are significantly related to offspring self-reported offending. However, these variables causing criminal behaviour does not refute the finding that they also - independently of their possible aetiological value - increase offspring conviction risk. The focus of the current study was on the discrepancy between offspring self-reported offending and offspring conviction risk. This discrepancy was operationalised as the reaction of official agencies. It is not surprising that variables that might cause criminal behaviour are also, whether explicitly or not, used to guide the behaviour of official agencies.

Some interesting patterns are visible in the results. Firstly, when examining the impact of biasing variables at different levels of self-reported offending (table 5.3), low family income and a father's poor job record do not have an impact on the risk of a conviction at the lowest level of self-reported offending, but they do at higher levels. This lowest category consisted of people who reported no committed offences between their 15th through 18th and 27th through 32nd birthday. Therefore, unless people are wrongly convicted, these individuals cannot be convicted.[39] It is not surprising that no official bias is visible in this group: when people commit no or little crime, there is little scope for the police to intervene. When people commit more crime,

---

[39] Two people were convicted for an offence when they were 16 years old which they did not report.

the police have more room to intervene or not, and to choose to apply their discretionary power.

Second, a parental conviction increased the risk of offspring convictions, but it also increased offspring's self-reported offending behaviour. The results in table 5.2 show that approximately 39% of sons whose parents had been convicted fall in the higher self-report category compared with approximately 21% of sons whose parents have not been convicted. This difference might be attributable to the process discussed previously and examined in this chapter where a parental conviction increases the risk of offspring convictions which subsequently increases offspring's offending behaviour through labelling or other collateral consequences of a conviction such as losing one's job (Van der Geest, 2011). It is also possible that other mechanisms of intergenerational transmission (as discussed in the Introduction of this dissertation) are partly responsible for intergenerational continuity of criminal behaviour. As previously mentioned, the explanations for intergenerational transmission are not mutually exclusive and they are empirically intertwined; a combination of these mechanisms could explain intergenerational transmission and the current results also show that official bias is not solely responsible for intergenerational continuity.

Finally, it is surprising that the significant impact of a conviction on someone's subsequent offending behaviour was only found for the people whose parents had been convicted, but not for the people whose parents had not been convicted. It appears that Labelling Theory only applies to people who are already disadvantaged by a convicted parent. There is a cumulative effect of having a convicted parent and being convicted yourself. As Bernburg and Krohn (2003, p. 1290) emphasised: 'Structural location, such as race or social class, may provide people with differential means to resist deviant labelling in the face of official intervention.' A conviction does not automatically lead to deviant labelling, but depends on other factors as well. When people are in a disadvantaged position 'deficits and disadvantages pile up faster' (Sampson & Laub, 1997, p. 153). The current study demonstrates strong support for this idea of differential labelling effects.

This study undoubtedly has limitations. Throughout the chapter it was assumed that self-reported offending is a valid and reliable measure of someone's offending behaviour. However, self-reports of offending behaviour obviously face challenges; people might forget, conceal or exaggerate their offending behaviour (Junger-Tas & Marshall, 1999). These issues pose a problem especially with long-term retrospective self-reports (Jolliffe et al., 2003). Furthermore, the willingness to commit offences, to forget, and to exaggerate might depend on characteristics of the respondent and of the crime. People seem to be less inclined to report sex and fraud offences, but sometimes exaggerate violent offences. It is possible that such characteristics of the respondent or the crime could explain differences between self-reported offending and official convictions. For example, offspring of convicted parents might feel a deviant label or stigmatisation and thus might be less inclined to present a pro-social image compared to individuals who feel they have more to lose (Junger-Tas & Marshall, 1999). However, this would predict a smaller difference between self-reported offending and official convictions for offspring of convicted parents which is not what was found in the current study. Even though numerous studies have shown that validity is high for prospective self-reports and white males as investigated in this sample, it is important to realise that we still do not know the true extent of offending behaviour. However, this is a recurrent problem in all criminological studies and the self-reports as used in this study can be perceived as the closest estimates of the respondents' true offending behaviour.

Furthermore, one could say that the increase found in self-reported offending after a conviction in the preceding period could be caused by an increased willingness to report offences rather than an increase in someone's offending behaviour. However, the respondents did not know that the researchers checked their criminal histories, therefore it seems unlikely that this knowledge could have influenced them. More importantly, previous analyses with the *CSDD* showed that, in general, the first self-report of an offence preceded the first conviction for it (Farrington, 1989). This implies that it is unlikely that the relationship found between a conviction and a subsequent increase in self-reported offending could be attributed to the tendency for convictions to make people more willing to admit offences in self-reports.

It is also possible that the observed difference between self-reported offending and official convictions varies between offspring with convicted parents and unconvicted parents for other reasons than official bias. Perhaps offspring of convicted parents and with poorer social circumstances are less likely to admit offending in self-reports. However, based on previous self-report validity research there is no evidence to suggest this.

An important limitation of this study is the low number of people involved in the analyses to investigate labelling. The group of offspring with a conviction and a convicted parent consists of only nine people. Hitherto the *CSDD* is the only study used to examine the topic of labelling in combination with a convicted parent. This highlights the need to replicate these analyses with large longitudinal data sets over multiple generations.

Unfortunately it was not possible investigate females. The *CSDD* has information on convictions for sisters of the original 411 men, but does not have self-reports for these women. It would be interesting to investigate official bias in intergenerational transmission and the impact of a conviction for daughters, because the attitude of official agencies might be different towards females. As mentioned previously, females are less likely to be arrested than males and females are at an advantage in several stages of delinquency case processing in the court (Bishop & Frazier, 1991; Sealock & Simpson, 1998;

Spohn & Beichner, 2000). It is unclear, however, how official bias might influence females. The "advantage" for females might eliminate the official bias against daughters of convicted parents. However, the advantage for females might apply to daughters of convicted as well as unconvicted parents, and official bias against certain families might still be noticeable. Alternatively, the combination of being female and coming from a criminal family might negatively change the attitude of official agencies, who do not show leniency with these women. Additionally, it would be interesting to examine whether females also report a similar increase in self-reported offending after being convicted. As discussed before (see page 36), women who commit crime are less common, and because of this, there might be more stigma for women who do commit crime. It would be desirable to replicate the current study using data on females to investigate whether similar conclusions apply to women.

Furthermore, it is important to realise that the results from this study might not be easily generalisable to today's situation or to other countries. This sample of men was born in London around 1953 and their offending behaviour was measured until age 32 (roughly 1986). Family structures, communities and police and justice organisations have changed. Nowadays, people move more often and move farther away. Police officers in the neighbourhood might not know people's parents or parents might have separated and one parent might live in a completely different neighbourhood, district or city relative to the child. Again, it would be advantageous to replicate this study using data from different periods and different countries to examine whether similar effects are visible.

What do these results mean to broader society? Apparently, certain people have a higher risk of conviction. Not necessarily because they commit more crime, but just because their parent(s) committed crime or because they grow up in poorer social circumstances. From an ethical point of view, this is obviously undesirable. We live in a democratic, fair society where everyone should be treated equally and thus official bias should be avoided. Furthermore, and this is more relevant from a practical point of view, this study showed an increase in these individuals' offending behaviour after official bias and labelling. Instead of decreasing or preventing crime, by their actions the official agencies appear to increase offending behaviour. As McAra & McVie (2005, p. 5, 2007a; 2007b) also demonstrated in their research in Edinburgh, the police appear to unfairly target certain categories of young people, the usual suspects, but thereby they 'serve to sustain and reproduce the very problems which the institution ostensibly attempts to contain or eradicate'. This is obviously an unwanted consequence of their actions. It is therefore important to make the police and courts aware of this bias so that they can try to avoid treating offenders' children unfairly.

Furthermore, it appears that children of convicted parents also report more criminal behaviour than children whose parents have not been convicted. Instead of increasing this behaviour even further by convicting these children disproportionally often, it is preferable to try to prevent the development of this behaviour. Energy and resources would be better spent on family-based prevention programs, such as parent education and parent management training. If special attention has to be focused on children of convicted parents, it would be better for it to be positive and effective by means of preventing the offending behaviour.

5.7 Summary

This chapter investigated to what extent children of convicted parents might have a higher risk of a conviction themselves because of bias against certain criminal families by official justice systems, such as the police and courts. Furthermore, I examined whether a conviction subsequently increased offending behaviour. Bias was measured using several variables: a convicted parent, low family income, low family socio-economic status, poor housing conditions and a father's poor employment record. The impact of a conviction between ages 19-26 on self-reported offending behaviour between 27-32 was investigated while controlling for previous self-reported behaviour between 15-18. A convicted parent as well as poorer social circumstances such as a father's poor job record, low family income and poor housing predicted an increased conviction risk while controlling for self-reported offending. Furthermore, a labelling effect was only visible among people whose parents had been convicted: people who had been convicted when they were between ages 19-26 reported significantly more offending between ages 27-32, while controlling for the level of self-reported offending between ages 15-18. The results support the official bias mechanism and labelling theory, but also suggest that other mechanisms are needed to explain intergenerational transmission.

Chapter 6

The relationship between parental imprisonment and offspring offending in England and the Netherlands*

'They call me names, sometimes about my dad being in prison, sometimes not. Sometimes I get into fights.'

(Lösel et al., 2011, p. 53)

6.1 Introduction

In the previous chapter I examined a possible impact of the justice system by investigating official bias and labelling. In this chapter, another aspect of the criminal justice system will be examined: the impact of parental imprisonment on offspring behaviour. In recent years imprisonment rates have increased enormously in Western Europe and the United States (Walmsley, 2009). As a consequence, today, an estimated 1.5 million children in the United States and 100,000 children in England[40] have an incarcerated par-

---

* An earlier version of this chapter was published as S. Besemer, V. van der Geest, J. Murray, C.C.J.H. Bijleveld, and D.P. Farrington (2011). The relationship between parental imprisonment and offspring offending in England and the Netherlands. *British Journal of Criminology*, 51, 413-437.

40 In this chapter, "England" is used as shorthand for "England and Wales".

ent (Murray & Farrington, 2008a).[41] There are no official figures for the prevalence of imprisoned parents and children in the Netherlands, although research on women in Dutch prisons estimates that at least between 800 to 1,200 children each year have an imprisoned mother (Slotboom, Bijleveld, Day & Van Giezen, 2008). It is clear that a substantial and increasing number of children experience parental imprisonment.

Earlier research suggests that parental imprisonment might have undesirable effects on children left behind: they exhibit more criminal behaviour and mental health problems than children whose parents were not imprisoned (Murray & Farrington, 2008a; Murray et al., 2009). Researchers have been unable to demonstrate what is causing this increased risk. The impact could be explained by the separation from the parent, or by collateral effects such as economic deprivation because of loss of family income. The increased risk could also be explained by the parent's criminal behaviour. It is extremely difficult to disentangle these influences without an experimental design. It is interesting, however, to see whether the impact of parental imprisonment varies by social and penal context. As explained in the Introduction, cross-national comparisons could help addressing the issue of whether risk factors or causes of delinquency are comparable in different settings (Farrington & Loeber, 1999).

Murray, Janson, and Farrington (2007) compared effects of parental imprisonment on children in Sweden and England. Children of imprisoned parents in England displayed more criminal behaviour than children whose parents were not imprisoned. In Sweden there was no difference between these groups after accounting for levels of parental criminality. Hitherto this is the only cross-national study of the impact of parental imprisonment on offspring offending. As Murray and Farrington (2008a, p. 186) stated: 'these results require replication'.

This chapter investigates the impact of parental imprisonment on children's criminal behaviour in a cross-national context. Specifically, it seeks an answer to the following questions: *Do children of prisoners display more criminal behaviour than children of convicted but not imprisoned parents?* And: *are the results different in the Netherlands and England?*

After the Second World War, the Netherlands developed tolerant, liberal social policies and a humane prison system and sentencing guidelines (Downes, 1988). The imprisonment rate dropped and was the lowest in Western Europe until the late 1980s (Downes & Van Swaaningen, 2007). As Downes and Van Swaaningen (2007, p. 32) stated, after the Second World War for three to four decades onwards, 'Dutch penal policy became a byword for humane prison conditions and sparing use of custody' where resocialization was the primary goal, while England developed a more repressive penal system. England had much higher imprisonment rates and longer sentences

---

41 These numbers are called the point prevalence and reflect the number of prisoners' children at one point in time.

(Downes, 1992). In the Netherlands, possibilities for families to visit prisoners were 'more liberally available' than in England (Downes, 1992, p. 201). Additionally, Dutch prisoners earned more money for their work in custody, which enabled more contact with their families, as phone calls and letters cost money. Furthermore, the 'generous welfare state' assured 'comprehensive social insurance over the life span' (Downes & Van Swaaningen, 2007, p. 38). This might have resulted in more financial support for prisoners' families. Moreover, because of the focus on punishment in England versus resocialization in the Netherlands, the social stigma for prisoners and their families might have been lower in the Netherlands. As I will describe later in this chapter, this stigma can result in problem behaviour in children (Hagan & Dinovitzer, 1999).

Recently, imprisonment rates increased in both countries, in the Netherlands much more so than in England. Although the Netherlands still has shorter imprisonments, prison life still appears less damaging and prison is more focused on resocialisation (see Kruttschnitt & Dirkzwager, 2011), today, the countries are more similar, both being more punitive than previously and having imprisonment rates that are among the highest in Western Europe (Downes, 1988; Tonry & Bijleveld, 2007b). Investigating these countries in the 1950s to the 1970s when they differed significantly in their criminal justice policies can yield important information for theories about the effects of parental imprisonment.

Earlier studies examined the impact of imprisonment (for an overview see Murray & Farrington, 2008a), but they investigated this by comparing prisoners' children to children without imprisoned parents. They failed to distinguish between children of convicted and non-convicted parents, making it difficult to differentiate between the effects of imprisonment and the effects of a parent's convictions on children (Murray et al., 2009). The current study focuses on the additional impact of parental imprisonment over and above parental conviction. Moreover, a comparison between the Netherlands and England on the relationship between parental imprisonment and offspring offending has never been done previously. In the present study, Dutch and English data is used on imprisonment and convictions of both parents and children. This enables comparing results cross-nationally and examining the independent impact of parental imprisonment and parental convictions on offspring offending. Before formulating hypotheses and explaining how the study was conducted, I will first discuss how and why parental imprisonment might affect children's behaviour.

6.2   Theoretical Background

Most studies on parental imprisonment conclude that it affects children unfavourably (Murray & Farrington, 2008a). Some authors, however, have pointed to the possibility that parental imprisonment could impact upon some children favourably, because removing an abusive parent from the home allows a child to develop positively (Eddy & Reid, 2003; Hagan & Dinovitzer, 1999). Below I discuss mechanisms that could explain unfavourable and favourable impacts of parental imprisonment and moderating factors that influence this relationship. It was not possible to study all of these mechanisms in the current study, but the theories provide a good starting point for interpreting the findings.

6.2.1 Unfavourable impact

One explanation for the unfavourable impact of parental imprisonment is that parental imprisonment is a stressful life event for children (Hagan & Dinovitzer, 1999). Separation from a parent might cause attachment problems which, in turn, can lead to problem behaviour (Bowlby, 1969, 1973, 1980). Moreover, because such children are less bonded to their parents, they may have fewer restraints to display antisocial behaviour (Hirschi, 1969). Hagan and Dinovitzer (1999, p. 125) stressed 'the importance of parental supervision, role models, and support in the childhood socialization process.' According to their 'socialization perspective', children will turn to their peers when they lack parental socialization (Hagan & Dinovitzer, 1999, p. 123). They will use their peers as role models which might lead to more delinquent behaviour (Warr, 2002).

A second possible explanation for an unfavourable impact of parental imprisonment is the stigma that prisoners' children carry in society. According to the 'stigmatization perspective' these children can experience bullying and teasing which might increase problem behaviour (Hagan & Dinovitzer, 1999, p. 126). Official bodies such as the police might be biased and pay more attention to prisoners' families (Farrington, 2011), something I investigated in the previous chapter (5). This connects to labelling theory, which posits that people will behave according to the label society attaches to them. According to Lemert (1967, p. v) 'social control leads to deviance'. Farrington previously demonstrated deviance amplification, an increase in self-reported deviant behaviour, after official action in the form of criminal convictions in the Cambridge Study (Farrington, 1977; Farrington et al., 1978). Sherman (1993, p. 459) hypothesized that persistent bullying, teasing, and official police action might lead to 'defiance', a 'proud and angry emotion' that can result in antisocial behaviour in children.

A third explanation concerns economic strain following a parent's imprisonment. Imprisonment often causes loss of income which can produce financial difficulties for the family (Bloom & Steinhart, 1993). According to the 'strain perspective' (Hagan & Dinovitzer, 1999, p. 124) this economic deprivation might lead to more problem behaviour in children.

As well as economic strain, when children lose a parent to prison, they lose 'human and social capital' (Hagan & Dinovitzer, 1999, p. 124). The remaining single parent, usually the mother, may be unable to devote sufficient time and energy to her children, especially as she suffers from the loss of her partner as well. Several studies suggest that children from single-parent families tend to display more problem behaviour (Amato, 2001; Juby & Farrington, 2001; Sigle-Rushton & McLanahan, 2004; Wells & Rankin, 1991). Furthermore, parental imprisonment often involves frequent caretaker changes which might also be related to increased problem behaviour and delinquency in offspring (Kjellstrand & Eddy, 2011a,b; Murray, Farrington & Sekol, 2012).

6.2.2 No impact

A further explanation for the correlation between parental imprisonment and offspring offending is that prisoners are often the most persistent and serious criminals (Murray & Murray, 2010). Based on theories and studies of intergenerational transmission one would expect stronger transmission of criminal behaviour from parent to child in the case of a more criminal parent (Farrington, 2011 and Chapter 3). Consequently, it may not be the parental imprisonment that is causing the offspring's offending behaviour, but the fact that the parent was criminal before the prison sentence. This 'selection perspective' (Hagan & Dinovitzer, 1999, p. 128) assumes 'that imprisoned parents and their children are already different from parents and their children who are not imprisoned, prior to the imposition of a prison sentence'. Murray and Farrington (2008a, p. 163) proposed as one hypothesis that 'parental criminality, parental mental illness, and other environmental risks before parental imprisonment might cause child behaviour problems, rather than parental imprisonment itself.' So, unlike the theories discussed previously that assume an unfavourable impact of parental imprisonment, this explanation proposes that parental imprisonment has no causal impact, but that an association between parental imprisonment and offspring offending can be explained by pre-existing differences. In their research on children of imprisoned mothers, Hissel, Bijleveld, and Kruttschnitt (2011) illustrated how these children experienced many negative life events already before the mother's imprisonment which was related to elevated levels of problem behaviour reported by the children.

6.2.3 Favourable impact

In some cases, parental imprisonment may have a favourable rather than an unfavourable impact on children. As Hagan and Dinovitzer (1999, p. 123) stated: 'there obviously are cases involving the imprisonment of negligent, violent, and abusive parents where the imprisonment of the parents benefits the children by removing serious risks of current and future harm.' In these cases, children's social capital might increase rather than decrease following a parent's imprisonment (Ezinga, Hissel, Slotboom & Bijleveld, 2009; Jaffee et al., 2003). This highlights the importance of obtaining knowledge regarding the family environment prior to parental imprisonment (Murray & Murray, 2010). Furthermore, the moment that parents get incarcerated might be the first time that social support organisations have contact with families. Parental imprisonment is rarely the only problem in a family; such families often have to cope with various difficulties, including unemployment, financial, and housing problems (Ezinga et al., 2009; Murray, 2005). These can go unnoticed for a long time, but parents being sent to prison could trigger the start of social service support. This could improve children's social and emotional development.

When a parent is imprisoned this might be an opportunity to restore contact with and supervision over children. The imprisonment may function as a turning point in the sense that relationships between prisoners and their children may be resumed since the imprisoned parent's life becomes more regular (Ezinga et al., 2009). Although incarcerated parents are greatly restricted in their contact with their children, prison allows time to reflect on their relationships and can increase motivation to focus attention on their children when parents are released (Ezinga et al., 2009). Some prisons also offer programs, often through non-profit organisations, to restore contact with children.[42]

It is difficult to disentangle the different explanations for favourable and unfavourable effects of parental imprisonment and currently there is little empirical evidence on these mechanisms (Murray & Farrington, 2008a). However, most studies conclude that parental imprisonment has an unfavourable rather than a favourable impact. As Hagan and Dinovitzer (1999, p. 125) state 'it is more likely imprisonment is harmful to children even in dysfunctional families, because imprisonment will more often compound than mitigate preexisting family problems'.

6.2.4 Moderators

Not all children are affected in the same way by parental imprisonment. Moderating variables may influence the way children respond to their parent's imprisonment (R. M. Baron & Kenny, 1986). Murray and Farrington (2008a) described several variables that may alter the impact of parental imprisonment. Below I only discuss those moderators that are examined in the current study: maternal versus paternal imprisonment, child's age, gender, and a country's prison policies and penal atmosphere.

---

42 Examples in the Netherlands are 'Gezin in Balans' (http://www.gezin-in-balans.nl/) by Humanitas and 'Ouders, kinderen en detentieproject' organised by stichting Exodus (http://www.exodus.nl/Ouders_kinderen_en_detentie-project_249.html) both of which help to maintain and improve contact between parents and children, for example with volunteers who take the children to visit their parent in prison. Examples in England are the Grassroots Family Days and Support Project which organises family days to maintain contact between prisoners and their families and Ormiston with services such as children's centres and visiting support services in prison (http://www.ormiston.org/). An example in the U.S. is the Horizon Program whose mission is 'to prepare prisoners to live responsibly with others' including restoring family relations (http://www.horizoncommunities.org/FactSheet.htm).

Researchers have suggested that maternal imprisonment is more disruptive than paternal imprisonment (Bloom, 1993; Bloom & Steinhart, 1993; Murray & Murray, 2010). Mothers are frequently the primary caretaker. When a mother is imprisoned and the father is already absent, children are often relocated with a new caregiver, home and school (Ezinga et al., 2009). Because there are fewer prisons for women, mothers are generally detained further away from their children than fathers, making it harder for the children to visit (Beckerman, 1989; Fishman, 1983; Hairston, 1991; Myers et al., 1999).

A child's age and developmental stage might also shape how parental imprisonment is experienced. Infants are particularly at risk of attachment problems (Bowlby, 1969, 1973, 1980). Due to early separation they might form insecure attachments which influence their later development. Two to six year olds have the highest chance of witnessing a parent's arrest, because they are too young to be at school (Johnston, 1995). Older children may experience the previously mentioned stigma of having an incarcerated parent (Ezinga et al., 2009). Teenagers who are developing self-identity and autonomy are at risk of associating with children from other problem families which might lead to delinquent behaviour (Myers et al., 1999).

Gender may also moderate the impact of parental imprisonment. Three prior studies on gender differences showed contradictory results (Friedman & Esselstyn, 1965; Gabel & Shindledecker, 1993; Murray et al., 2007). As I discussed in Chapter 3 (see page 56), an explanation for differences might be that boys and girls react differently to stressful life events such as parental imprisonment (Murray & Farrington, 2008a). In general, boys display more externalizing problem behaviour such as delinquency, while girls have more internalizing problems such as anxiety and depression (Capaldi et al., 2002; Robins, 1966, 1986).

Finally, the previously mentioned country's social policies and penal atmosphere can influence the impact of parental imprisonment. National policies dictate the opportunities for children to visit their parents, the means and frequency of communication during imprisonment, and the amount of welfare support and social security that such families receive. Furthermore, both social stigma and official bias might vary between countries. As mentioned previously, Murray et al. (2007) demonstrated an unfavourable effect of parental imprisonment on children in England, but found no effect in Sweden. They speculated that this was caused by differences in national policies and public perceptions of imprisonment and prisoners; Sweden had shorter prison sentences, a welfare-oriented juvenile justice system, more family friendly prison policies, an extended welfare system and more sympathetic public attitudes towards offenders and punishment. This highlights the importance of context which can be investigated using cross-national studies of the impact of imprisonment as this study does for the Netherlands and England.

6.2.5 Hypotheses

The following hypotheses will be studied in this chapter:

1. Parental imprisonment between the child's birth and nineteenth birthday predicts more criminal behaviour than parental conviction.

2. This relationship is found in England as well as in the Netherlands.

3. This relationship is similar for boys and girls.

4. Maternal imprisonment is more disruptive than paternal imprisonment.

5. Parental imprisonment between birth and eighteen predicts more offspring convictions than parental imprisonment before the birth of the child.

6. The impact of parental imprisonment will be different at different ages of the child.[43]

7. There is a relationship between the frequency and length of parental imprisonment and offspring convictions (i.e. the more often and/or the longer a parent has been imprisoned, the more convictions the child will have).

8. Parental imprisonment still predicts offspring convictions after controlling for the number of parental convictions, for parental violent offending, and for risk factors for crime.

6.3 Method

6.3.1 Sample

For the analyses in this chapter, the *Cambridge Study in Delinquent Development* (*CSDD*) and the *NSCR-Transfive study* (Transfive) were used (see page 13 for more information).

Previously, the effects of parental imprisonment on the 411 original participants (all male) in the *CSDD* were investigated by Murray and Farrington (2005; 2008a) and compared with Sweden (Murray et al., 2007). However, the current manuscript is the first time that results on parental imprisonment for the brothers and sisters of the 411 boys are being reported.

For comparison of these datasets, a comparable sample was taken from both: offspring born between January 1946 and September 1962 (see page 14 for more information).

---

[43] Given the paucity of research in this area and theories that predict different effects at all ages, a priori hypotheses about the age at which parental imprisonment would impact most strongly were not developed.

6.3.2 Measures

Outcome Variable

The outcome variable was the offspring's conviction rate, defined as the number of convictions for crimes committed between the 19th and 40th birthday. As described below, parental imprisonment was measured up until the 19th birthday and therefore, offspring offending was measured after this date.

Predictor Variable

To examine whether parental imprisonment affected children more strongly than parental convictions, two mutually exclusive groups were compared and a dichotomous variable of parental imprisonment was created. The first group, the prisoners' children group, consisted of children whose parents had been imprisoned at least once between the children's birth and their 19th birthday. The second group, the convicted parents group, consisted of children whose parents were never imprisoned up to the child's 19th birthday, also not before birth, but were convicted between the child's birth and 19th birthday. In the *CSDD*, the prisoners' children group consisted of 143 children, the convicted parents group of 185. In *Transfive*, 82 children were in the prisoners' children group and 87 in the convicted parents group. For hypothesis 7, two continuous variables of parental imprisonment were used: the number and length of parental imprisonment. Only offspring of prisoners and of convicted parents were included. This meant that offspring in the convicted parents group had a value of 0 on the predictor variable, while the prisoners' children group varied according to the number of times the parent had been imprisoned or the length. The maximum length of parental imprisonment offspring experienced was used so as not to confound this analysis with the previous one that looked at the frequency of parental imprisonment.

Criminal Convictions

See the section on Criminal convictions on page 15 for information on how criminal convictions were collected and operationalised.

6.3.3 Data analysis

Negative binomial regression analysis was used in Generalized Estimating Equations (GEE) (see the Introduction, page 16 for more information).

6.4 Results

Prisoners' children had more convictions than children whose parents were never convicted, in England (mean 2.23 versus 0.35, B=1.83, $p < .001$) as

Table 6.1: Parental imprisonment and parental conviction versus offspring conviction rate - England and the Netherlands

	PC when offspring 0-18		PI when offspring 0-18				
	N	offspring CR 19-39	N	offspring CR 19-39	B	95 % CI B	p
England all	185	1.32	143	2.23	0.47	-0.08-1.01	.095
EN sons	126	1.63	92	3.17	0.58	0.01-1.16	.049*
EN daughters	59	0.66	51	0.53	-0.24	-1.26-0.78	.642
Netherlands all	87	1.16	82	0.91	-0.24	-1.03-0.56	.557
NL sons	38	2.26	34	1.50	-0.38	-1.15-0.40	.340
NL daughters	49	0.31	48	0.50	0.48	-1.21-2.17	.578

* $p < .05$; 95 % CI, 95 % Confidence interval; PC, parental conviction; PI, parental imprisonment; CR, conviction rate.

well as in the Netherlands (mean 0.91 versus 0.28, B=1.17, $p = .001$).[44] As pointed out previously, however, it is important to distinguish between the impact of parental imprisonment and conviction. The main question of this chapter, therefore, was whether prisoners' children displayed more criminal behaviour than children whose parents were convicted. Results from the regression analyses to answer this question are presented in table 6.1.

In England, prisoners' sons had significantly more convictions (mean=3.17) than sons whose parents were convicted but not imprisoned (mean=1.63) (B=0.58, $p = .049$).[45] There was no significant difference for daughters in England. In the Netherlands, prisoners' children had a lower conviction rate than children of convicted parents, but this difference was not statistically significant. Only the results for English males support hypothesis 1 that parental imprisonment between the child's birth and nineteenth birthday predicts more criminal behaviour than parental conviction in this age range. The results do not support hypothesis 2 that the relationship between

---

44 In the group children of non-convicted parents five outliers were excluded with respectively 36, 51, 59, 61 and 88 convictions. Including these outliers yielded a non-significant difference in conviction rate between prisoners' children and children from non-convicted parents, while risk analyses demonstrated that prisoners' children had a significantly higher risk to develop criminal behaviour than children of non-convicted parents (OR=1.87, 95 % CI=1.08-3.25).

45 The original *CSDD* men and their male siblings were also analysed separately while looking at prevalence and conviction rate independently. Male siblings whose parents had been imprisoned offended significantly more often (mean=3.29) than male siblings whose parents had been convicted only (mean=1.28) (B=0.92, $p = .014$). This difference was smaller for the original men (prisoners children's mean=3.14 versus mean children from convicted parents=2.04) and not significant (B=0.43, $p = .179$). Looking at prevalence, however, the relationship was much stronger for the original men: 75 % of prisoners' children offended compared with 40% of children of convicted parents, leading to an OR of 4.50 (95 % CI=1.64-12.37). When looking at male siblings only, 45.2 % of prisoners' children offended compared with 37.7 % of children of convicted parents, which results in an OR of 1.32 (95 % CI=0.60-2.88). This illustrates that the relationship for the original men is driven by a larger difference in prevalence and the relationship for the male siblings by a larger difference in conviction rate. Both groups, however, display the same pattern: prisoners' children have a higher risk of and exhibit more criminal behaviour than children of convicted parents.

parental imprisonment and offspring is found in the Netherlands as well as in England.

6.4.1 Moderators

As mentioned previously, the following moderating variables were studied: offspring gender, maternal versus paternal imprisonment, and offspring age at the time of parental imprisonment. Furthermore, information about the times and lengths of parental imprisonment was available. Moderating analyses were run for male and female offspring together and separately. None of the moderating analyses for the Netherlands or for female offspring in England was significant. In discussing the results, I therefore focus on the analyses for male offspring in England.

Offspring Gender

A significant relationship was found for sons but not for daughters in the *CSDD*. This is not enough evidence to say that there is a difference between males and females. Therefore a regression analysis was run for the *CSDD* sample of male and female offspring together where the interaction of gender * parental imprisonment was added as a predictor. Both gender (B=-0.99, p = .018) and whether the parent was imprisoned or convicted (B=1.49, p = .044) were significant predictors in this analysis, but the interaction effect was not significant (B=-0.91, p = .121). Although the interaction effect was not significant, the large difference between male and female offspring shown in table 6.1 does suggest that the impact of parental imprisonment is different for males and females. It is possible that the interaction effect was not significant primarily because of the small number of females. Although we cannot be absolutely certain, the results suggest that hypothesis 3, that the relationship between parental imprisonment and offspring offending is similar for boys and girls, should be rejected.

Paternal versus Maternal Imprisonment

Based on the theories it was expected that maternal imprisonment would be more strongly related to criminal behaviour than paternal imprisonment. Separate analyses were run for children who had their mother versus their father imprisoned. Children who experienced both paternal and maternal imprisonment were excluded from these analyses. Next, children who had their mother imprisoned were compared directly with children who had their father imprisoned. The results are presented in table 6.2.

These results show a similar pattern as was visible in table 6.1. Although none of the relationships is significant, the effect sizes are of similar strength. The non-significance is most likely due to lower numbers in the analyses, especially for mothers. The results revealed no significant difference between the impact of maternal versus paternal imprisonment on children's offending

Table 6.2: Impact of paternal versus maternal imprisonment on offspring offending - England

	PaC	PaI	MaC	MaI		Pac-PaI	Mac-MaI	PaI-MaI
Son 0 to 18								
N	89	74	51	12	B	0.65	0.52	0.01
Offspring CR 19-39	1.60	3.20	1.65	3.17	95 % CI B	-0.03-1.33	-0.72-0.67	-1.18-1.19
					(p)	(.060)	(.412)	(.997)
Daughter 0 to 18								
N	48	38	22	6	B	-0.40	-0.26	-0.59
Offspring CR 19-39	0.81	0.55	1.32	1.00	95 % CI B	-1.44-0.63	-1.77-1.26	-2.00-0.82
					(p)	(.446)	(.739)	(.410)

* $p < .05$; 95 % CI, 95 % Confidence interval; PaC, paternal conviction, no imprisonment; PaI, paternal imprisonment; MaC, maternal conviction, no imprisonment; MaI, Maternal Imprisonment; CR, conviction rate.

and therefore do not support hypothesis 4 that maternal imprisonment is more disruptive than paternal imprisonment.

Age at Parental Imprisonment

To analyse the influence of age at the time of parental imprisonment, four mutually exclusive groups of offspring were compared: sons whose parents were imprisoned before their birth, between their birth and seventh birthday, between their seventh and thirteenth birthday and between their thirteenth and nineteenth birthday.[46] Each of these groups was compared with sons whose parents were not imprisoned, but convicted at some point up until the son's nineteenth birthday including before birth.[47] The results are presented in table 6.3.

There was no difference in offending between sons of convicted parents and sons whose parents were imprisoned before birth or between birth and their seventh birthday. Sons whose parents had been imprisoned between their seventh and thirteenth or between their thirteenth and nineteenth birthday had significantly more convictions than sons whose parents had been convicted only. Each of these two "significant" groups were then compared with each of the two "non-significant" groups. Sons whose parents

---

46 The age cut-off points were chosen to create groups with a similar age interval. First, children who experienced parental imprisonment in more than one age range were excluded from the analyses to clearly compare parental imprisonment in different age periods. After running these first analyses, in the next analyses these children were added to the age group in which their parent was last imprisoned. For example, the group of children who experienced parental imprisonment between ages 13 to 18 could possibly have had their parent imprisoned before age 13 as well and so on for the other two groups. Doing this increased the group size. The results were similar, apart from two comparisons. When comparing 'clear' groups parental imprisonment between ages 7 to 12 was not significantly different from parental imprisonment between ages 0 to 6 (B=0.653, $p = .173$) or ages 13 to 18 (B=0.490, $p = .222$).
47 This control group was different from the control group in the other analyses (in table 6.1, 6.2 and 6.4-6.7), because it also included offspring whose parents were convicted before their birth. This group was chosen for the analyses in table 6.3, because they were compared with offspring whose parents were imprisoned before their birth. Conversely, in the other analyses only parental imprisonment and conviction after the child's birth was taken into account.

Table 6.3: Sons' age at parental imprisonment and sons' conviction rate - England

		PC up to son 18	Parental Imprisonment				
			up to son 18	before birth	son 0-6	son 7-12	son 13-18
N		173	130	38	35	28	29
Son CR 19-39		1.62	2.55	1.05	1.06	3.04	5.86
	B	Reference group	0.44	-0.54	-0.41	0.67*	1.25*
	95 % CI B		-0.08-0.96	-1.30-0.21	-1.04-0.23	0.04-1.29	0.66-1.85
	(p)		(.095)	(.159)	(.212)	(.037)	(.001)
PI son 7-12	B	-			1.24*	1.05*	-
	95 % CI B	-			0.37-2.10	0.31-1.80	
	(p)				(.005)	(.006)	
PI son 13-18	B	-			1.83*	1.59*	0.56*
	95 % CI B	-			0.98-2.67	0.94-2.25	0.02-1.09	-
	(p)				(.001)	(.001)	(.040)

* $p < .05$; 95 % CI, 95 % Confidence interval; PC, parental conviction; PI, parental imprisonment; CR, conviction rate.

had been imprisoned between their seventh and thirteenth or between their thirteenth and nineteenth birthday had significantly more convictions than sons whose parents had been imprisoned before their birth or between their birth and seventh birthday. Furthermore, sons whose parents were imprisoned between their thirteenth and nineteenth birthday had significantly more convictions than sons whose parents had been imprisoned between their seventh and thirteenth birthday. These results suggest that parental imprisonment has a larger impact on sons' offending behaviour when sons experience this at an older age. Parental imprisonment before the seventh birthday did not predict more offspring convictions than parental conviction. These results support hypothesis 5 that parental imprisonment between birth and eighteen predicts more offspring offending than parental imprisonment before the child's birth. Additionally, the results support hypothesis 6 stating that the impact of parental imprisonment will be different at different ages of the child.

Number of Parental Imprisonments

Next, sons' conviction rate was regressed on the number of times the parent had been imprisoned between the son's birth and nineteenth birthday. The results are presented in table 6.4.

The more often a parent had been imprisoned, the more convictions the son had (see figure 6.1). The regression coefficient in this relationship was significant (B=0.29, $p < .001$). This result, however, could be explained by the fact that parents who had been imprisoned more often had more convictions (B=0.20, $p = .002$).[48] The amount of parental criminality rather than

---

[48] This was analysed separately and is not presented in table 6.4.

Table 6.4: Number and length of parental imprisonment - England

Prediction of sons' conviction rate 19-39			
Variable	B	95 % CI B	p
Step 1 - number PI			
Number of PI when son 0-18	0.29	0.13- 0.45	.001 *
Step 2 - number PI			
Number of PI when son 0-18	0.29	0.08- 0.49	.007 *
Number of PC when son 0-18	0.01	-0.10- 0.11	.915
Step 1 - length PI			
(maximum) length of PI when son 0-18	0.05	0.03- 0.07	.001 *
Step 2 - length PI			
(maximum) length of PI when son 0-18	0.05	0.02- 0.07	.001 *
Number of PC when son 0-18	0.03	-0.06- 0.12	.574

* $p < .05$; 95 % CI, 95 % Confidence interval; PC, parental conviction; PI, parental imprisonment.

Figure 6.1: Number of parental imprisonments and son's conviction rate 19-39 - England

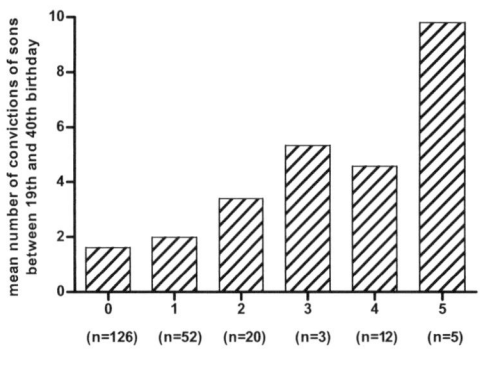

the number of parental imprisonments would then explain offspring offending. Therefore the regression analyses were run again and the number of parental convictions was added as a predictor. After doing this, the number of parental imprisonments was still significantly related to sons' conviction rate (B=0.29, p = .007). These results suggest that the more often children experienced parental imprisonment, the larger the impact.

Length of Parental Imprisonment

Next, the relationship between the length of parental imprisonment (actual time served) and sons' conviction rate was analysed. Table 6.4 shows that there was a significant relationship between the length of parental imprisonment and a son's conviction rate, also when controlling for the number of parental convictions. These results support hypothesis 7 stating that there is a relationship between frequency and length of parental imprisonment and offspring offending.

6.4.2 Multivariate Regression Analyses

Next, multivariate regression analyses were run to check for confounding factors and a possible counterbalancing effect. As discussed previously, unfavourable impacts of parental imprisonment might be counterbalanced by favourable impacts such as decreased exposure to a criminal parent. If this were true, one would expect to find that children of violent parents especially "benefited" from parental imprisonment: while children of burglars need not be exposed to the offending behaviour of their parents, parents who commit violent offences may be expected to - on average - also be aggressive in the home. I therefore wanted to test whether the relationship between parental imprisonment and offspring offending was different for violent and non-violent parents. Unfortunately it was not possible to test this interaction in a regression analysis in GEE, because violent parents who had not been to prison did not have convicted children. Looking at the mean conviction rates for these children (table 6.5), however, there does not seem to be such an interaction effect. Children of violent as well as non-violent parents who had been to prison had more convictions than children whose parents had not been imprisoned.

Table 6.5: Parental imprisonment and parental conviction for violent and non-violent parents versus sons' conviction rate - England

	PC when offspring 0-18		PI when offspring 0-18	
	N	Son conviction rate 19-39	N	Son conviction rate 19-39
Violent parents	11	0	27	2.56
Non-violent parents	115	1.78	65	3.43

PC, parental conviction; PI, parental imprisonment.

In addition, parental violence and the number of parental convictions were included in the regression models to investigate the impact of parental imprisonment over and above these possible confounders. First, a dichotomous variable was used indicating whether the parent had been convicted of a violent offence between the son's birth and nineteenth birthday. Second, a variable for the number of parental violent convictions in this period was used. The results are presented in table 6.6. Step 1 repeats values from the main analysis in table 6.1 where offspring offending was regressed on the dichotomous variable of parental imprisonment. Step 2 and 3 present values when parental violence was added. Adding parental violence to the regression analysis does not remove the significant relationship between parental imprisonment and sons' conviction rate.

As mentioned previously, imprisoned parents had significantly more convictions than parents who were convicted but not imprisoned. It is important to control for this to ensure that the difference between parental imprisonment and convictions should not be explained by the amount of

Table 6.6: Multivariate regression analyses predicting sons' conviction rate by parental imprisonment controlling for parental convictions and violence - England

Prediction of sons' conviction rate 19-39			
Variable	B	95 % CI B	p
Step 1 - main analysis (table 6.1)			
PI vs. PC when son 0-18	0.58	0.01- 1.16	.049*
Step 2 - parental violence			
PI vs. PC when son 0-18	0.74	0.18- 1.29	.009*
PV when son 0-18	-0.67	-1.46- 0.13	.099
Step 3 - parental violence			
PI vs. PC when son 0-18	0.62	0.03- 1.21	.038*
Number of PV when son 0-18	-0.06	-0.28- 0.15	.561
Step 4 - parental convictions			
PI vs. PC when son 0-18	0.36	-0.23- 0.95	.228
Number of PC when son 0-18	0.10	-0.01- 0.95	.082
Step 5 - interaction			
PI vs. PC when son 0-18	0.38	-0.50- 1.26	.392
Number of PC when son 0-18	0.11	-0.27- 0.49	.569
PI vs. PC x number of PC	-0.02	-0.41- 0.37	.935

* $p < .05$; 95 % CI, 95 % Confidence interval; PC, parental conviction; PI, parental imprisonment; PV, parental violence conviction.

parental criminality. Above, parental criminality was added as a control in the relationships where parental imprisonment was measured continuously, but I did not control for this in the main analysis where parental imprisonment was measured dichotomously. Therefore a multivariate regression analysis was run with the dichotomous variable of parental imprisonment and the number of parental convictions as predictor variables. Step 4 in table 6.6 shows that adding the number of parental convictions removes the significant relationship between the dichotomous variable of parental imprisonment and sons' conviction rate. It seems that the relationship between parental imprisonment and offspring offending can be partly explained by parental criminality. However, as shown previously in table 6.4, a relationship remained between the number of parental imprisonments and offspring offending when controlling for the number of parental convictions. This shows that the continuous variable for parental imprisonment predicts offspring offending better than the dichotomous variable.

Next, several variables known to be risk factors for criminal behaviour were added as control variables(Farrington & Painter, 2004). I first investigated which risk factors were significantly related to the outcome variable, conviction rate between the 19th and 40th birthday. The following seven variables were significant predictors of sons' conviction rate: low family SES, low family income, large family size, teen mother at birth first child, parental conflict, parents' interest in education, and poor job record of father (for more details on how these were measured, see Farrington & Painter, 2004). Previous research showed a cumulative effect of multiple risk factors; the more risk factors, the more problem behaviour (Farrington et al., 2009; Loe-

Table 6.7: Multivariate regression analyses predicting sons' conviction rate by parental imprisonment controlling for risk factors - England

Prediction of sons' conviction rate 19-39			
Variable	B	95 % CI B	p
Dichotomous variable PI			
Step 1 - PI vs. PC (table 6.1)			
PI vs. PC when son 0-18	0.58	0.01- 1.16	.049*
Step 2 - PI vs. PC			
PI vs. PC when son 0-18	0.44	-0.22- 1.10	.195
Risk factors	1.13	0.25- 2.02	.012*
Continuous variable PI			
Step 1 - number PI (table 6.4)			
Number of PI when son 0-18	0.29	0.13- 0.45	.001*
Step 2 - number PI			
Number of PI when son 0-18	0.26	0.06- 0.46	.010*
Risk factors	1.09	0.29- 1.89	.008*
Step 3 - number PI			
Number of PI when son 0-18	0.28	0.05- 0.52	.018*
Number of PC when son 0-18	-.020	-0.13- 0.09	.725
Risk factors	1.11	0.30- 1.92	.007*

* $p < .05$; 95 % CI, 95 % Confidence interval; PC, parental conviction; PI, parental imprisonment.

ber et al., 1998; Thornberry et al., 2003). Furthermore, the seven variables correlated with each other. Therefore, these risk factors were summarised by taking the mean value. This risk factor mean was included in a regression analysis with the dichotomous as well as with the continuous variable of parental imprisonment. The results are presented in table 6.7.

Adding the risk factors removed the significant relationship between the dichotomous variable of parental imprisonment and sons' conviction rate. However, the relationship between the number of parental imprisonments and sons' conviction rate remained when risk factors were added. Again, the continuous variable for parental imprisonment is a more significant predictor of offspring offending than the dichotomous variable. Even when both the number of parental convictions and risk factors were added as predictors (step 3 in table 6.7), the number of parental imprisonments remained a significant predictor of sons' conviction rate. Our results support hypothesis 8 that parental imprisonment still predicts offspring offending after controlling for the number of parental convictions, for parental violent offending and for other risk factors.

6.5 Discussion

This study investigated the relationship between parental imprisonment and offspring offending in England and the Netherlands using prospective longitudinal data from the Cambridge Study in Delinquent Development and the

NSCR Transfive Study. In the Netherlands, no significant relationship was found between parental imprisonment and offspring offending. In England, a significant relationship between parental imprisonment and offspring offending was only visible for sons. The relationship between the number of parental imprisonments and sons' conviction rate remained significant when controlling for the number of parental convictions, parental violence and risk factors for crime. No difference was found between paternal and maternal imprisonment, parental imprisonment was only significantly related to son's offending when the son experienced this after the seventh birthday, and the more often and longer a son experienced parental imprisonment, the more often he offended. Furthermore, it seems that the relationship between parental imprisonment and son's offending can be partly explained by parental criminality.

These are surprising results. Why were no significant relationships found in the Netherlands and only for boys in England, while many previous studies led one to expect that an effect would be found in both countries? An explanation is that few previous studies investigated differences between parental imprisonment and parental conviction. To look at the net impact of imprisonment, over and above the impact of convictions, the analyses need to be designed in the way that this study did. These analyses illustrate that, in fact, it may have been the impact of frequent parental conviction, rather than parental imprisonment, that generated the findings in these previous studies.

Second, why were the few effects found mostly in England, but not in the Netherlands? In the Introduction of this chapter I described several possible explanations for the relationship between parental imprisonment and children's offending. Some of these factors will be similar in England and the Netherlands, such as the possibility that prisoners are the most criminal parents, and the trauma and social strain that children experience when their parent is incarcerated. Other mechanisms, however, will not be the same, because the situation in the two countries was different. Dutch prisons were far more humane than English ones in the period when this study's subjects experienced parental imprisonment (1946-1981). Dutch prisoners had considerably more opportunities for contact with their children. Not only were prisons more humane, but penal policy in general focussed much more on resocialisation in the Netherlands and on punishment in England. The social stigma for prisoners' children might have been a bigger problem in England than in the Netherlands which could have led to more problem behaviour and adult offending in these children. In the Netherlands, up until the beginning of the 1970s, a large proportion of the people who were imprisoned were sentenced for drunk driving and received relatively short sentences (two to three weeks). As a result, imprisonment might have been associated less with social stigma in the Netherlands and had less impact on the prisoner's children.

An example of the strong influence of penal and political environment on reactions to crime and stigma is described by Green (2008a,b) who studied this in relation to the subject of child-on-child homicide. He compared the English and Norwegian criminal justice systems and the public response to the cases of James Bulger and Silje Redergard. In Norway, the young killers were shielded from the public and carefully reintegrated into the community because it was believed that this was a tragic one-off accident, while in England, James Bulger's killers experienced extreme press and public antagonism. In England, harsh public attitudes created great stigma for these young people. Similarly, greater public stigma might affect children of imprisoned parents in England than in other countries. Green shows how stigmatization can differ vastly according to the penal and political environment.

In addition, it is expected that the children of Dutch prisoners experienced less economic strain, because the Netherlands had a more generous social security system than England (Dixon, 1998; Kaim-Caudle, 1973). Prisoners' families in England often experienced a 'considerable reduction in income, and in some cases acute poverty' (Morris, 1965, p. 293). This is not to say that prisoners' families in the Netherlands did not have economic problems, but the 'generous welfare state' might have softened the economic strain a bit (Downes & Van Swaaningen, 2007, p. 38). Furthermore, prison sentences in England were considerably longer than in the Netherlands and this study demonstrated a relationship between the length of parental imprisonment and offspring offending (Downes, 1992).

This study only looked at offspring offending after the nineteenth birthday, because I wanted parental imprisonment to precede offspring offending. This does mean, however, that a large part of offspring offending is missing, since the prevalence of offending peaks in the teenage years (Blumstein et al., 1986; Farrington, 1986; Piquero et al., 2007). This could possibly explain why a relationship was found in England, but not in the Netherlands. It could be that prisoners' children in the Netherlands desisted after adolescence, while in England they continued offending. A possible difference in desistance after adolescence could be linked to variation in class distinctions between the two countries. In England geographical and cultural class boundaries were - and are - much more pronounced than in the Netherlands, where birth class has a much weaker forecasting effect on children's life-path (Blanden et al., 2005; Breen, 2004; Musterd, 2005). Although research on the relationship between social class and crime produces inconsistent results and one could argue that people from higher social classes might commit different offences not always measured in crime studies, research in the United Kingdom demonstrates that people from a lower social class offend more often (Braithwaite, 1981; Farrington & Welsh, 2007; Wadsworth, 1979). The impact of parental imprisonment in the Netherlands might have evaporated after adolescence because people were able to *escape* the lower class environment, while in England parental imprisonment and associated factors may have sustained risk factors for crime further in life because they are much more connected to social and cultural class factors. It was not possible to examine this and it is uncertain that this happened, but this could be a possible explanation for the difference between England and the Netherlands.

Third, a relationship was found between parental imprisonment and the offending of sons, not of daughters. This is in line with the possibility that boys and girls react differently to stressful life events, with boys showing externalizing problem behaviour including criminal behaviour while girls have more internalizing problems (Murray & Farrington, 2008a). Another possible explanation for this gender difference could be that behaviour is more strongly transmitted in same-gender relationships (Farrington, Barnes & Lambert, 1996). However, this study revealed no difference between the impact of paternal and maternal imprisonment on sons or daughters and therefore does not support the idea of stronger same-gender transmission. It is also possible that relationships for girls were not significant, because of lower numbers of girls and mothers who were convicted and imprisoned.

Fourth, it is interesting to see that parental imprisonment between offspring ages seven and eighteen is more strongly related to sons' offending than parental imprisonment before that age. This does not support Bowlby's attachment theory stating that separation from a parent in the first few years of life will cause attachment problems and subsequent behaviour problems including offending behaviour. The finding that parental imprisonment impacts more strongly on older children is consistent with the previously mentioned stigma that these older children have to deal with, that one would expect to be stronger in England.

Analyses comparing parental imprisonment before and after birth can be used as a way of controlling for unmeasured variance. Many factors could influence the relationship between parental imprisonment and offspring offending. A way to control for these influences is to compare children whose parents were imprisoned before and after their birth. These two groups both have parents that were imprisoned at some point, so one could expect that associated risk factors are comparable. The only known difference here is the actual exposure of the child to the parent's imprisonment. By comparing these two groups confounding factors were held constant. Sons whose parents were imprisoned after birth had a significantly higher conviction rate than sons whose parents were imprisoned before birth. This suggests that the actual exposure to the parent's imprisonment was important in the relationship between parental imprisonment and a son's offending behaviour. However, there might be other differences between these two groups of parents that could account for the differences in offspring offending such as the possibility that parents who were imprisoned only before their child's birth might have experienced parenthood or marriage preceding parenthood as a "turning point" towards a less active criminal career (Sampson & Laub, 2005; Theobald & Farrington, 2009). Nevertheless, the finding that offspring offending increased with the length and the number of times parents had been imprisoned also suggests that the actual event of parental imprisonment impacts children and the more often this happens and the longer the event, the larger the impact on children.

Finally, the difference between prisoners' children and children of convicted parents disappeared when controlling for the number of parental convictions and several risk factors for crime. However, the relationships for length and number of parental imprisonments and offspring offending were robust and did not disappear when controlling for the number of parental convictions and for risk factors. This shows a clear impact of parental imprisonment on boys' offending, over and above the predictive effect of parental conviction and other risk factors.

This research undoubtedly has limitations and several other interpretations of the results should be considered. The study sample is relatively small, especially for females. This led to non-significant results where the effect size was relatively large. A larger sample would have shown more significant results. Furthermore, this is a quantitative study and in that sense a complex reality was simplified to a few variables. As Ezinga et al. (2009) have demonstrated, prisoners' children experience manifold and intricate problems. It is difficult to investigate the processes through which children may be positively or negatively affected by a parent's imprisonment through quantitative research only. Much more research, and also more qualitative research, is needed to understand these processes.

In addition, it was not possible to investigate genetic mechanisms of intergenerational transmission and the influence of this on the relationship between parental imprisonment and offspring offending. Adoption and twin studies, or direct investigation of genetic factors, would be needed to examine this. Furthermore, it was not certain that subjects who experienced parental imprisonment were not permanently separated from their parents before the event. Murray and Farrington (2005) knew this when they studied the original *CSDD* men, but this information was not available for the siblings used in this study. We can only assume that this information is similar for siblings older than the original men. In *Transfive*, information was available about divorces and analyses were run corrected and uncorrected for divorce, but the results were the same.

I tested whether parental imprisonment still predicted offspring offending after controlling for the number of parental convictions. This reduced the relationship between parental imprisonment and offspring offending and I concluded that parental offending plays a large role in this association. However, controlling for parental convictions in this way might have resulted in underestimating the impact of parental imprisonment on children. No attention was paid to whether parental imprisonment or parental convictions came first. An alternative explanation could be that parental imprisonment causes worse parental criminal behaviour (Nieuwbeerta, Nagin & Blokland,

2009; Wermink, Blokland, Nieuwbeerta & Tollenaar, 2009), which in turn causes more child crime.

Nevertheless, this is the first comparative study of parental imprisonment and offspring offending in the Netherlands and England. For both countries, longitudinal prospective datasets were used that followed high-risk groups for a long time. Such datasets are rare, and in that sense the comparison is unique. Through the design, method disparities were ruled out, and because parental imprisonment always occurred before offending by the child, the causal order was right. Also, because prisoners' children were compared with children whose parents were convicted but not imprisoned, the additional impact of parental imprisonment was examined. This is an improvement on earlier studies into the impact of parental imprisonment on children's behaviour.

What do these results mean for policy makers? The relationship between parental imprisonment and offspring offending differs considerably between the Netherlands and England. It is not certain, but a likely explanation for this is the previously described difference in the penal landscape. Today, the penal landscape in both countries has become more punitive with higher imprisonment rates, longer sentences, more women being imprisoned than before, and more drug offenders being prosecuted. The current results are not easily generalisable to today's situation. Yet, with today's more punitive landscape and the 'reinvention of the prison' (Garland, 2001, p. 14), this topic is even more relevant today, because more children experience parental imprisonment. Policy makers could design crime prevention programmes specifically targeted at families where a parent has been sent to prison. They could expand opportunities for contact between prisoners and their children, through special children's visits, affordable phone calls, schemes to record and playback stories and messages. They could offer financial support for prisoners' families. Social support organisations should especially pay attention to older children and adolescents who experience parental imprisonment. Moreover, children who experience many and longer parental imprisonments should be especially targeted for support.

It is important to investigate the relationship between parental imprisonment and offspring offending in today's more punitive societies. Since we do not know how parental imprisonment affects today's children, it would be good to closely monitor and study children whose parents are currently imprisoned. It would be especially interesting to examine this topic in the United States, an exceptionally punitive society, where the number of children with a parent in prison is enormous. Factors such as the opportunities for contact and visits and the amount of economic strain should be studied in a (quasi-)experimental design, wherever ethically possible. Killias, Aebi, and Ribeaud (2000) compared the effect of community services versus imprisonment on subsequent offending behaviour in an experimental design. Similarly, it would be good to randomly assign convicted people to imprisonment or community service and investigate their children's offending behaviour. Furthermore, it would be good to investigate parental imprisonment in more cross-national studies. Finally, though, it is important to investigate these issues in longitudinal studies including knowledge about the situation before parental imprisonment, as explained by Murray and Murray (2010).

6.6 Summary

This study examined whether prisoners' children have more adult convictions than children whose parents were convicted but not imprisoned. Parental imprisonment was investigated in England and the Netherlands from 1946-1981 using the *Cambridge Study in Delinquent Development* and the *NSCR Transfive Study*. In the Netherlands, no significant relationship was found between parental imprisonment and offspring offending. In England, a relationship was found for sons only. This association can be partly explained by parental criminality. However, after controlling for number of parental convictions and other childhood risk factors, a significant relationship remained between number of parental imprisonments and son's offending. When parental imprisonment at different ages was examined, parental imprisonment only significantly predicted sons' offending when it happened after the sons' seventh birthday.

Chapter 7

Discussion

'Sometimes they say I'm just like my mum and that makes me mad.'
(Ormiston, 2007, p. 17)

This study investigated mechanisms of intergenerational transmission of criminal behaviour. In this final chapter I will give an overview of the findings, discuss strengths and limitations of the study and consider implications for future research and for policy and politics. I will first provide a summary of the main results, followed by a discussion of the theoretical implications of these results.

7.1 What we know now

7.1.1 Intergenerational specialisation of violence

The first question of this dissertation was whether parents who have been convicted of a violent offence transmit criminal and violent behaviour more strongly than parents who were convicted, but never for violence. To answer this question a traditional and a statistically more advanced approach (Latent Class Analysis) were used. Both approaches demonstrated a higher risk for sons of violent fathers to have violent convictions, but this risk was only significantly higher for *CSDD* sons when applying Latent Class Analysis. The results demonstrated that violent parents do not transmit general offending behaviour more strongly, but that they do transmit violent offending more strongly. By demonstrating that specialisation in intergenerational transmission exists, these results support theories of specialisation of violent offending.

7.1.2 Timing and frequency of parental crime in the child's life and risk factors

In the second empirical chapter I investigated transmission of general criminal behaviour - including violence - in more detail by focusing on the timing and frequency of parental crime as well as on risk factors related to criminal behaviour. Frequency of parent and offspring crime was significantly related: offspring of parents with more convictions had an increased conviction rate. The second conclusion of this chapter was that children of parents who had only been convicted before birth had more convictions than children whose parents had never been convicted before or during the offspring's childhood. Furthermore, children whose parents had been convicted after the child's birth had even more convictions than those whose parents had only been convicted before their birth. When risk factors were taken into account, the difference between children whose parents had never been convicted versus children whose parents had been convicted before the child's birth remained significant. However, the difference between this last group and children whose parents had been convicted after their birth was not significant anymore when risk factors were taken into account. Risk factors were stronger predictors of the offspring's offending than the observation whether the parents had been convicted before versus after the child's birth. Children whose parents had been convicted when the children were between age 7 and 12 had the highest conviction rate, but none of the differences comparing the impact of parental conviction at different ages was significant. There does not appear to be a *sensitive* period for the impact of parental criminal behaviour.

7.1.3 Intergenerational continuity of conviction trajectories

In the third chapter so-called developmental trajectories of criminal behaviour were estimated for fathers as well as offspring. Among fathers three separate conviction trajectories could be identified: non-offenders, low chronic or sporadic offenders, and chronic offenders. Three groups were also identified among the *CSDD* daughters: non-offenders, low desisters, and chronic offenders. Among *CSDD* sons two additional groups were identified: low chronic offenders and high desisters. Among *Transfive* sons similar offending groups as among *CSDD* sons were identified, although there was no clear non-offending group among *Transfive*. It was not possible to estimate trajectory models for mothers in either dataset or for daughters in *Transfive*.

Surprisingly, although non-offending fathers significantly predict non-offending children, offspring of more persistent offending fathers do not have more convictions than offspring of sporadically offending fathers. Furthermore, although it seems as though father and offspring trajectories are related, the significant relationship can be explained by the observation that non-offending father trajectories tend to predict non-offending child trajectories. Chronic offending (CO) fathers do not predict chronic offending (CO) or high desisting (HD) sons significantly better than sporadic (LC) fathers. The results demonstrate a strong intergenerational transmission of criminal behaviour, but the fact that fathers have a conviction is more related to offspring convictions than is their conviction trajectory.

It is possible, however, that no significant relationships were found because the numbers involved in the analyses to test intergenerational transmission were relatively low. For example, the effect sizes for the difference in proportion of LC or HD sons among LC fathers and CO fathers (see page 73) are relatively high for the *CSDD* (odds ratios of 1.9 and 2.4) but not significant. It is possible that significant relationships will be found with larger samples.

7.1.4 Official bias and labelling

The fourth empirical chapter of this dissertation investigated whether official bias and labelling could explain intergenerational continuity of criminal behaviour. A convicted parent as well as a father's poor job record, low family income and poor housing were biasing variables; they increased the risk of offspring conviction taking into account the level of self-reported offending. Low family socio-economic status did not significantly predict convictions when controlling for self-reported offending. Furthermore, a conviction subsequently increased an individual's self-reported offending behaviour. However, this labelling effect was only visible for people whose parents have been convicted and not among the offspring whose parents have never been convicted.

7.1.5 Parental imprisonment

The final empirical chapter concentrated on the question whether offspring of prisoners display more criminal behaviour than offspring of convicted but not imprisoned parents. The additional impact of parental imprisonment over and above parental convictions was investigated specifically. In the Netherlands prisoners' offspring did not have more convictions than offspring of convicted parents, but in England a significant relationship was visible between parental imprisonment and offspring offending for sons. After controlling for the number of parental convictions, parental violence and risk factors for crime, a significant relationship remained between the number of parental imprisonments and a son's offending. There was no difference between a father's or a mother's imprisonment; parental imprisonment was only significantly related to son's offending when the son experienced this after the seventh birthday; and the more often and longer a son experienced parental imprisonment, the more often he offended. Furthermore, it appears that the relationship between parental imprisonment and a son's offending can be partly explained by parental criminality.

7.1.6 Cross-national comparison: England and the Netherlands

As discussed in the introduction, replication of results was the main motivation to compare the results for the analyses in Chapters 2 and 4 on specialisation and trajectory analyses, while the comparison in Chapter 6 was interesting from a policy perspective. In this section, I will provide a brief overview of the comparability of the data sets and differences and similarities in results.

The samples used in this study are comparable in the sense that the subjects were born in the same period: 1946-1962. They also come from a relatively high-risk group. A difference between the samples is that the English sample is larger. The *CSDD* sample included 1184 subjects of which 782 were male and 402 were female. These subjects came from 397 families (the 411 original men include 14 brother pairs). The 804 subjects in *Transfive* came from 351 families; 412 were male and 392 were female. The smaller sample for *Transfive* could have resulted in less statistical power to detect statistical differences.

In terms of offending, a larger proportion of offspring has been convicted in the English sample compared with the Dutch sample: 41.3% of *CSDD* males has ever been convicted between their 12th and 40th birthday compared with 34.2% of *Transfive* males; and 12.4% of *CSDD* daughters has been convicted compared with 9.4% in *Transfive*. Moreover, the average number of convictions is higher for *CSDD* males (4.56) than for *Transfive* (3.25).[49] This number is comparable for daughters: 2.66 for *CSDD* daughters compared to 2.50 for *Transfive* daughters.

Results from Chapter 2 on specialisation reveal strikingly similar patterns in the Netherlands and England. The extent of intergenerational specialisation using the traditional method is similar in the English and Dutch samples (OR 1.60 versus 1.83). Interestingly, the LCA solutions are also quite similar for both samples: two classes of which one can be characterised as a theft and the other as a violence-other class. Transmission of violence using LCA is stronger for the English sample, but the Dutch sample shows a pattern in the same direction.

In Chapter 4 I investigated intergenerational transmission using trajectory analyses in both England and the Netherlands. Trajectories for fathers were remarkably similar in both countries. Offspring trajectories also looked similar, although they are higher for the English sample. This is not surprising taking into account the observation that the English males had a higher average number of convictions than the Dutch males.

---

49 Excluding the earlier mentioned outliers, see page 70

Looking at offspring behaviour per father trajectory the patterns are comparable in both countries, although the extent of intergenerational transmission appears stronger in England. The conviction rates are higher in the English sample, but the difference between children of the different father groups is also larger. Although this chapter did not compare whether intergenerational transmission was stronger in England or the Netherlands, it is possible to hypothesize what could explain stronger transmission in England. In the Netherlands police registrations and prison sentences were at a low level in the 1950s to 1970s, the period of study of this dissertation (Bijleveld & Wijkman, 2009; Tonry & Bijleveld, 2007a). The Netherlands offered a mild penal environment in this period. Furthermore, this period was characterised by increased opportunities and access to higher education for individuals of all social classes. These factors could explain why intergenerational transmission might have been stronger in England compared with the Netherlands. The conclusion from this chapter that there is no significant difference between children of the different offending father trajectories is similar in both countries though.

The third comparison of England and the Netherlands focused on parental imprisonment. It is interesting that a difference was found between the impact of parental imprisonment in England versus the Netherlands. This could possibly be explained by the difference in penal and prison policies of these countries in the period for which parental imprisonment was investigated (1946-1981). The Netherlands was known as an extremely humane, tolerant and liberal country where imprisonment rates were low and prison sentences short. England, in contrast, had much higher imprisonment rates, longer sentences and fewer opportunities for contact with families. I also hypothesized that stigma for prisoners' children might have been lower in the Netherlands compared with England. These results suggest that a more punitive penal landscape impacts more strongly on the children of those at whom the penal policies are aimed. In the section on Implications for policy and politics I will further discuss policy implications.

7.2 Implications for theories on intergenerational transmission

How can we explain intergenerational transmission of criminal behaviour: Does it matter how often parents offend? What kind of crime parents commit? When parents offend? What their criminal career looks like? And does it matter whether and how parents get sentenced for criminal behaviour? These questions are of central concern to criminologists as well as policy makers. The current section relates the empirical findings to the theories and mechanisms discussed in the Introduction.

One could ask which mechanisms contribute more strongly to intergenerational transmission compared with others. A simple comparison of these mechanisms was not possible with the data used in this study. Moreover, each mechanism appears to be relevant and the mechanisms are also likely to interact with each other. It is important to stress that the study design - not being experimental - did not enable the drawing of conclusions about causal relationships. However, it is possible to relate this study's findings to theories and discuss where the results support or disprove mechanisms of intergenerational transmission. In doing this, I will follow the structure used in the Introduction.

7.2.1 Risk factors: a criminogenic environment

The first explanation for intergenerational transmission was that continuity of criminal behaviour over generations could be explained by a criminogenic environment. The behaviour is not necessarily transmitted, but children of criminal parents grow up in an environment characterised by many risk factors for crime. Criminal behaviour is not isolated from the rest of someone's life, and people committing crime often exhibit problems in other realms of life. They are more likely to use drugs, to be unemployed, experience poverty and live in poor accommodation and/or bad neighbourhoods. Criminal parents thus increase the odds of their children growing up in an environment where these circumstances feature, which in turn will increase the risk for offspring developing criminal behaviour.

The findings of this study support this mechanism. Analyses in Chapter 3 demonstrated that offspring whose parents offended before versus after their birth differed in terms of risk factors. Children whose parents had been convicted after the child's birth were more likely to come from backgrounds characterised by low family income, large family size, fathers with a poor job record, and less interest in education by parents. These risk factors better explained the difference in offspring offending between these two groups than the observation that parents offended before versus after the offspring's birth. Similarly, analyses from Chapter 6 demonstrated that risk factors were stronger predictors of offspring offending than whether the parent had been sent to prison or not.

In the Introduction (see pages 4-5) I discussed how these risk factors can be defined as risk markers, causal risk factors or mediating factors. Although this study was unable to investigate which of these scenarios is the best explanation for this phenomenon, this study's findings do demonstrate that risk factors play an important role in intergenerational continuity. It is not just behaviour that is transmitted, and even if behaviour was transmitted, this does not happen in a vacuum. Parental offending might influence these risk factors and vice versa and, similarly, offspring offending and these risk factors might also interact with each other. This, then, links back to Thornberry and Krohn's Interactional Theory of Offending which states that offending

Implications for theories on intergenerational transmission

will interact with other spheres of life (Thornberry, 2005; Thornberry & Krohn, 2001, 2005, see page 8 of this dissertation). Thornberry discusses how people involved in antisocial behaviour might have problems making successful transitions into adult roles, including parenthood, and thereby might have problems in raising their children. Even though this study did not test this mediating path via the quality and effectiveness of parenting, the findings demonstrate that people involved in antisocial behaviour do have problems with adult roles such as having a job and providing their family with a stable income. Instead of providing their offspring with an environment that encourages prosocial behaviour, they bestow upon them a risky environment. In sum, the risk factor mechanism as well as the intergenerational extension to the Interactional Theory are supported by findings from this dissertation.

7.2.2 Social learning: imitating behaviour

Imitation of behaviour is an explanation offered intuitively by (lay) people when talking about intergenerational continuity. Children will observe their parents' criminal or noncriminal behaviour and copy these behaviours. Social Learning theory suggests that this imitation could occur directly as well as indirectly. The first type of learning occurs when a parent directly conveys attitudes or other information about how to commit crime. Crime is broadly defined here and could include minor behaviours such as hurting others, taking things from others, or using alcohol or drugs. Indirect social learning is more subtle, although opportunities for this type of transmission possibly occur on a more everyday basis. For example, while a parent might not necessarily demonstrate stealing in front of the child, the child could learn that it is acceptable to try and go through the turnstile with two people at a time when using public transport.

The findings of this study do not necessarily support the idea of direct social learning. In Chapter 3 I demonstrated how, after controlling for other risk factors for crime, there was no significant difference in criminal behaviour between children whose parents had only been convicted before versus after the child's birth. For direct social learning, one would expect that it would be important for the parent to commit criminal behaviour when the child could observe this. One would thus expect that children whose parents had been convicted after the child's birth would show more antisocial behaviour. The findings do not support this hypothesis. It is important to realise, however, that this sample did not enable the study of actual social learning processes, and it is uncertain whether children whose parents had been convicted after the child's birth actually experienced or observed their parents committing crime.

It is possible that parents who did not commit criminal behaviour after the child was born, but did so before the child's birth, still had some (minor) antisocial attitudes or customs that they indirectly communicated to their children. The fact that no significant difference was found between these two groups of children when controlling for risk factors could actually fit with the idea of indirect social learning. Akers' (1977; 2002) Social Learning theory focuses particularly on reinforcement and suggests that children will learn much through reinforcement. For example, the child will learn, from the parent's reaction, whether it is acceptable to come home while intoxicated. A parent who does not respond negatively or disapprovingly will convey that this behaviour is tolerable. Other studies such as Giordano (2010) have demonstrated support for the transmission of such values and attitudes.

Furthermore, a distinction can be made between specific and generalised social learning. Specific social learning posits that people will copy the exact same behaviour as their model, while generalised social learning suggests transmission of a more general antisocial behaviour pattern or an accepting attitude towards violent or criminal behaviour (see also page 22). The findings from Chapter 2 on specialisation in intergenerational transmission would support the idea of specific social learning, because the offspring of violent fathers were more likely to commit violent crime. However, both fathers and offspring also committed other types of crime, and a group of people who committed only violence could not be identified. This demonstrates that it is also likely that a more general attitude, acceptance, or pattern of antisocial behaviour is transmitted.

7.2.3 Genetic or biological transmission

Another intuitive explanation for intergenerational transmission suggests that the criminal behaviour of both generations could be explained by biological or genetic mechanisms. Due to the absence of a twin- or adoption design and lack of biological/genetic measurements, it was even harder to investigate this mechanism in the current study. However, the findings from this study do not disprove biological or genetic measurements. Results from Chapter 2 on specialisation would confirm the idea that violent behaviour could have a different or stronger biological origin than other types of criminal behaviour, because offspring of violent parents had a higher risk of exhibiting violent behaviour in particular. Results from Chapter 3 on timing of parental crime demonstrated that offspring whose parents had been convicted before the child's birth committed more crime than offspring whose parents had never been convicted. Part of the difference between these two groups of children could be explained by differences in risk factors, but a significant part also remained unexplained. An explanation for this unmeasured variance could be a genetic or biological process.

7.2.4 The impact of sentencing of parents on intergenerational transmission

The official bias mechanism suggests that people are more likely to get convicted when their parents are known to the police. Offspring of convicted parents thus turn into 'the usual suspects'.[50] The findings of Chapter 5 demonstrated support for this official bias. Having a convicted parent or growing up in poorer social circumstances means that people are more likely to get convicted compared with others with a similar level of self-reported offending but without these characteristics. These poorer social circumstances are characterised by a father with a poor job record, low family income and poor housing. The quantitative analyses from this dissertation confirm more qualitative analyses by McAra and McVie (2005; 2007a; 2007b) concluding that individuals are more likely to be targeted when they are perceived as less respectable.

Furthermore, analyses in this chapter also demonstrated labelling effects: self-reported offending behaviour increased when people had been convicted, but decreased (naturally) when they did not experience conviction. Labelling theory (see also page 82) proposes that a conviction will amplify someone's offending behaviour either through a change in the individual's self-perception (by conforming to the criminal stereotype) or through blocked opportunities for a non-criminal life (because it is difficult to find a job with a criminal record and hard to sustain important relationships while in prison). Although this study did not examine such mediating labelling processes (but others did, see for example: Bernburg & Krohn, 2003; Bernburg et al., 2006; Murray et al., forthcoming; Van der Geest, 2011), it does demonstrate support for labelling effects.

Moreover, I demonstrated an interaction effect: when considering whether parents had a conviction, the findings demonstrate a strong labelling effect for children with a convicted parent, but no labelling effect for people without a convicted parent. A cumulative effect is taking place: the impact of someone's own conviction is much stronger when someone has a convicted parent. In a sense, disadvantages pile up, and one could hypothesize the amplification of offending behaviour via both labelling routes: a) already felt stigma of being a criminal's child will increase when someone is labelled as a criminal, and b) when people grow up with a convicted parent, and thus in a more than average criminogenic environment, they will have fewer opportunities for a non-criminal life compared with someone who grew up in an environment full of opportunities for a conventional life. This accumulation of official bias and labelling is a novel and important finding.

Another aspect of sentencing of parents that I investigated was whether parental imprisonment entails a risk in addition to a parent's conviction. I discussed how parental imprisonment can impact on offspring's offending, mental health and well-being according to several theoretical perspectives (see page 107). Interestingly, no significant impact of parental imprisonment on offspring offending was found in the Netherlands, but such an impact was found in England. This demonstrates that parental imprisonment does

---

50 A term coined by McAra and McVie (2005, p. 5) in their research on the police 'unfairly targeting certain categories of young people.'

not necessarily have a negative impact on offspring offending. As I also discussed in Chapter 6, circumstances before, during, and after a parental imprisonment are likely to determine the impact of a parent's imprisonment as well (see also Murray & Murray, 2010). As other studies have demonstrated (e.g. Giordano, 2010; Hissel et al., 2011) parental imprisonment is not the only negative life event children of incarcerated parents experience. These children often grow up in an unstable environment consisting of constantly changing care-giving arrangements, shifts of schools, living in less-than-desirable neighbourhoods, and thus parental imprisonment might be just one more negative event. However, the finding that parental imprisonment was significantly related to offspring offending in England, even when controlling for risk factors for criminal behaviour, does suggest an impact of this sentencing of parents on offspring. I proposed that the penal climate and possibly greater levels of stigma in England could explain the difference between the two countries. This is an important issue, because it would also mean that policies might influence the possible impact of sentencing on the children of those who are sentenced.

In this dissertation I investigated the impact of sentencing of parents on offspring offending in two ways: via official bias and labelling and via parental imprisonment. The results of both these chapters demonstrate that sentencing of parents is likely to impact on children of these offenders. Much research and theorising exists on the impact of sentencing on offenders in the form of labelling research, and also on the consequences of imprisonment. Research investigating the impact of sentencing on offenders' *offspring* often focuses on the impact of parental imprisonment (for an overview see Murray & Farrington, 2008a; Murray et al., 2009). This dissertation added to this knowledge by not only examining the impact of parental imprisonment, but also by investigating official bias. It supports conclusions by McAra and McVie (2005) that penal policies may in fact augment these problems that they aim to reduce. By employing policies aimed at reducing offending behaviour, we run the risk of increasing offending behaviour in the next generation. This conclusion has important policy implications that I will discuss below.

7.3 Strengths and limitations of the present research

In each chapter I have already discussed relevant strengths and limitations, but I will reiterate those which span the whole dissertation.

7.3.1 Strengths

The major strength of this dissertation is the combination of two prospective, longitudinal datasets with information on the development of criminal behaviour for a large number of people.

The *Cambridge Study in Delinquent Development* is an extremely rich dataset that includes information on official offending, self-reported offending, and several risk factors for criminal behaviour. The study design has many strengths, such as the long-term follow-up, high retention rates, few missing data, information from multiple sources such as official records, the males and their parents, and information on a wide variety of relevant constructs related to antisocial behaviour, such as parental child-rearing methods, socio-economic status, impulsiveness, environmental risk factors, and so on. The study's males have been interviewed nine times over a period of 40 years, and the sample size of 411 males allows for detailed statistical analyses, case histories and face-to-face interviews (Farrington et al., 2006). Including the siblings of these males increased statistical power and enabled investigating females.

The strength of the *NSCR Transfive Study* is its long-term follow up of several generations of people in the Netherlands, resulting in a large number of study subjects, even though in the current study only participants born between 1946 and 1962 and their parents were investigated. *Transfive* has traced all descendants of the original study males and thus has a 100% retrieval rate. Next to official records of criminal behaviour, the study has information on demographic variables such as marriage, divorce, death and child bearing.

The combination of both datasets enabled comparison of the validity of risk factors for criminal behaviour in different times and places as well as replication of results using exactly the same operationalisation of constructs. Another strength is the use of a variety of (advanced) statistical techniques to quantitatively investigate the topic of intergenerational transmission. One of these methods, trajectory analysis, has been applied to intergenerational transmission only once before. Latent Class Analysis has never been employed before to study intergenerational transmission. By utilising this technique in a new field of study this dissertation has filled a methodological gap and thereby will hopefully reinvigorate the study of specialisation in intergenerational transmission.

7.3.2 Limitations

Although this study has several strengths, there are also important limitations.

First, as I have already discussed in the empirical chapters, only official convictions were used, with the exception of Chapter 5, where self-reported offending was included to study official bias. For *Transfive* and for parents and siblings in the *CSDD*, only official data are available and therefore I was unable to study intergenerational transmission using measures of self-reported offending. Official measures show only a part of offending behaviour and suffer from a *dark number*, the other part of offending that cannot be measured using official statistics. Examining official data and not self-reported offending could have impacted on the results in several ways as stated in the discussions in the empirical chapters.

Second, to examine mechanisms of intergenerational transmission, I had to investigate specific subgroups of the sample. This sometimes resulted in small groups of subjects, especially for females (daughters as well as mothers). This reduced the statistical power of the analyses, and consequently the reliability of the results.

Third, although I used a variety of (advanced) statistical techniques to study intergenerational transmission, these mechanisms were not observed in interactions or specifically discussed in interviews with the research subjects. The quantitative analyses reveal important insights in intergenerational transmission, but these analyses also simplify a complex reality. Qualitative analyses such as those done by Giordano (2010) are important to investigate more specifically the process of intergenerational transmission.

Fourth, it is important to realise that the data used are non-experimental. No causal inferences can be drawn from the analyses in this dissertation: it is unknown whether parental convictions or imprisonment and the other risk factors are causal factors or markers. It is possible that other processes, and not so much parental conviction or imprisonment, are causing offspring of convicted parents to have a higher risk of conviction. Furthermore, I was unable to study the influence children had on their parents' offending behaviour or the reciprocal relationships between parent and offspring's behaviour (Pardini, Fite & Burke, 2008; Bell, 1968; Belsky, 1984; Belsky & Vondra, 1989; Patterson, 1995, 2002). It is possible that the relationship between parent and offspring offending can be partly explained by parents and offspring reciprocally influencing each other's behaviour.

Fifth, following on from the previous limitations and reflecting a general issue in social science research, in this study I could not include every relevant factor related to intergenerational transmission or the development of criminal behaviour. Individuals are not only affected by experiences at home, but school and peers will also impact on their development (Harris, 1995, 1998). It is important to realise the limited scope of influence of parental conviction and imprisonment on offending behaviour.

Finally, the children investigated in this dissertation were born between 1946 and 1962. As I have discussed in the discussions of the empirical chapters, results from these analyses cannot be easily generalised to today's children. The penal environment in England as well as the Netherlands has become more punitive, the role and structure of the family has changed, and society has changed in general. It might also be easier for someone to escape their socio-economic background, and thus the impact of intergenerational transmission might be weaker. However, the more punitive environment would suggest that more children experience parental conviction and imprisonment, and this could imply that the scope of intergenerational transmission has grown larger.

Bonferroni correction

In the research for this dissertation I have used several statistical comparisons. Bonferroni corrections for a more stringent criterion than the conventional $p<.05$ were not applied. Some have argued that Bonferroni adjustments are necessary, because multiple statistical comparisons increase the chance of Type 1 errors, where one would falsely reject the null hypothesis (and conclude that there is a statistical difference when in reality there is no difference). However, as Perneger (1998) and Feise (2002) argue, there are a number of problems with such Bonferroni adjustments. Coming back to the type I error, a Bonferroni adjustment might decrease this error, but simultaneously increase type II error, the acceptance of the null hypothesis when the alternative is true. Furthermore, Perneger (1998) has suggested that Bonferroni adjustments challenge common sense in that comparisons should be interpreted differently according to the number of tests performed. As Perneger (1998, p. 1236) states 'evidence in data is what the data say – other considerations such as how many other tests are performed, are irrelevant'. Moreover, it is unclear how many tests should be included when applying a Bonferroni adjustment. Finally though, when performing statistical analyses, the emphasis should be more on effect sizes than on significance. In light of these arguments, I decided not to apply Bonferroni adjustments.

7.4 Implications for future research

Given the limitations discussed above, several future prospects and suggestions for future research can be formulated.

7.4.1 Intergenerational transmission with self-reported offending behaviour

A limitation of the current study and of many studies into intergenerational transmission of criminal behaviour is the reliance on official convictions. Not only do official convictions face a dark number, this difference between official convictions and someone's real offending behaviour might vary for different types of offenders. Some smart offenders might know better how to stay out of the police's hands, and these people might also transmit this behaviour differently to their offspring. In any case, it is vital to study intergenerational transmission using self-reported data and particularly with aspects that have not been studied previously using self-reported data, such as specialisation in intergenerational transmission and intergenerational resemblance of offending trajectories.

7.4.2 Intergenerational transmission for females

One of the limitations of this study highlights the need for similar analysis to focus on women. It is possible that behaviour is more strongly transmitted in same-gender relationships (Farrington, Barnes & Lambert, 1996), and therefore it is important to study transmission from both parents. Furthermore, especially in the sample investigated in this dissertation, most children will spend more time with their mother and will thus be more exposed to their mother's behaviour. I also discussed how convicted and violent women are less common than convicted and violent men and how this might lead to more stigma in society and possible official bias. These women may also be labelled as disturbed rather than criminal (Hedderman & Gelsthorpe, 1997). In line with this, one might expect intergenerational transmission of criminal behaviour from mothers to be stronger than from fathers. Therefore, it would be desirable to replicate this research with a dataset that includes more females. This would be especially informative for aspects that have not been studied previously, such as specialisation in intergenerational transmission and continuity of offending trajectories.

7.4.3 Intergenerational specialisation of violence

Given the paucity of research into specialisation in intergenerational transmission, it would also be informative to apply the other recent approach to study specialisation, item response theory (IRT) in a multilevel regression framework (Osgood & Schreck, 2007; Sullivan et al., 2009), to intergenerational transmission (see page 20). This method also utilises a latent variable to define specialisation. Furthermore, by using a multilevel model, it takes into account the immanent confounds with the frequency of offending and measures specialisation taking into account the base rates of each offence. It is thereby possible to a) gauge the extent and significance of specialisation, b) estimate the stability of this specialisation and c) measure associations of specialisation with other variables. IRT in a multilevel framework is thus a statistical approach with greater sensitivity that incorporates all available information combined with suitable modelling including these measures of offending frequency and offence base rates (Osgood & Schreck, 2007). Because of the statistical advantages, it would be extremely interesting to utilise this method in the study of specialisation in intergenerational transmission.

7.4.4 Intergenerational resemblance of conviction trajectories

It would be particularly desirable to replicate the trajectory analyses with a larger sample. The current study was the first to test specifically the resemblance between father and offspring trajectories using Adjusted Standardised Residuals (ASRs) and Odds Ratios (ORs). It is important to know whether the non-significant results are due to the relatively low number of people in each trajectory group or because there is no relationship. For example, the Dutch Criminal Career and Life Course Study (CCLS) used by Van de Rakt et al. (2008) would be a good source to investigate this. Van de Rakt et al. (2008) estimated trajectories for fathers and offspring, but failed to provide effect sizes for the strength of the relationships between trajectories or whether these relationships are significantly related. Their sample would be excellent to calculate these values and examine this issue, because the sample contains about 3,500 fathers and their 7,987 children.

7.4.5 Experimental designs

An important gap in the knowledge on intergenerational transmission and the impact of parental imprisonment is whether parental conviction and transmission are *causing* offspring criminal behaviour. To examine this, one ideally needs an experimental design or a randomised control trial. Killias et al. (2000) used a randomised experiment in Switzerland to compare the effect of community services versus imprisonment on subsequent offending behaviour and to compare the impact of community services versus electronic monitoring (Killias, Gilliéron, Kissling & Villettaz, 2010). It is desirable to use a comparable design where people are randomly assigned to imprisonment, community service, and/or electronic monitoring and subsequently their children are compared. It is somewhat more difficult with such a design to investigate the impact of parental convictions, because it is ethically harder not to convict certain people as part of a randomised control trial. However, electronic monitoring could be a good option here, because the impact is likely to be less than a prison or community service sentence. Another option would be to use cautions instead of a sentence. People who would normally receive a sentence could be randomly assigned to such a warning instead of a more intrusive sentence.

Experiments such as these are difficult to realise, not only because they require measurement over a long time span, but also because the law needs to enable experiments. The Switzerland experiment (Killias et al., 2000), for example, was performed while the law was changing. The Swiss Criminal Code provided an option to evaluate innovative ways of correctional treatment such as community services versus prison sentences in a pilot project. Sometimes situations arise in which a natural or pseudo-experiment can take place. For example, in the Netherlands, with the marriage of H.R.H. Princess Beatrix in 1966, the then Queen Juliana remitted sentences for a large group of offenders (Van der Werff, 1979). This enabled comparison of a group of convicted offenders who had their sentence remitted completely with a group of offenders who had to serve their sentence normally. This last group had either already served their sentence by the time the royal order of remission was announced or was sentenced after the remission date (10th of March 1966). This led to a methodologically unique situation since the groups were comparable in background and other factors, but arbitrarily had to serve their short prison sentence or not. Such circumstances do not arise often, but provide interesting opportunities to investigate the impact of sentences.[51]

Alternatively, it would be useful to employ a quasi-experimental design. In comparison to a real experiment, the quasi-experiment would lack random assignment. Instead, it would carefully assess before and after measures of offspring behaviour and include appropriately matched control subjects. This relates to the use of longitudinal studies including knowledge about the situation before and after parental conviction or imprisonment. Longitudinal studies also adhere to the logic of quasi-experimental designs. It is important to replicate analyses in this study using other large scale longitudinal studies.

To examine biological or genetic mechanisms of intergenerational transmission, adoption or twin designs could be used. Such designs enable drawing conclusions about the relative impact of someone's environment versus genetic make-up (DiLalla & Gottesman, 1991). Genetic factors explain a considerable fraction of the variance in criminal and violent behaviour (see page 6). Therefore it is important to consider these influences when studying intergenerational transmission.

7.4.6 Reciprocal relationships

By using longitudinal designs that measure parent and offspring behaviour at regular intervals over a long period of time, it would also be possible to study reciprocal relationships between parents' and offspring's antisocial behaviour. The impact of parents' behaviour on offspring problem behaviour has been investigated extensively. It is also recognised that children's behaviour might impact on parenting practices, but empirical research examining the mutual influences of parents and children on each other is a relatively recent phenomenon. Several studies have demonstrated these mutual influences: parents whose children develop conduct problems tend to worsen their parenting techniques over time (Pardini et al., 2008; Bell, 1968; Belsky, 1984; Belsky & Vondra, 1989; Patterson, 1995, 2002). Capaldi et al. (2002, p. 129) also stated that 'an additional stress factor that can affect par-

---

51 Van der Werff (1979) compared recidivism for traffic, property, and aggressive offenders. There were no significant differences between offenders who did and did not serve their term of imprisonment in the proportion of reconviction within six years after their conviction, in the number of convictions nor in the speed with which they reoffended.

ental mood states and diminish parenting is the child's antisocial behaviour itself.' For example, 'interactions charged with negative emotion and parental rejection diminish family management skills, including discipline and supervision, and result in further increases in the boys' antisocial behaviour' (Capaldi et al., 2002, p. 130). However, most of these studies have focused on parenting practices and antisocial behaviour, not on criminal behaviour. It is crucial to investigate what the impact of delinquent teenagers would be on parental parenting practices and criminal behaviour and vice versa.

7.4.7 Peers and school environment

Similarly, it would be interesting to investigate the interaction between parental offending on offspring offending and other relevant environmental influences such as peers and school. For example, Harris (1995, 1998, 2000) has suggested that research tends to overestimate the influence parents have on their children. She proposes that a great deal of socialisation takes place outside the home in children and adolescents' peer groups. It would be valuable simultaneously to investigate the impact and interaction of peers and parents.

7.4.8 Other settings

Finally, it is vital that the validity of this study's results be tested using information from other countries and more contemporary samples. In the Introduction, I started by explaining how important cross-national comparisons are to investigate whether causes and risk factors for criminal behaviour are comparable in different times and places. As Farrington (1999, p. 163) stated:

> An advantage of cross-national comparative studies is that they would help to establish how far criminal careers, risk factors, and intervention effects are the same or different in participating countries. To the extent that results are similar, they might strengthen our confidence in universal findings and theories. To the extent that results are different, the challenge would be to explain the differences, perhaps by reference to features of national contexts.

Studying the Netherlands and England has produced valuable knowledge about intergenerational transmission and the impact of the national context. However, it is unknown how far these results generalise to contemporary societies and other countries. It would be especially informative to study the topic of intergenerational transmission and the impact of policies on this in the United States, because the U.S. is an example of an exceptionally punitive society.

7.5 Implications for policy and politics

Criminological research is vital in informing policy makers and politicians about what we know about what works to reduce criminal behaviour. The research in this dissertation provides a compelling case for the existence of intergenerational transmission and for the need to intervene in this cycle of violence and offending.

It is desirable to focus attention on the children of convicted parents to try and stop this intergenerational transmission. A first suggestion would be to provide family-based intervention programs, such as parent education and parent management training. These have been shown to be effective in reducing offspring offending behaviour (Farrington & Welsh, 2007). Parent education involves educating parents about the health of their children, but also serves to improve parents' and children's well being. Parent management training involves training parents to alter their child's behaviour (Kazdin, 1997). The results from this study demonstrate that these prevention programmes would be desirable for all offspring with convicted parents, but especially for offspring whose parents are convicted more often and whose parents have been sent to prison.

In the case of parental imprisonment, several specific issues could be improved. Policy makers could expand opportunities for contact between prisoners and their children, through special children's visits, affordable phone calls, schemes to record and playback stories and messages. Special child-centred visits remove a great deal of the stress involved in visiting parents in prison. Searching methods for normal visits vary for every prison, but can be rigorous and stressful for children; they range from walking through an electronic portal, taking off shoes, to walking past a drug dog, and some prisons require fingerprinting for all visitors (Ormiston, 2007). During normal visits, children and parents need to stay seated in their own chairs. Family visits take place in rooms specifically fitted for leisure time, parents can move around freely, children can play, run around, and sit on their parent's lap. Such visits can be used to build family bonds and create positive experiences for parents and children. Children also show preference for such visits: 'I like it when he doesn't have to wear the red vest because he is like my dad not like a prisoner' (Lösel et al., 2011, p. 54).

A specific prevention program focused on prisoners and their children is *Betere Start* - Better beginnings - which supports incarcerated mothers in the last three months of their detention and afterwards. The program, based on the internationally recognised training program *Incredible Years* (Webster-Stratton, 1992), focuses on parent training and education. Preliminary results from the randomised controlled trial in the Netherlands show that children of incarcerated mothers involved in the program show less problem behaviour and score lower on risk factors for delinquent behaviour compared with children of incarcerated mothers who were not involved in *Betere Start*

(De Castro, October 2011). The final results of this randomised controlled trial will be published mid-2012, so conclusions are still preliminary, but such a program might be effective in decreasing the risk of future criminal involvement for prisoners' offspring.

Furthermore, financial support for prisoners' families could be offered. Social support organisations should particularly pay attention to older children and adolescents who experience parental imprisonment. Moreover, children who experience many and longer parental imprisonments should be specifically targeted for support.

This study also demonstrated that risk factors appear important in the intergenerational transmission of criminal behaviour. Some of these risk factors, such as a large family or having a mother who was a teenager when her first child was born, are static and therefore harder to change. Others are dynamic and hence more open to change, such as low family income, poor housing, poor job record of father and low interest in education by parents. Even though the current study was unable to examine whether these risk factors are *causing* the offspring's criminal behaviour, these factors likely add to the risk and might be an opportunity to intervene in the cycle of intergenerational transmission. For example, improving someone's employability might not only decrease that person's criminal behaviour (as demonstrated by Van der Geest et al., 2011; Verbruggen et al., 2011) but also their offspring's future criminal behaviour. Even the more static factors, such as teenage motherhood, are open to intervention through the use of programs to reduce teenage pregnancy. When trying to reduce or prevent criminal behaviour, it is important to focus not only on this behaviour itself, but also on areas of life that might interactively impact on each other. As Farrington (2011, p. 133) suggested, we should perceive intergenerational transmission as 'a larger cycle of deprivation and antisocial behaviour'. The results from this study provide justification for targeting interventions at this larger cycle of deprivation.

Furthermore, the results from this study suggest an impact of penal, police, and prison policies on offspring of offenders. It appears that offspring of convicted parents are more likely to be convicted. This is not necessarily because they commit more crime, but because their parents are known offenders and because they live in poorer social circumstances characterised by having a father with a poor job record, low family income and poor housing. These offspring also tend to commit more criminal behaviour than offspring with unconvicted parents and offspring who do not grow up in these poorer social circumstances, but if we take this into account, these individuals still have a higher risk of getting convicted. This is a crucial finding, and at the same time ethically undesirable. This finding conflicts with the UN Convention on the Rights of the Child (United Nations General Assembly, 1989). Article 2 of this convention states that:

> States Parties shall respect and ensure the rights set forth in the present Convention to each child within their jurisdiction without discrimination of any kind, irrespective of the child's or his or her parent's or legal guardian's race, colour, sex, language, religion, political or other opinion, national, ethnic or social origin, property, disability, birth or other status.

And

> States Parties shall take all appropriate measures to ensure that the child is protected against all forms of discrimination or punishment on the basis of the status, activities, expressed opinions, or beliefs of the child's parents, legal guardians, or family members.

Furthermore, article 3 of the convention posits:

> In all actions concerning children, whether undertaken by public or private social welfare institutions, courts of law, administrative authorities or legislative bodies, the best interests of the child shall be a primary consideration.

Thus, according to this convention, the state should protect children from discrimination or punishment based on the status or activities of the child's parents. Moreover, the 'the best interests of the child' should be the 'primary consideration.' When children of convicted parents are disproportionally convicted, this clashes with the convention just quoted.

Official agencies might not be aware of their possible bias against these individuals. In social interaction and when perceiving information, people use schemas, or 'cognitive frameworks for organising, interpreting, and recalling information' (R. A. Baron, Byrne & Johnson, 1998, p. 127). Prejudice and stereotypes help us to perceive the world around us, a world with often too much information to handle easily. Stereotypes conserve energy and save cognitive resources. The biasing variables are also risk factors for criminal behaviour, so it is not surprising that police and other justice agencies might use these to focus their attention on. These stereotypes work, because people whose parents have been convicted and live in poor housing do have a higher risk to commit criminal behaviour. However, it is vital that the police and courts are aware of this bias and that, in their decision making, they try to reduce the impact of this bias. Furthermore, instead of convicting these people disproportionally often, it might be more fruitful to intervene on these poorer social circumstances. For example, housing or neighbourhood improvement programmes, and again improving someone's employability would be ethically more appropriate and possibly also more effective interventions.

This study also demonstrated that offspring of convicted parents increased their offending behaviour after they themselves had been convicted.

Even though this study only found a significant effect for children of convicted parents and not for children of unconvicted parents, previous research has demonstrated evidence for this labelling effect as well. It is critical that politicians and policy makers are aware of this phenomenon. Penal policies aim to reduce criminal behaviour, but by their actions, they actually increase the behaviour that they want to decrease.

When comparing the impact of parental imprisonment in the Netherlands versus England, no additional impact of parental imprisonment was found in the Netherlands, but a strong impact was found in England. These results suggest that a country's penal policy might impact on offenders' children. Again, when trying to reduce criminal behaviour, offending appears to increase in the next generation by these policies. By creating a less punitive penal atmosphere the impact of parental imprisonment on children might ease. This could be achieved by the earlier mentioned opportunities for child-friendly visits, but also by a more general shift towards prevention and rehabilitation instead of the emphasis on punishment. Instead of the current exclusion of offenders and their children (see also Garland, 2001; Micklewright, 2002; Murray, 2006; Young, 1999), we should strive to offer offenders opportunities out of crime and thereby also offer their offspring better opportunities. The message from this research would be that by developing and enforcing penal and prison policies the consequences for offenders' children should be of vital importance. It is crucial that this knowledge is communicated to the general public and politicians, so they can design interventions for crime that might actually decrease criminal behaviour.

7.6 Conclusion

With the research in this dissertation I have attempted to increase our knowledge of mechanisms of intergenerational continuity of offending and on the impact of sentencing of parents on offspring offending. Particularly the results on official bias and parental imprisonment are cause for concern, as they show that conviction of parents might actually increase offending behaviour in the next generation. There is a clear need for replication studies to determine whether these findings are replicable, generalisable and whether parental conviction and imprisonment have a causal impact on offspring offending. This dissertation also provides points of intervention in the cycle of intergenerational offending. It highlights how changes in research, practice, and policy could assist to reduce the part of intergenerational continuity that appears to originate in collateral consequences of parental conviction and imprisonment.

References

Agnew, R. (1992). Foundation for a general strain theory of crime and delinquency. *Criminology, 30,* 47-87.

Agnew, R. (1997). Stability and change in crime over the life course: A strain theory explanation. In T. P. Thornberry (Ed.), *Advances in criminological theory. vol 7: Developmental theories of crime and delinquency* (p. 101-132). New Brunswick, NJ: Transaction.

Agresti, A. & Agresti, B. F. (1978). Statistical analysis of qualitative variation. *Sociological Methodology, 9,* 204-237.

Aiken, L. S. & West, S. G. (1991). *Multiple regression: Testing and interpreting interactions.* London: Sage.

Akers, R. L. (1977). *Deviant Behavior: A Social Learning Approach.* Belmont, CA: Wadsworth.

Akers, R. L. (2002). A social learning theory of crime. In S. Cote (Ed.), *Criminological Theories: Bridging the Past to the Future* (p. 135-143). Thousand Oaks, CA: Sage.

Amato, P. R. (2001). Children of divorce in the 1990s: An update of the Amato and Keith (1991) meta-analysis. *Journal of Family Psychology, 15,* 355-370.

Ananth, C. V., Platt, R. W. & Savitz, D. A. (2005). Regression models for clustered binary responses: Implications of ignoring the intracluster correlation in an analysis of perinatal mortality in twin gestations. *Annals of Epidemiology, 15,* 293-301.

Avakame, E. F. (1998a). Intergenerational transmission of violence and psychological aggression against wives. *Canadian Journal of Behavioural Science, 30*(3), 193-202.

Avakame, E. F. (1998b). Intergenerational transmission of violence, self-control, and conjugal violence: A comparative analysis of physical violence and psychological aggression. *Violence and Victims, 13*(3), 301-316.

Bailey, J. A., Hill, K. G., Oesterle, S. & Hawkins, J. D. (2006). Linking substance use and problem behavior across three generations. *Journal of Abnormal Child Psychology, 34,* 273–292.

Bailey, J. A., Hill, K. G., Oesterle, S. & Hawkins, J. D. (2009). Parenting practices and problem behavior across three generations: Monitoring, harsh discipline, and drug use in the intergenerational transmission of externalizing behavior. *Developmental Psychology, 45,* 1214-1226.

Bandura, A. (1971). Social learning theory of aggression. In J. F. Knutson (Ed.), *Control of aggression: Implications from basic research.* Englewood Cliffs, NJ: Prentice-Hall.

Bandura, A. (1973). *Aggression. A social learning analysis.* Englewood Cliffs, NJ: Prentice Hall.

Bandura, A. (1977). *Social learning theory.* Englewood Cliffs, NJ: Prentice Hall.

Baron, R. A., Byrne, D. & Johnson, B. T. (1998). *Exploring social psychology.* Needham Heights, MA: Allyn and Bacon.

Baron, R. M. & Kenny, D. A. (1986). The moderator-mediator variable distinction in social psychological research: Conceptual, strategic, and statistical considerations. *Journal of Personality and Social Psychology, 51*, 1173-1182.

Becker, H. S. (1963). *Outsiders*. London: Free Press.

Beckerman, A. (1989). Incarcerated mothers and their children in foster care: The dilemma of visitation. *Children and Youth Services Review, 11*, 175-183.

Bell, R. Q. (1968). A reinterpretation of the direction of effects in studies of socialization. *Psychological Review, 75*, 81-95.

Belsky, J. (1984). The determinants of parenting: A process model. *Child Development, 55*, 83-96.

Belsky, J. & Vondra, J. (1989). Lessons from child abuse: The determinants of parenting. In D. Cicchetti & V. Carlson (Eds.), *Child maltreatment: Theory and research on the causes and consequences of child abuse and neglect* (p. 153-202). Cambridge: Cambridge University Press.

Berk, L. E. (2009). *Child development*. Boston: Pearson.

Bernburg, J. G. (2009). Labeling theory. In M. D. Krohn, A. J. Lizotte & G. P. Hall (Eds.), *Handbook on crime and deviance* (p. 187-207). Dordrecht, the Netherlands: Springer.

Bernburg, J. G. & Krohn, M. D. (2003). Labeling, life chances, and adult crime: The direct and indirect effects of official intervention in adolescence on crime in early adulthood. *Criminology, 41*, 1287-1318.

Bernburg, J. G., Krohn, M. D. & Rivera, C. J. (2006). Official labeling, criminal embeddedness, and subsequent delinquency. *Journal of Research in Crime and Delinquency, 43*, 67-88.

Besemer, S. & Farrington, D. P. (2012). Intergenerational transmission of criminal behaviour: Conviction trajectories of fathers and their children. *European Journal of Criminology, 9*, 120-141.

Besemer, S., Van der Geest, V. R., Murray, J., Bijleveld, C. C. J. H. & Farrington, D. P. (2011). The relationship between parental imprisonment and offspring offending in England and the Netherlands. *British Journal of Criminology, 51*, 413-437.

Besjes, G. & Van Gaalen, R. (2008). Jong geleerd, fout gedaan? [Learned young, done wrong?]. *Bevolkingstrends [population trends], 2*, 23-31.

Bijleveld, C. C. J. H. (2007). *Methoden en technieken van onderzoek in de criminologie / druk 3 [Methods and techniques for research in criminology / 3rd edition]*. Den Haag: Boom Juridische Uitgevers.

Bijleveld, C. C. J. H. & Wijkman, M. (2009). Intergenerational continuity in convictions: A five-generation study. *Criminal Behaviour and Mental Health, 19*, 142-155.

Bijleveld, C. C. J. H., Wijkman, M. & Stuifbergen, J. A. (2007). *198 boefjes? [198 rascals?]* Leiden, the Netherlands: NSCR.

Bishop, D. M. (2005). The role of race and ethnicity in juvenile justice processing. In D. F. Hawkins & K. Kempf-Leonard (Eds.), *Our children, their children. Confronting racial and ethnic differences in American juvenile justice.* (p. 23-82). Chicago: The University of Chicago Press.

Bishop, D. M. & Frazier, C. E. (1991). Gender bias in juvenile justice processing: Implications of the JJDP Act. *Journal of Criminal Law and Criminology, 82*, 1162-1186.

Bishop, D. M. & Frazier, C. E. (1996). Race effects in juvenile justice decision-making: Findings of a statewide analysis. *Journal of Criminal Law and Criminology, 86*, 392-414.

Black, D. S., Sussman, S. & Unger, J. B. (2010). A further look at the intergenerational transmission of violence: Witnessing interparental violence in emerging adulthood. *Journal of Interpersonal Violence, 25*, 1022-1042.

Blanden, J., Gregg, P. & Machin, S. (2005). *Intergenerational mobility in Europe and North America*. London: Sutton Trust.

Blokland, A. A. J., Nagin, D. S. & Nieuwbeerta, P. (2005). Life span offending trajectories of a Dutch conviction cohort. *Criminology, 43*, 919-954.

Blonigen, D. M., Hicks, B. M., Krueger, R. F., Patrick, C. J. & Iacono, W. G. (2005). Psychopathic personality traits: Heritability and genetic overlap with internalizing and externalizing psychopathology. *Psychological Medicine, 35*, 637-648.

Bloom, B. (1993). Incarcerated mothers and their children: Maintaining family ties. In A. C. Association (Ed.), *Female offenders: Meeting needs of a neglected population* (p. 60-68). Baltimore, MD: United Book Press.

Bloom, B. & Steinhart, D. (1993). *Why punish the children? A reappraisal of the children of incarcerated mothers in America*. San Francisco: National Council on Crime and Delinquency.

Blumstein, A., Cohen, J. M., Roth, J. A. & Visher, C. A. (1986). *Criminal careers and "career criminals"*. Washington, DC: National Academy Press.

Bornstein, M. H. (1989). Sensitive periods in development: Structural characteristics and causal interpretations. *Psychological Bulletin, 105*, 179-197.

Bouchard, T. J. (2004). Genetic influence on human psychological traits. *Current Directions in Psychological Science, 13*, 148-151.

Bouchard, T. J. & Loehlin, J. C. (2001). Genes, evolution, and personality. *Behavior Genetics, 31*, 243-273.

Bouffard, L. A., Wright, K. A., Muftic, L. R. & Bouffard, J. A. (2008). Gender differences in specialization in intimate partner violence: Comparing the gender symmetry and violent resistance perspectives. *Justice Quarterly, 25*, 570-594.

Bowlby, J. (1969). *Attachment and loss: Volume 1: Attachment*. London: Hogarth Press.

Bowlby, J. (1973). *Attachment and loss: Volume 2: Separation, anxiety and anger*. London: Hogarth Press and the Institute of Psycho-Analysis.

Bowlby, J. (1980). *Attachment and loss: Volume 3: Loss, sadness and depression*. London: Hogarth Press and the Institute of Psycho-Analysis.

Bowles, S. & Gintis, H. (2002). The inheritance of inequality. *The Journal of Economic Perspectives, 16*, 3-30.

Braithwaite, J. (1981). The myth of social class and criminality reconsidered. *American Sociological Review, 46*, 36-57.

Breen, R. (2004). *Social mobility in Europe*. Oxford: Oxford University Press.

Brendgen, M., Dionne, G., Girard, A., Boivin, M., Frank, V. & Pérusse. (2005). Examining genetic and environmental effects on social aggression: A study of 6-year-old twins. *Child Development, 76*, 930-946.

Brennan, P. A., Mednick, B. R. & Mednick, S. A. (1993). Parental psychopathology, congenital factors, and violence. In S. Hodgins (Ed.), *Mental disorder and crime* (p. 244-261). Newbury Park, CA: Sage.

Brennan, P. A. & Raine, A. (1997). Biosocial bases of antisocial behavior: psychophysiological, neurological, and cognitive factors. *Clinical Psychology Review, 17*, 589-604.

Brennan, P. K. & Spohn, C. (2008). Race/ethnicity and sentencing outcomes among drug offenders in North Carolina. *Journal of Contemporary Criminal Justice, 24*, 371-398.

Bridges, G. S. & Crutchfield, R. D. (1988). Law, social standing and racial disparities in imprisonment. *Social Forces, 66*, 699-724.

Bukatko, D. & Daehler, M. W. (2001). *Child development: A thematic approach*. Boston: Houghton Mifflin Company.

Bursik, R. J. (1980). The dynamics of specialization in juvenile offenses. *Social Forces, 58*, 851-864.

Bushway, S. D., Thornberry, T. P. & Krohn, M. D. (2003). Desistance as a developmental process: A comparison of static and dynamic approaches. *Journal of Quantitative Criminology, 19*, 129-153.

Cadoret, R. J., Leve, L. D. & Devor, E. (1997). Genetics of aggressive and violent behavior. *Psychiatric Clinics of North America, 20*, 301-322.

Capaldi, D. M., DeGarmo, D., Patterson, G. R. & Forgatch, M. (2002). Contextual risk across the early life span and association with antisocial behavior. In J. B. Reid, G. R. Patterson & J. Snyder (Eds.), *Antisocial behavior in children and adolescents: A developmental analysis and model for intervention* (p. 123-145). Washington, DC: American Psychological Association.

Capaldi, D. M. & Patterson, G. R. (1996). Can violent offenders be distinguished from frequent offenders: Prediction from childhood to adolescence. *Journal of Research in Crime and Delinquency, 33*, 206-231.

Capaldi, D. M., Pears, K. C., Patterson, G. R. & Owen, L. D. (2003). Continuity of parenting practices across generations in an at-risk sample: A prospective comparison of direct and mediated associations. *Journal of Abnormal Child Psychology, 31*, 127-142.

Caspi, A., McClay, J., Moffitt, T. E., Mill, J., Martin, J., Craig, I. W. et al. (2002). Role of genotype in the cycle of violence in maltreated children. *Science, 297*, 851-854.

Catalano, R. F. & Hawkins, J. D. (1996). The social development model: A theory of antisocial behavior. In J. D. Hawkins (Ed.), *Delinquency and crime: Current theories* (p. 149-197). Cambridge: Cambridge University Press.

Chaplin, R., Flatley, J. & Smith, K. (2011). *Crime in England and Wales 2010/11*. London: Home Office.

Christiansen, K. O. (1974). Seriousness of criminality and concordance among Danish twins. In R. Hood (Ed.), *Crime, criminology, and public policy* (p. 63-77). London: Heinemann.

Cohen, J. M. (1986). Research on criminal careers: Individual frequency rates and offense seriousness. In A. Blumstein, J. M. Cohen, J. A. Roth & C. A. Visher (Eds.), *Criminal careers and "career criminals"* (Vol. II, p. 292-418). Washington, DC: National Academy Press.

Compact Oxford English Dictionary of Current English. (2005). Oxford: Oxford University Press.

Compas, B. E. (1987). Coping with stress during childhood and adolescence. *Psychological Bulletin, 101*, 393-403.

Compas, B. E., Connor-Smith, J. K., Saltzman, H., Thomsen, A. H. & Wadsworth, M. E. (2001). Coping with stress during childhood and adolescence: Problems, progress, and potential in theory and research. *Psychological Bulletin, 127*, 87-127.

Conger, R. D., Neppl, T., Jeong Kim, K. & Scaramella, L. V. (2003). Angry and aggressive behavior across three generations: A prospective, longitudinal study of parents and children. *Journal of Abnormal Child Psychology, 31*, 143-160.

Crick, N. R. & Dodge, K. A. (1994). A review and reformulation of social information-processing mechanisms in children's social adjustment. *Psychological Bulletin, 115*, 74-101.

Cukier, W. & Chapdelaine, A. (2001). Small arms: A major public health hazard. *Medicine and Global Survival, 7*, 26-32.

Daly, K. (1989). Neither conflict nor labeling nor paternalism will suffice: Intersections of race, ethnicity, gender, and family in criminal court decisions. *Crime and Delinquency, 35*, 136-168.

Daly, K. (1994). *Gender, crime, and punishment*. New Haven: Yale University Press.

De Castro, B. O. (October 2011). *Betere start - presentation given at the symposium vrouwen in detentie [women in detention]*. Penitentiaire Inrichting Ter Peel, the

Netherlands.

De Li, S. (1999). Legal sanctions and youths' status achievement: A longitudinal study. *Justice Quarterly, 16*, 377-401.

DiLalla, L. F. (2002). Behavior genetics of aggression in children: Review and future directions. *Developmental Review, 22*, 593-622.

DiLalla, L. F. & Gottesman, I. I. (1991). Biological and genetic contributors to violence: Widom's untold tale. *Psychological Bulletin, 109*, 125-129.

Dixon, J. (1998). Comparative social security: The challenge of evaluation. *Journal of Comparative Policy Analysis: Research and Practice, 1*, 61-95.

Downes, D. (1988). *Contrasts in tolerance: Post-war penal policy in the Netherlands and England and Wales*. Oxford: Clarendon Press.

Downes, D. (1992). The case for going Dutch. *Tijdschrift voor Criminologie, 34*, 198-209.

Downes, D. & Van Swaaningen, R. (2007). The road to dystopia? Changes in the penal climate of the Netherlands. In M. Tonry & C. C. J. H. Bijleveld (Eds.), *Crime and justice in the netherlands* (p. 31-71). Chicago: University of Chicago Press.

D'Unger, A. V., Land, K. C., McCall, P. L. & Nagin, D. S. (1998). How many latent classes of delinquent / criminal careers? Results from mixed Poisson regression analyses. *American Journal of Sociology, 103*, 1593-630.

Eckenrode, J., Zielinski, D., Smith, E., Marcynyszyn, L. A., Henderson, C. R., Kitzman, H. et al. (2001). Child maltreatment and the early onset of problem behaviors: Can a program of nurse home visitation break the link? *Development and Psychopathology, 13*, 873-890.

Eddy, J. M. & Reid, J. B. (2003). Adolescent children of incarcerated parents. A developmental perspective. In J. Travis & M. Waul (Eds.), *Prisoners once removed: The impact of incarceration and reentry on children, families, and communities* (p. 233-258). Washington, DC: The Urban Institute Press.

Eggleston, E. P., Laub, J. H. & Sampson, R. J. (2004). Methodological sensitivities to latent class analysis of long-term criminal trajectories. *Journal of Quantitative Criminology, 20*, 1-26.

Ezinga, M. A., Hissel, S. C. E. M., Slotboom, A.-M. & Bijleveld, C. C. J. H. (2009). *Kinderen van gedetineerde moeders [children of imprisoned mothers]*. Amsterdam: Vrije Universiteit.

Farrington, D. P. (1977). The effects of public labelling. *British Journal of Criminology, 17*, 112-125.

Farrington, D. P. (1979). Environmental stress, delinquent behavior, and convictions. In I. G. Sarason & C. D. Spielberger (Eds.), *Stress and anxiety (volume 6)* (p. 93-107). Washington DC: Hemisphere Publishing Corporation.

Farrington, D. P. (1986). Age and crime. In M. Tonry & N. Morris (Eds.), *Crime and justice* (Vol. 7, p. 189-250). Chicago: University press.

Farrington, D. P. (1989). Self-reported and official offending from adolescence to adulthood. In M. W. Klein (Ed.), *Cross-national research in self-reported crime and delinquency* (p. 399-423). Dordrecht, the Netherlands: Kluwer.

Farrington, D. P. (1991). Childhood aggression and adult violence: Early precursors and later-life outcomes. In D. J. Pepler & K. H. Rubin (Eds.), *The development and treatment of childhood aggression* (p. 5-29). Hillsdale, NJ: Lawrence Erlbaum.

Farrington, D. P. (1995). The development of offending and antisocial behaviour from childhood: Key findings from the Cambridge Study in Delinquent Development. *Journal of Child Psychology and Psychiatry, 36*, 929-964.

Farrington, D. P. (1997). Human development and criminal careers. In M. Maguire, R. Morgan & R. Reiner (Eds.), *The Oxford handbook of criminology* (Second ed., p. 361-408). Oxford: Oxford University Press.

Farrington, D. P. (1999). A criminological research agenda for the next millennium. *International Journal of Offender Therapy and Comparative Criminology, 43*, 154-167.

Farrington, D. P. (2001a). Predicting adult official and self-reported violence. In G.-F. Pinard & L. Pagani (Eds.), *Clinical assessment of dangerousness* (p. 66-88). Cambridge: Cambridge University Press.

Farrington, D. P. (2001b). *What has been learned from self-reports about criminal careers and the causes of offending?* London: Home Office (online report).

Farrington, D. P. (2003a). Developmental and life-course criminology: Key theoretical and empirical issues - The American Society of Criminology 2002 Sutherland address. *Criminology, 41*, 221-255.

Farrington, D. P. (2003b). Key results from the first forty years of the Cambridge Study in Delinquent Development. In T. P. Thornberry & M. D. Krohn (Eds.), *Taking stock of delinquency: An overview of findings from contemporary longitudinal studies* (p. 137-183). New York: Kluwer.

Farrington, D. P. (2007). Origins of violent behavior over the life span. In D. J. Flannery, A. T. Vazsonyi & I. D. Waldman (Eds.), *The Cambridge handbook of violent behavior and aggression* (p. 19-48). Cambridge: Cambridge University Press.

Farrington, D. P. (2011). Families and crime. In J. Q. Wilson & J. Petersilia (Eds.), *Crime and public policy* (p. 130-157). New York: Oxford University press.

Farrington, D. P., Barnes, G. C. & Lambert, S. (1996). The concentration of offending in families. *Legal and Criminological Psychology, 1*, 47-63.

Farrington, D. P., Coid, J. W., Harnett, L., Jolliffe, D., Soteriou, N., Turner, R. et al. (2006). *Criminal careers up to age 50 and life success up to age 48: New findings from the Cambridge Study in Delinquent Development.* London: Home Office (Home Office Research Study No. 299).

Farrington, D. P., Coid, J. W. & West, D. J. (2009). The development of offending from age 8 to age 50: Recent findings from the Cambridge Study in Delinquent Development. *Monatsschrift für Kriminologie und Strafrechtsreform [Journal of Criminology and Penal Reform], 92*, 160-173.

Farrington, D. P., Gundry, G. & West, D. J. (1975). The familial transmission of criminality. *Medicine, Science and the Law, 15*(3), 177-186.

Farrington, D. P., Jolliffe, D., Hawkins, J. D., Catalano, R. F., Hill, K. G. & Kosterman, R. (2003). Comparing delinquency careers in court-records and self-reports. *Criminology, 41*, 933-958.

Farrington, D. P., Jolliffe, D., Loeber, R., Stouthamer-Loeber, M. & Kalb, L. M. (2001). The concentration of offenders in families, and family criminality in the prediction of boys' delinquency. *Journal of Adolescence, 24*, 579-596.

Farrington, D. P. & Loeber, R. (1999). Transatlantic replicability of risk factors in the development of delinquency. In P. Cohen, C. Slomkowski & L. N. Robins (Eds.), *Historical and geographical influences on psychopathology.* Mahwah, NJ: Lawrence Erlbaum.

Farrington, D. P., Loeber, R., Stouthamer-Loeber, M., Van Kammen, W. B. & Schmidt, L. (1996). Self-reported delinquency and a combined delinquency seriousness scale based on boys, mothers, and teachers: concurrent and predictive validity for African-Americans and Caucasians. *Criminology, 34*, 493-517.

Farrington, D. P., Osborn, S. G. & West, D. J. (1978). The persistence of labelling effects. *British Journal of Criminology, 18*, 277-284.

Farrington, D. P. & Painter, K. A. (2004). *Gender differences in offending: Implications for risk-focused prevention.* London: Home Office. (Online report 09/04).

Farrington, D. P., Snyder, H. N. & Finnegan, T. A. (1988). Specialization in juvenile court careers. *Criminology, 26*, 461-487.

Farrington, D. P. & Welsh, B. C. (2007). *Saving children from a life of crime. Early risk factors and effective interventions*. Oxford: Oxford University Press.

Farrington, D. P. & West, D. J. (1990). The Cambridge Study in Delinquent Development: A long-term follow-up of 411 London males. In H.-J. Kerner & G. Kaiser (Eds.), *Kriminalität: Personlichkeit, lebensgeschichte und verhalten [criminality: Personality, life history and criminal behaviour]* (p. 115-138). Berlin: Springer-Verlag.

Feise, R. (2002). Do multiple outcome measures require p-value adjustment? *BMC Medical Research Methodology, 2*, 1-4.

Felson, R. B. (2009). Violence, crime, and violent crime. *International Journal of Conflict and Violence, 3*, 23-39.

Ferguson, T. (1952). *The young delinquent in his social setting: a Glasgow study*. London: Oxford University Press.

Fergusson, D. M., Horwood, L. J. & Nagin, D. S. (2000). Offending trajectories in a New Zealand birth cohort. *Criminology, 38*, 525-552.

Field, A. (2005). *Discovering statistics using SPSS (and sex, drugs and rock 'n' roll)* (second ed.). London: Sage.

Fisher, G. & Ross, S. (2006). Beggarman or thief: methodological issues in offender specialisation research. *The Australian and New Zealand Journal of Criminology, 39*, 151-170.

Fishman, S. H. (1983). The impact of incarceration on children of offenders. *Journal of Children in Contemporary Society, 15*, 89-99.

Francis, B., Soothill, K. & Fligelstone, R. (2004). Identifying patterns and pathways of offending behaviour: A new approach to typologies of crime. *European Journal of Criminology, 1*, 47-87.

Friedman, S. & Esselstyn, T. C. (1965). The adjustment of children of jail inmates. *Federal Probation, 29*, 55-59.

Gabel, S. & Shindledecker, R. (1993). Characteristics of children whose parents have been incarcerated. *Hospital and Community Psychiatry, 44*, 656-660.

Gamoran, A. (2001). American schooling and educational inequality: A forecast for the 21st century. *Sociology of Education, 74*, 135-153.

Garbarino, J. (1989). Troubled youth, troubled families: Understanding families at risk for adolescent maltreatment. In V. Carlson & D. Cicchetti (Eds.), *Child maltreatment: Theory and research on the causes and consequences of child abuse and neglect* (p. 685-706). Cambridge: Cambridge University Press.

Garland, D. W. (2001). *The culture of control*. Oxford: Oxford University Press.

Gibson, H. B., Morrison, S. & West, D. J. (1970). The confession of known offences in response to a self-reported delinquency schedule. *British Journal of Criminology, 10*, 277-287.

Giordano, P. C. (2010). *Legacies of crime. A follow-up of the children of highly delinquent girls and boys*. Cambridge: Cambridge University Press.

Goodman, L. A. (2007). On the assignment of individuals to latent classes. *Sociological Methodology, 37*, 1-22.

Goodman, S. H. & Gotlib, I. H. (1999). Risk for psychopathology in the children of depressed mothers: A developmental model for understanding mechanisms of transmission. *Psychological Review, 106*, 458-490.

Gorman-Smith, D., Tolan, P. H., Loeber, R. & Henry, D. B. (1998). Relation of family problems to patterns of delinquent involvement among urban youth. *Journal of Abnormal Child Psychology, 26*, 319-333.

Gottfredson, M. R. & Hirschi, T. (1990). *A general theory of crime*. Stanford, CA: Stanford University Press.

Green, D. A. (2008a). Suitable vehicles: Framing blame and justice when children kill a child. *Crime, Media, Culture, 4*, 197-220.

Green, D. A. (2008b). *When children kill children: Penal populism and political culture.* Oxford: Oxford University Press.

Grove, W., Eckert, E., Heston, L., Bouchard Jr, T., Segal, N. & Lykken, D. T. (1990). Heritability of substance abuse and antisocial behavior: a study of monozygotic twins reared apart. *Biological Psychiatry, 27,* 1293-1304.

Haberman, S. J. (1973). The analysis of residuals in cross-classified tables. *Biometrics, 29,* 205-220.

Hagan, J. (1974). Extra-legal attributes and criminal sentencing: An assessment of a sociological viewpoint. *Law and Society Review, 8,* 357-383.

Hagan, J. & Dinovitzer, R. (1999). Collateral consequences of imprisonment for children, communities and prisoners. In M. Tonry & J. Petersilia (Eds.), *Prisons* (p. 121-162). Chicago: University of Chicago Press.

Hagan, J. & Palloni, A. (1990). The social reproduction of a criminal class in working-class London, circa 1950-1980. *The American Journal of Sociology, 96,* 265-299.

Hairston, C. F. (1991). Mothers in jail: Parent-child separation and jail visitation. *Affilia, 6,* 9-27.

Hanley, J. A., Negassa, A., Edwardes, M. D. d. & Forrester, J. E. (2003). Statistical analysis of correlated data using generalized estimating equations: An orientation. *American Journal of Epidemiology, 157,* 364-375.

Harley, B. & Wang, W. (1997). The critical period hypothesis: Where are we now? In A. M. de Groot & J. F. Kroll (Eds.), *Tutorials in bilingualism. Psycholinguistic perspectives* (p. 19-52). Mahwah, NJ: Lawrence Erlbaum Associates.

Harris, J. R. (1995). Where is the child's environment? a group socialization theory of development. *Psychological review, 102,* 458-489.

Harris, J. R. (1998). *The nurture assumption. why children turn out the way they do.* London: Bloomsbury.

Harris, J. R. (2000). The outcome of parenting: What do we really know? *Journal of Personality, 68,* 625-637.

Hearold, S. (1986). A synthesis of 1043 effects of television on social behavior. In G. A. Comstock (Ed.), *Public communication and behavior (vol. 1)* (p. 65-133). San Diego: Academic Press.

Hedderman, C. & Gelsthorpe, L. (1997). *Understanding the sentencing of women.* London: Home Office Research and Statistics Directorate (Home Office Research Study No. 170).

Hindelang, M. J., Hirschi, T. & Weiss, J. G. (1981). *Measuring delinquency.* Beverly Hills, CA: Sage.

Hirschi, T. (1969). *Causes of delinquency.* Berkeley, CA: University of California Press.

Hirschi, T. & Gottfredson, M. R. (1993). Commentary: Testing the general theory of crime. *Journal of Research in Crime and Delinquency, 30,* 47-54.

Hissel, S. C. E. M., Bijleveld, C. C. J. H. & Kruttschnitt, C. (2011). The well-being of children of incarcerated mothers: An exploratory study for the Netherlands. *European Journal of Criminology, 8,* 346-360.

Hudziak, J., Van Beijsterveldt, C., Bartels, M., Rietveld, M. J. H., Rettew, D. C., Derks, E. M. et al. (2003). Individual differences in aggression: Genetic analyses by age, gender, and informant in 3-, 7-, and 10-year old Dutch twins. *Behavior Genetics, 33,* 575-589.

Huesmann, L. R., Eron, L. D., Lefkowitz, M. M. & Walder, L. O. (1984). Stability of aggression over time and generations. *Developmental Psychology, 20,* 1120-1134.

Huizinga, D. H. & Elliott, D. S. (1986). Reassessing the reliability and validity of self-report delinquency measures. *Journal of Quantitative Criminology, 2,* 293-327.

Huizinga, D. H., Thornberry, T. P., Knight, K. E., Lovegrove, P. J., Loeber, R., Hill, K. G. et al. (2007). *Disproportionate minority contact in the juvenile justice system:*

A study of differential minority arrest/referral to court in three cities. Washington, DC: U.S. Department of Justice.

Huschek, D. & Bijleveld, C. C. J. H. (2011). *Standard and deviant family life sequences and offending. findings for a mid 20th century high-risk cohort.* Paper presented at NVK congres - Annual conference of Dutch Society of Criminology, Leiden, the Netherlands.

Ireland, T. O., Smith, C. A. & Thornberry, T. P. (2002). Developmental issues in the impact of child maltreatment on later delinquency and drug use. *Criminology, 40,* 359-400.

Jaffee, S. R., Caspi, A., Moffitt, T. E., Dodge, K. A., Rutter, M., Taylor, A. et al. (2005). Nature x nurture: Genetic vulnerabilities interact with physical maltreatment to promote conduct problems. *Development and Psychopathology, 17,* 67-84.

Jaffee, S. R., Moffitt, T. E., Caspi, A. & Taylor, A. (2003). Life with (or without) father: The benefits of living with two biological parents depend on the father's antisocial behavior. *Child Development, 74,* 109-126.

Johnston, D. (1995). Jailed mothers. In K. Gabel & D. Johnston (Eds.), *Children of incarcerated parents* (p. 41-55). New York: Lexington Books.

Jolliffe, D., Farrington, D. P., Hawkins, J. D., Catalano, R. F., Hill, K. G. & Kosterman, R. (2003). Predictive, concurrent, prospective and retrospective validity of self-reported delinquency. *Criminal Behaviour and Mental Health, 13,* 179-197.

Jones, B. L. & Nagin, D. S. (2007). Advances in group-based trajectory modeling and an SAS procedure for estimating them. *Sociological Methods and Research, 35,* 542-571.

Jones, B. L., Nagin, D. S. & Roeder, K. (2001). A SAS procedure based on mixture models for estimating developmental trajectories. *Sociological Methods and Research, 29,* 374-393.

Juby, H. & Farrington, D. P. (2001). Disentangling the link between disrupted families and delinquency. *British Journal of Criminology, 41,* 22-40.

Junger, M. (1990). *Delinquency and ethnicity. An investigation on social factors relating to delinquency among Moroccan, Turkish, Surinamese and Dutch boys.* Doctoral dissertation, Vrije Universiteit, Amsterdam.

Junger-Tas, J. & Marshall, I. H. (1999). The self-report methodology in crime research. *Crime and Justice, 25,* 291-367.

Kaim-Caudle, P. R. (1973). *Comparative social policy and social security.* New York: Dunellen.

Kalidien, S. N. & De Heer-de Lange, N. (2011). *Criminaliteit en rechtshandhaving 2010. Ontwikkelingen en samenhangen. [Crime and law enforcement 2010. Developments and connections].* Den Haag: Boom Juridische Uitgevers.

Kalmuss, D. (1984). The intergenerational transmission of marital aggression. *Journal of Marriage and the Family, 46,* 11-19.

Kazdin, A. E. (1997). Parent management training: Evidence, outcomes, and issues. *Journal of American Academy of Child and Adolescent Psychiatry, 36,* 1349-1356.

Kazdin, A. E., Kraemer, H. C., Kessler, R. C., Kupfer, D. J. & Offord, D. R. (1997). Contributions of risk-factor research to developmental psychopathology. *Clinical Psychology Review, 17,* 375-406.

Killias, M., Aebi, M. & Ribeaud, D. (2000). Does community service rehabilitate better than short-term imprisonment?: Results of a controlled experiment. *The Howard Journal of Criminal Justice, 39,* 40-57.

Killias, M., Gilliéron, G., Kissling, I. & Villettaz, P. (2010). Community service versus electronic monitoring–what works better?: Results of a randomized trial. *British Journal of Criminology, 50*(6), 1155-1170.

Kim, H. K., Capaldi, D. M., Pears, K. C., Kerr, D. C. & Owen, L. D. (2009). Intergenerational transmission of internalising and externalising behaviours across three generations: Gender-specific pathways. *Criminal Behaviour and Mental Health*, *19*(2), 125-141.

Kim-Cohen, J., Caspi, A., Taylor, A., Williams, B., Newcombe, R., Craig, I. W. et al. (2006). MAOA, maltreatment, and gene-environment interaction predicting children's mental health: new evidence and a meta-analysis. *Molecular Psychiatry*, *11*, 903-913.

Kjellstrand, J. M. & Eddy, J. M. (2011a). Mediators of the effect of parental incarceration on adolescent externalizing behaviors. *Journal of Community Psychology*, *39*, 551-565.

Kjellstrand, J. M. & Eddy, J. M. (2011b). Parental incarceration during childhood, family context, and youth problem behavior across adolescence. *Journal of Offender Rehabilitation*, *50*, 18-36.

Knudsen, E. I. (2004). Sensitive periods in the development of the brain and behavior. *Journal of Cognitive Neuroscience*, *16*, 1412-1425.

Kokko, K. & Pulkkinen, L. (2005). Stability of aggressive behavior from childhood to middle age in women and men. *Aggressive Behavior*, *31*, 485-497.

Kraemer, H. C., Kazdin, A. E., Offord, D. R., Kessler, R. C., Jensen, P. S. & Kupfer, D. J. (1997). Coming to terms with the terms of risk. *Archives of General Psychiatry*, *54*, 337-343.

Kraemer, H. C., Stice, E., Kazdin, A. E., Offord, D. R. & Kupfer, D. J. (2001). How do risk factors work together? mediators, moderators, and independent, overlapping, and proxy risk factors. *American Journal of Psychiatry*, *158*, 848-856.

Krahn, H., Hartnagel, T. F. & Gartrell, J. W. (1986). Income equality and homicide rates: Cross-national data and criminological theories. *Criminology*, *24*, 269-295.

Krueger, R. F., Moffitt, T. E., Caspi, A., Bleske, A. & Silva, P. A. (1998). Assortative mating for antisocial behavior: Developmental and methodological implications. *Behavior Genetics*, *28*, 173-186.

Kruttschnitt, C. & Dirkzwager, A. (2011). Are there still contrasts in tolerance? imprisonment in the Netherlands and England 20 years later. *Punishment and Society*, *13*, 283–306.

Lanier, M. M. & Henry, S. (2004). *Essential criminology*. Boulder, CO: Westview Press.

Larson, R. & Asmussen, L. (1991). Anger, worry, and hurt in early adolescence: An enlarging world of negative emotions. In M. E. Colten & S. Gore (Eds.), *Adolescent stress: Causes and consequences* (p. 21-41). New York: Aldine de Gruyter.

Larson, R. & Ham, M. (1993). Stress and "storm and stress" in early adolescence: The relationship of negative events with dysphoric affect. *Developmental Psychology*, *29*, 130-140.

Leiber, M. J. & Johnson, J. D. (2008). Being young and black: What are their effects on juvenile justice decision making? *Crime and Delinquency*, *54*, 560-581.

Lemert, E. M. (1967). *Human deviance, social problems, and social control*. Englewood Cliffs, NJ: Prentice-Hall.

Lenneberg, E. H. (1967). *Biological foundations of language*. New York: Wiley.

Liang, K.-Y. & Zeger, S. L. (1993). Regression analysis for correlated data. *Annual Review of Public Health*, *14*, 43-68.

Liefbroer, A. C. (2005). *Valt de appel nog steeds niet ver van de boom? Over intergenerationele overdracht van demografisch gedrag [Is the apple still not falling far from the tree? About intergenerational transmission of demographic behaviour]*. Inaugurele rede Vrije Universiteit Amsterdam.

Lipsitz, S. R., Laird, N. M. & Harrington, D. P. (1991). Generalized estimating equations for correlated binary data: Using the odds ratio as a measure of association. *Biometrika*, *78*, 153-160.

Loeber, R. (1988). Natural histories of conduct problems, delinquency, and associated substance use: Evidence for developmental progressions. In B. B. Lahey & A. E. Kazdin (Eds.), *Advances in clinical child psychology* (p. 73-124). New York: Plenum.

Loeber, R., Farrington, D. P., Stouthamer-Loeber, M. & Van Kammen, W. B. (1998). Multiple risk factors for multi-problem boys: Co-occurrence of delinquency, substance use, attention deficit, conduct problems, physical aggression, covert behavior, depressed mood, and shy/withdrawn behavior. In R. Jessor (Ed.), *New perspectives on adolescent risk behavior* (p. 90-149). New York: Cambridge University Press.

Loeber, R. & Stouthamer-Loeber, M. (1998). Development of juvenile aggression and violence: Some common misconceptions and controversies. *American Psychologist, 53,* 242-259.

Lösel, F., Bliesener, T. & Bender, D. (2007). Social information processing, experiences of aggression in social contexts, and aggressive behavior in adolescents. *Criminal Justice and Behavior, 34,* 330-347.

Lösel, F., Pugh, G., Markson, L., Souza, K. A. & Lanskey, C. (2011). *Risk and protective factors as predictors of fathers' resettlement and families' adjustment.* Cambridge: Report for the Project Conference, 30 November 2011.

Maguire, M. (2007). Crime data and statistics. In M. Maguire, R. Morgan & R. Reiner (Eds.), *The Oxford handbook of criminology* (fourth ed., p. 241-301). Oxford: Oxford University Press.

Mason, D. A. & Frick, P. J. (1994). The heritability of antisocial behavior: A meta-analysis of twin and adoption studies. *Journal of Psychopathology and Behavioral Assessment, 16,* 301-323.

Maxfield, M. G., Weiler, B. L. & Widom, C. S. (2000). Comparing self-reports and official records of arrests. *Journal of Quantitative Criminology, 16,* 87-110.

Mazerolle, P., Brame, R., Paternoster, R., Piquero, A. R. & Dean, C. W. (2000). Onset age, persistence, and offending versatility: Comparisons across gender. *Criminology, 38,* 1143-1172.

McAra, L. & McVie, S. (2005). The usual suspects?: Street-life, young people and the police. *Criminology and Criminal Justice, 5*(1), 5-36.

McAra, L. & McVie, S. (2007a). Criminal justice transitions. In *Edinburgh study of youth transitions and crime* (Research Digest No. 14 ed.). Edinburgh: Centre for Law and Society.

McAra, L. & McVie, S. (2007b). Youth justice? the impact of system contact on patterns of desistance from offending. *European Journal of Criminology, 4,* 315-345.

McCord, J. (1977). A comparative study of two generations of native americans. In R. F. Meier (Ed.), *Theory in criminology. contemporary views* (p. 83-92). Beverly Hills: Sage.

McCord, J. (1988). Parental behavior in the cycle of aggression. *Psychiatry, 51*(1), 14-23.

McCutcheon, A. L. (1987). *Latent class analysis.* Newbury Park, CA: Sage.

McGloin, J. M., Sullivan, C. J. & Piquero, A. R. (2009). Aggregating to versatility?: Transitions among offender types in the short term. *British Journal of Criminology, 49,* 243.

Mednick, S. A. & Kandel, E. (1988). Genetic and perinatal factors in violence. In S. Mednick & T. E. Moffitt (Eds.), *Biological contributions to crime causation* (p. 121-134). Dordrecht, the Netherlands: Martinus Nijhoff.

Mednick, S. A., Moffitt, T. E. & Stack, S. A. (1987). *The causes of crime: New biological approaches.* Cambridge: Cambridge University Press.

Messner, S. F. (1989). Economic discrimination and societal homicide rates: Further evidence on the cost of inequality. *American Sociological Review, 54*, 597-611.

Michael, J. & Adler, M. J. (1933). *Crime, law and social science*. New York: Harcourt, Brace and Company.

Micklewright, J. (2002). *Social exclusion and children: A european view for a us debate, casepaper 51*. London: Centre for Analysis of Social Exclusion, London School of Economics.

Mitchell, O. (2005). A meta-analysis of race and sentencing research: Explaining the inconsistencies. *Journal of Quantitative Criminology, 21*, 439-466.

Moffitt, T. E. (1993). Adolescence-limited and life-course-persistent antisocial behavior: A developmental taxonomy. *Psychological Review, 100*, 674-701.

Moffitt, T. E., Caspi, A., Rutter, M. & Silva, P. A. (2001). *Sex differences in antisocial behaviour: Conduct disorder, delinquency, and violence in the Dunedin Longitudinal Study*. Cambridge: Cambridge University Press.

Morris, P. (1965). *Prisoners and their families*. London: George Allen and Unwin.

Murray, J. (2005). The effects of imprisonment on families and children of prisoners. In A. Liebling & S. Maruna (Eds.), *The effects of imprisonment* (p. 442-462). Cullompton, Devon: Willan.

Murray, J. (2006). *Parental imprisonment: Effects on children's antisocial behaviour and mental health through the life-course*. Doctoral dissertation, University of Cambridge, United Kingdom.

Murray, J., Blokland, A. A. J., Farrington, D. P. & Theobald, D. (forthcoming). Long term effects of conviction and incarceration on men in the Cambridge Study in Delinquent Development. In D. P. Farrington & J. Murray (Eds.), *Labeling theory: Empirical tests (advances in criminological theory volume 18)*. New Brunswick, NJ: Transaction Publishers.

Murray, J. & Farrington, D. P. (2005). Parental imprisonment: Effects on boys' antisocial behaviour and delinquency through the life-course. *Journal of Child Psychology and Psychiatry, 46*, 1269-1278.

Murray, J. & Farrington, D. P. (2008a). Effects of parental imprisonment on children. In M. Tonry (Ed.), *Crime and justice* (Vol. 37, p. 133-206). Chicago: University of Chicago Press.

Murray, J. & Farrington, D. P. (2008b). Parental imprisonment: Long-lasting effects on boys' internalizing problems through the life course. *Development and Psychopathology, 20*, 273-290.

Murray, J., Farrington, D. P. & Sekol, I. (2012). Children's antisocial behavior, mental health, drug use, and educational performance after parental incarceration: A systematic review and meta-analysis. *Psychological Bulletin, 138*, 175-200.

Murray, J., Farrington, D. P., Sekol, I. & Olsen, R. F. (2009). *Effects of parental imprisonment on child antisocial behaviour and mental health: A systematic review*. Campbell Systematic Reviews: 2009: 4.

Murray, J., Janson, C.-G. & Farrington, D. P. (2007). Crime in adult offspring of prisoners: A cross-national comparison of two longitudinal samples. *Criminal Justice and Behavior, 34*, 133-149.

Murray, J. & Murray, L. (2010). Parental incarceration, attachment, and child psychopathology. *Attachment and Human Development, 12*, 289-309.

Musterd, S. (2005). Social and ethnic segregation in Europe: Levels, causes, and effects. *Journal of Urban Affairs, 27*, 331-348.

Muthén, L. K. & Muthén, B. O. (1998-2009). *Mplus user's guide* (fifth ed.). Los Angeles, CA: Muthén and Muthén.

Myers, B. J., Smarsh, T. M., Amlund-Hagen, K. & Kennon, S. (1999). Children of incarcerated mothers. *Journal of Child and Family Studies, 8*, 11-25.

Nagin, D. S. (2004a). Response to "methodological sensitivities to latent class analysis of long-term criminal trajectories". *Journal of Quantitative Criminology*, *20*, 27-35.

Nagin, D. S. (2004b). A semi-parametric, group-based approach for analysing trajectories of developement: a non-technical overview. In G. Bruinsma, H. Elffers & J. de Keijser (Eds.), *Punishment, places and perpetrators: Developments in criminology and criminal justice research* (p. 247-259). Collumpton, Devon: Willan.

Nagin, D. S. (2005). *Group-based modeling of development*. Cambridge, MA: Harvard University Press.

Nagin, D. S., Farrington, D. P. & Moffitt, T. E. (1995). Life-course trajectories of different types of offenders. *Criminology*, *33*, 111-139.

Nagin, D. S. & Land, K. C. (1993). Age, criminal careers, and population heterogeneity: Specification and estimation of a nonparametric, mixed Poisson model. *Criminology*, *31*, 327-362.

Nagin, D. S. & Paternoster, R. (1991). On the relationship of past to future participation in delinquency. *Criminology*, *29*, 163-189.

Nagin, D. S. & Paternoster, R. (2000). Population heterogeneity and state dependence: State of the evidence and directions for future research. *Journal of Quantitative Criminology*, *16*, 117-144.

Nagin, D. S. & Tremblay, R. E. (2005a). Developmental trajectory groups: fact or a useful statistical fiction? *Criminology*, *43*, 873-904.

Nagin, D. S. & Tremblay, R. E. (2005b). What has been learned from group-based trajectory modeling? Examples from physical aggression and other problem behaviors. *Annals of the American Academy of Political and Social Science*, *602*, 82-117.

Neapolitan, J. L. (1994). Cross-national variation in homicides: The case of Latin America. *International Criminal Justice Review*, *4*, 4-22.

Neapolitan, J. L. (1995). Differing theoretical perspectives and cross-national variation in thefts in less developed nations. *International Criminal Justice Review*, *5*, 17-31.

Neapolitan, J. L. (1997). *Cross-national crime*. Westport, CT: Greenwood Press.

Nelson, J. F. (1994). A dollar or a day: Sentencing misdemeanants in new york state. *Journal of Research in Crime and Delinquency*, *31*, 183-201.

Nieuwbeerta, P., Nagin, D. S. & Blokland, A. A. J. (2009). Assessing the impact of first-time imprisonment on offenders' subsequent criminal career development: A matched samples comparison. *Journal of Quantitative Criminology*, *25*, 227-257.

Nijhof, K. S., Engels, R. C., Wientjes, J. A. & Kemp, R. A. d. (2007). Crimineel gedrag van ouders en kinderen. [Criminal behaviour of parents and children]. *Pedagogiek [Pedagogy]*, *16*, 29-44.

Nylund, K. L., Asparouhov, T. & Muthén, B. O. (2007). Deciding on the number of classes in latent class analysis and growth mixture modeling: A Monte Carlo simulation study. *Structural Equation Modeling*, *14*, 535-569.

Olweus, D. (1979). Stability of aggressive reaction patterns in males: A review. *Psychological Bulletin*, *86*, 852-875.

Olweus, D. (1987). Testosterone and adrenaline: Aggressive antisocial behavior in normal adolescent males. In S. A. Mednick, T. E. Moffitt & S. A. Stack (Eds.), *The causes of crime: New biological approaches* (p. 263-282). Cambridge: Cambridge University Press.

Ormiston. (2007). *Working with children and families of prisoners*. Ipswich, UK: Ormiston Children and Family Trust.

Osborn, S. G. & West, D. J. (1979). Conviction records of father and sons compared. *British Journal of Criminology*, *19*(2), 120-133.

Osgood, D. W. & Schreck, C. J. (2007). A new method for studying the extent, stability, and predictors of individual specialization in violence. *Criminology*, *45*, 273-312.

Pardini, D. A., Fite, P. J. & Burke, J. D. (2008). Bidirectional associations between parenting practices and conduct problems in boys from childhood to adolescence: The moderating effect of age and African-American ethnicity. *Journal of Abnormal Child Psychology, 36*, 647-662.

Paternoster, R. & Iovanni, L. (1989). The labeling perspective and delinquency: An elaboration of the theory and an assessment of the evidence. *Justice Quarterly, 6*, 359-394.

Patterson, G. R. (1995). Coercion as a basis for early age of onset for arrest. In J. McCord (Ed.), *Coercion and punishment in long-term perspectives* (p. 81-105). New York: Cambridge University Press.

Patterson, G. R. (2002). The early development of coercive family process. In J. B. Reid, G. R. Patterson & J. J. Snyder (Eds.), *Antisocial behavior in children and adolescents: A developmental analysis and the oregon model for intervention* (p. 25-44). Washington, DC: American Psychological Association.

Penfield, W. & Roberts, L. (1959). *Speech and brain mechanisms*. Princeton, N.J.: Princeton University Press.

Perneger, T. V. (1998). What's wrong with Bonferroni adjustments. *British Medical Journal, 316*, 1236–1238.

Petersilia, J. (1983). *Racial disparities in the criminal justice system*. Santa Monica, CA: Rand Corporation.

Petersilia, J. (1985). Racial disparities in the criminal justice system: A summary. *Crime and Delinquency, 31*, 15-34.

Piquero, A. R. (2000). Frequency, specialization, and violence in offending careers. *Journal of Research in Crime and Delinquency, 37*, 392-418.

Piquero, A. R. (2008). Taking stock of developmental trajectories of criminal activity over the life course. In A. M. Liberman (Ed.), *The long view of crime: A synthesis of longitudinal research* (p. 23-78). New York: Springer.

Piquero, A. R., Blumstein, A., Brame, R., Haapanen, R., Mulvey, E. P. & Nagin, D. S. (2001). Assessing the impact of exposure time and incapacitation on longitudinal trajectories of criminal offending. *Journal of Adolescent Research, 16*(1), 54-74.

Piquero, A. R., Farrington, D. P. & Blumstein, A. (2007). *Key issues in criminal career research. New analyses of the Cambridge Study in Delinquent Development*. Cambridge: Cambridge University Press.

Piquero, A. R., Paternoster, R., Mazerolle, P., Brame, R. & Dean, C. W. (1999). Onset age and offense specialization. *Journal of Research in Crime and Delinquency, 36*, 275-299.

Pratt, T. C. (1998). Race and sentencing: A meta-analysis of conflicting empirical research results. *Journal of Criminal Justice, 26*, 513-523.

Pruitt, C. R. & Wilson, J. Q. (1983). A longitudinal study of the effect of race on sentencing. *Law and Society Review, 17*, 613-635.

Putnam, F. W. (1997). *Dissociation in children and adolescents: A developmental perspective*. New York: Guildford Press.

Raine, A. (2002a). Annotation: The role of prefrontal deficits, low autonomic arousal, and early health factors in the development of antisocial and aggressive behavior in children. *Journal of Child Psychology and Psychiatry, 43*, 417-434.

Raine, A. (2002b). Biosocial studies of antisocial and violent behavior in children and adults: A review. *Journal of Abnormal Child Psychology, 30*, 311-326.

Raine, A., Brennan, P. A., Farrington, D. P. & Mednick, S. A. (1997). *Biosocial bases of violence (proceedings of a NATO ASI held in Rhodes, Greece, May 12-21, 1996)*. New York: Plenum Press.

Reiss, A. J. & Farrington, D. P. (1991). Advancing knowledge about co-offending: Results from a prospective longitudinal survey of London males. *Journal of Criminal Law and Criminology, 82*, 360-395.

Research Development and Statistics Directorate. (1998). *Offenders index codebook*. London: Home Office.

Rhee, S. H. & Waldman, I. D. (2002). Genetic and environmental influences on antisocial behavior: A meta-analysis of twin and adoption studies. *Psychological Bulletin, 128*, 490-529.

Robins, L. N. (1966). *Deviant children grown up: a sociological and psychiatric study of sociopathic personality*. Baltimore: Williams and Wilkins.

Robins, L. N. (1986). The consequences of antisocial behavior in girls. In D. Olweus, J. Block & M. Radke-Yarrow (Eds.), *Development of antisocial and prosocial behavior: research, theories, and issues* (p. 385-414). Orlando, FL: Academic Press.

Rowe, D. C. & Farrington, D. P. (1997). The familial transmission of criminal convictions. *Criminology, 35*, 177-201.

Rutter, M. (2007). Gene-environment interdependence. *Developmental Science, 10*, 12-18.

Sampson, R. J. & Laub, J. H. (1993). *Crime in the making: Pathways and turning points through life*. Cambridge, MA: Harvard University Press.

Sampson, R. J. & Laub, J. H. (1997). A life-course theory of cumulative disadvantage and the stability of delinquency. In T. P. Thornberry (Ed.), *Developmental theories of crime and delinquency* (p. 133-162). New Brunswick, NJ: Transaction.

Sampson, R. J. & Laub, J. H. (2005). A general age-graded theory of crime: Lessons learned and the future of life-course criminology. In D. P. Farrington (Ed.), *Integrated developmental and life-course theories of offending* (p. 165-181). New Brunswick, NJ: Transaction.

Scott, J. P. (1962). Critical periods in behavioral development. *Science, 138*, 949-958.

Sealock, M. D. & Simpson, S. S. (1998). Unraveling bias in arrest decisions: The role of juvenile offender type-scripts. *Justice Quarterly, 15*, 427-457.

Serbin, L. A., Cooperman, J. A., Peters, P. L., Lehoux, P. M., Stack, D. M. & Schwartzman, A. E. (1998). Intergenerational transfer of psychosocial risk in women with childhood histories of aggression, withdrawal, or aggression and withdrawal. *Developmental Psychology, 34*(6), 1246-1262.

Shaffer, A., Hurt, K. B., Obradović, J., Herbers, J. E. & Masten, A. S. (2009). Intergenerational continuity in parenting quality: The mediating role of social competence. *Developmental Psychology, 45*, 1227-1240.

Sharkey, P. (2008). The intergenerational transmission of context. *American Journal of Sociology, 113*, 931-969.

Sherman, L. W. (1993). Defiance, deterrence, and irrelevance: A theory of the criminal sanction. *Journal of Research in Crime and Delinquency, 30*, 445-473.

Shorter Oxford English Dictionary. (2002). Oxford: Oxford University Press.

Sigle-Rushton, W. & McLanahan, S. (2004). Father absence and child well-being: A critical review. In D. P. Moynihan, T. M. Smeeding & L. Rainwater (Eds.), *The future of the family* (p. 116-155). New York: Russel Sage.

Simons, R. L., Wu, C.-i., Johnson, C. & Conger, R. D. (1995). A test of various perspectives on the intergenerational transmission of domestic violence. *Criminology, 33*, 141-172.

Skardhamar, T. (2010). Distinguishing facts and artifacts in group-based modeling. *Criminology, 48*(1), 295-320.

Slotboom, A.-M., Bijleveld, C. C. J. H., Day, S. & Van Giezen, A. (2008). *Gedetineerde vrouwen in Nederland; over import- en deprivatiefactoren bij detentieschade [detained women in the Netherlands; about import and deprivation factors caused by detention]*. Amsterdam: Vrije Universiteit.

Slutske, W., Lyons, M., True, W., Eisen, S., Goldberg, J. & Tsuang, M. (July 1997). *Testing a developmental taxonomy of antisocial behavior*. Paper presented at the meeting of the Behavior Genetics Association, Toronto, Ontario, Canada.

Smith, C. A., Ireland, T. O. & Thornberry, T. P. (2005). Adolescent maltreatment and its impact on young adult antisocial behavior. *Child Abuse and Neglect, 29*, 1099-1119.

Solon, G. (1992). Intergenerational income mobility in the United States. *The American Economic Review, 82*, 393-408.

Soothill, K., Francis, B. & Fligelstone, R. (2002). *Patterns of offending behaviour: A new approach*. London: Home Office.

Spohn, C. & Beichner, D. (2000). Is preferential treatment of female offenders a thing of the past? a multisite study of gender, race, and imprisonment. *Criminal Justice Policy Review, 11*, 149-184.

Sroufe, L. A. & Rutter, M. (1984). The domain of developmental psychopathology. *Child Development, 55*, 17-29.

Stewart, E. A., Simons, R. L., Conger, R. D. & Scaramella, L. V. (2002). Beyond the interactional relationship between delinquency and parenting practices: The contribution of legal sanctions. *Journal of Research in Crime and Delinquency, 39*, 36-59.

Sullivan, C. J., McGloin, J. M., Pratt, T. C. & Piquero, A. R. (2006). Rethinking the "norm" of offender generality: Investigating specialization in the short term. *Criminology, 44*, 199-233.

Sullivan, C. J., McGloin, J. M., Ray, J. V. & Caudy, M. S. (2009). Detecting specialization in offending: comparing analytic approaches. *Journal of Quantitative Criminology, 25*, 419-441.

Sutherland, E. H. & Cressey, D. R. (1955). *Principles of criminology*. Chicago: J.C. Lippincott.

Tabachnick, B. G. & Fidell, L. S. (2007). *Using multivariate statistics (5th ed.)*. London: Pearson Education.

Theobald, D. & Farrington, D. P. (2009). Effects of getting married on offending: Results from a prospective longitudinal survey of males. *European Journal of Criminology, 6*, 496-516.

Thornberry, T. P. (2005). Explaining multiple patterns of offending across the life course and across generations. *Annals of the American Academy of Political and Social Science, 602*, 156-195.

Thornberry, T. P. (2009). The apple doesn't fall far from the tree (or does it?): Intergenerational patterns of antisocial behavior - The American Society of Criminology 2008 Sutherland address. *Criminology, 47*, 297-325.

Thornberry, T. P., Freeman-Gallant, A., Lizotte, A. J., Krohn, M. D. & Smith, C. A. (2003). Linked lives: The intergenerational transmission of antisocial behavior. *Journal of Abnormal Child Psychology, 31*, 171-184.

Thornberry, T. P., Freeman-Gallant, A. & Lovegrove, P. J. (2009). Intergenerational linkages in antisocial behaviour. *Criminal Behaviour and Mental Health, 19*, 80-93.

Thornberry, T. P., Ireland, T. O. & Smith, C. A. (2001). The importance of timing: The varying impact of childhood and adolescent maltreatment on multiple problem outcomes. *Development and Psychopathology, 13*, 957-979.

Thornberry, T. P. & Krohn, M. D. (2001). The development of delinquency. An interactional perspective. In S. O. White (Ed.), *Handbook of youth and justice* (p. 289-305). New York: Kluwer Academic - Plenum Publishers.

Thornberry, T. P. & Krohn, M. D. (2005). Applying interactional theory to the explanation of continuity and change in antisocial behavior. In D. P. Farrington (Ed.), *Integrated developmental and life-course theories of offending* (p. 183-209). London: Transaction Publishers.

Tofighi, D. & Enders, C. K. (2008). Identifying the correct number of classes in growth mixture models. In G. R. Hancock & K. M. Samuelsen (Eds.), *Advances in latent variable mixture models* (p. 317-341). Charlotte NC: Information Age

Publishing.

Tonry, M. & Bijleveld, C. C. J. H. (2007a). *Crime and justice in the Netherlands*. Chicago: University of Chicago Press.

Tonry, M. & Bijleveld, C. C. J. H. (2007b). Crime, justice, and criminology in the Netherlands. In M. Tonry & C. C. J. H. Bijleveld (Eds.), *Crime and justice in the Netherlands* (p. 1-30). Chicago: University of Chicago Press.

Tremblay, R. E. (2000). The development of aggressive behaviour during childhood: What have we learned in the past century? *International Journal of Behavioral Development, 24*, 129-141.

United Nations General Assembly. (1989). *The convention on the rights of the child*. New York: United Nations.

Van de Rakt, M. G., Nieuwbeerta, P. & Apel, R. (2009). Association of criminal convictions between family members: Effects of siblings, fathers and mothers. *Criminal Behaviour and Mental Health, 19*, 94-108.

Van de Rakt, M. G., Nieuwbeerta, P. & de Graaf, N. D. (2008). Like father, like son: The relationships between conviction trajectories of fathers and their sons and daughters. *British Journal of Criminology, 48*, 538-556.

Van de Rakt, M. G., Ruiter, S., de Graaf, N. D. & Nieuwbeerta, P. (2010). When does the apple fall from the tree? Static versus dynamic theories predicting intergenerational transmission of convictions. *Journal of Quantitative Criminology, 26*, 371-389.

Van der Geest, V. R. (2011). *Working their way into adulthood. delinquency and employment in high-risk boys to age 32*. Doctoral dissertation, Vrije Universiteit Amsterdam.

Van der Geest, V. R., Bijleveld, C. C. J. H. & Blokland, A. A. J. (2011). The effects of employment on longitudinal trajectories of offending: A follow up of high risk youth from 18 to 32 years of age. *Criminology, 49*, 1195-1234.

Van der Geest, V. R., Blokland, A. A. J. & Bijleveld, C. C. J. H. (2009). Delinquent development in a sample of high-risk youth: Shape, content, and predictors of delinquent trajectories from age 12 to 32. *Journal of Research in Crime and Delinquency, 46*, 111-143.

Van der Werff, C. (1979). *Speciale preventie, een penologisch onderzoek [special prevention, a penological study]*. Doctoral dissertation, University of Amsterdam.

Verbruggen, J., Blokland, A. A. J. & Van der Geest, V. R. (2011). Werk, werkduur en criminaliteit [Employment, employment duration and crime]. *Tijdschrift voor Criminologie, 53*, 116-139.

Wadsworth, M. E. (1979). *Roots of delinquency: Infancy, adolescence, and crime*. London: Martin Robertson.

Waldman, I. D., Levy, F. & Hay, D. A. (1995). Multivariate genetic analyses of the overlap among DSM-III-R disruptive behavior disorder symptoms. *Behavior Genetics, 25*, 293-294.

Waldman, I. D. & Rhee, S. H. (2006). Genetic and environmental influences on psychopathy and antisocial behavior. In C. J. Patrick (Ed.), *Handbook of psychopathy* (p. 205-228). New York: The Guildford Press.

Walmsley, R. (2009). *World prison population list* (8th ed.). London: International Centre for Prison Studies, King's College.

Warr, M. (2002). *Companions in crime: The social aspects of criminal conduct*. Cambridge: Cambridge University Press.

Webster-Stratton, C. (1992). *The incredible years: A trouble-shooting guide for parents of children ages 3-8 years*. Toronto: Umbrella Press.

Wells, L. E. & Rankin, J. H. (1991). Families and delinquency: A meta-analysis of the impact of broken homes. *Social Problems, 38*, 71-93.

Wermink, H. T., Blokland, A. A. J., Nieuwbeerta, P. & Tollenaar, N. (2009). Recidive na werkstraffen en na gevangenisstraffen: Een gematchte vergelijking [Recidivism after community service: A matched samples comparison]. *Tijdschrift voor Criminologie, 51*, 211-227.

West, D. J. (1969). *Present conduct and future delinquency*. London: Heinemann.

West, D. J. (1982). *Delinquency: Its roots, careers and prospects*. London: Heinemann.

West, D. J. & Farrington, D. P. (1973). *Who becomes delinquent?* London: Heinemann.

West, D. J. & Farrington, D. P. (1977). *The delinquent way of life*. London: Heinemann.

Wiesner, M. & Windle, M. (2004). Assessing covariates of adolescent delinquency trajectories: A latent growth mixture modeling approach. *Journal of Youth and Adolescence, 33*, 431-442.

Wilson, H. (1975). Juvenile delinquency, parental criminality and social handicap. *British Journal of Criminology, 15*, 241-250.

Wilson, J. Q. & Herrnstein, R. J. (1985). *Crime and human nature*. New York: Simon and Schuster.

Wright, K. A., Pratt, T. C. & Delisi, M. (2008). Examining offending specialization in a sample of male multiple homicide offenders. *Homicide Studies, 12*, 381-398.

Wu, B. & Fuentes, A. I. (1998). Juvenile justice processing: The entangled effects of race and urban poverty. *Juvenile and Family Court Journal, 49*(2), 41-54.

Yang, C.-C. (2006). Evaluating latent class analysis models in qualitative phenotype identification. *Computational Statistics and Data Analysis, 50*, 1090-1104.

Young, J. (1999). *The exclusive society*. London: Macmillan.

Zedner, L. (2002). Victims. In M. Maguire, R. Morgan & R. Reiner (Eds.), *The Oxford handbook of criminology* (Third ed., p. 419-456). Oxford: Clarendon Press.

Zeger, S. L. & Liang, K.-Y. (1992). An overview of methods for the analysis of longitudinal data. *Statistics in Medicine, 11*, 1825-1839.

Summary

In this dissertation, I have investigated mechanisms that might explain why children with criminal parents have a higher risk of committing crime. Several explanations for this intergenerational transmission have been contrasted, such as social learning (imitation of behaviour), official bias against certain families, and transmission of risk factors. I have investigated this in England as well as in the Netherlands.

Some of the questions answered in my dissertation are: does it matter when the parents committed crime in the child's life? Do more persistent offenders transmit crime more than sporadic offenders? Do violent offenders specifically transmit violent behaviour or general crime to their children? Might the police and courts be biased against certain families? Might continuity of a criminogenic environment explain why parents as well as children show criminal behaviour? Does parental imprisonment pose an extra risk?

I find some support for social learning and strong support for the transmission of a criminogenic environment and official bias. It does not matter at what point in the offspring's youth parents commit crime; the risk of transmission is similar at different ages. Contrary to predictions, persistent offenders do not necessarily have more criminally active children than sporadic offenders, but violent offenders do specifically transmit violent offending. Official agencies appear to target offenders' children more and thereby these children have a higher risk of being convicted, regardless of their level of offending. Subsequently, these children appear to increase their offending after being convicted. Growing up in an environment with many risk factors for crime seems to be an important explanation for why children of criminals have a higher risk to commit crime. Finally, parental imprisonment increases offspring offending in England, but not in the Netherlands. This could possibly be explained by the fact that, comparatively, Dutch prisons and penal policy were much more humane and liberal in the period during which our subjects experienced parental imprisonment (1946-81).

This dissertation is the first study to specifically investigate these mechanisms of intergenerational continuity. The study is scientifically relevant because of its breadth, integration of conviction data as well as data on self-reported offending and environmental risk factors, its comparative design and the long periods over which transmission is investigated. Furthermore, the dissertation has important policy implications. It demonstrates how penal policy designed to reduce criminal behaviour might actually increase this behaviour in the next generation. This is especially important since Western countries such as the United Kingdom and the Netherlands show an increasing trend towards more punitive policies.

Appendix

Table 1: Appendix - Bayesian Information Criterion (BIC) Values per model
-1 = zero trajectory, 0 = flat, 1 = linear, 2 = quadratic

Model	Low N BIC	High N BIC
England		
Fathers - no. of groups (all quadratic)		
3	-969.52	-987.83
4	-965.22	-990.20
5	-974.70	-1006.34
Fathers - order of the trajectories		
2 2 2	-969.52	-987.83
0 2 2	-963.75	-978.74
-1 2 2	-969.52	-987.83
0 0 2	-958.38	-970.04
-1 0 2	-955.39	-965.38
-1 0 1	-956.34	-964.66
The Netherlands		
Fathers - no. of groups (all quadratic)		
3	-984.28	-1002.59
4	-978.63	-1003.60
5	-984.31	-1015.93
Fathers - order of the trajectories		
2 2 2	-984.28	-1002.59
0 2 2	-979.32	-994.30
-1 2 2	-978.89	-992.21
0 0 2	-982.01	-993.66
-1 0 2	-979.08	-989.06
England		
Sons - no. of groups (all quadratic)		
3	-4281.62	-4299.88
4	-4218.06	-4242.96
5	-4196.86	-4228.40
6	-4209.66	-4247.85
	Continued on next page	

Model	Low N BIC	High N BIC
England		
Sons - order of the trajectories		
2 2 2 2 2	-4196.86	-4228.40
0 2 2 2 2	-4192.94	-4221.16
0 2 0 2 2	-4187.88	-4212.78
-1 2 0 2 2	-4241.45	-4264.69
The Netherlands		
Sons - no. of groups (all quadratic)		
3	-1641.90	-1660.20
4	-1636.98	-1661.93
5	-1631.78	-1663.39
6	-1639.21	-1677.47
Sons - no. of groups (one intercept-only group)		
3	-1661.59	-1676.56
4	-1633.83	-1655.45
5	-1627.42	-1655.70
6	-1636.37	-1671.30
Sons - 4 group models - order of the trajectories		
2 2 2 2	-1636.98	-1661.93
0 2 2 2	-1633.83	-1655.45
-1 2 2 2	-1639.59	-1659.55
0 1 2 2	-1639.48	-1659.44
0 0 2 2	-1641.72	-1660.01
1 -1 2 2	-1641.51	-1659.81
Sons - 3 group models - order of the trajectories		
2 2 2	-1641.90	-1660.20
0 2 2	-1661.59	-1676.56
1 2 2	-1654.15	-1670.79
2 1 2	-1639.44	-1656.08

Subject Index

Age
    parental conviction, 54
    parental imprisonment, 116
Assortative mating, 7–8

Betere Start - Better Beginnings, 146
BIC - Bayesian Information Criterion, 27–28, 64
Biological mechanisms, see also Genetic mechanisms, 6–7, 136
BLRT - Bootstrap Likelihood Ratio Test, 27–28

Cambridge Study in Delinquent Development
    description, 13
Cognitive frameworks, 148
Conviction rate, 46–47
Conviction trajectories, 59–80
CR ratio, Conviction rate ratio, 49
Critical period, see Sensitive period

Dark number, 36
Definitions
    Aggression, 3
    Crime, 2–3
    Intergenerational transmission, 2
    Violence, 3

England and Wales
    policy, 106–107, 122–123

GEE - Generalized Estimating Equations, 16–17
Gender, 56
    parental imprisonment, 115
Genetic mechanisms, see also Biological mechanisms, 6–7, 136
Group-Based Trajectory Modelling, 59, 63–65

Interactional theory of intergenerational transmission, 8–9

Labelling theory, 82, 84–85
LCA - Latent Class Analysis, 26–28, 34–35

Mechanisms, 3
    assortative mating, see Assortative mating
    biological mechanisms, see Biological mechanisms
    genetic mechanisms, see Genetic mechanisms
    official bias, see Official bias
    risk factors, see Risk factors
    social learning, see Social learning
Methodology, 12–17

Natural experiment, 143–144

Official bias, 7, 81–103, 136–138
Outline of dissertation, 9

Parental imprisonment, 105–127, 136–138
Population heterogeneity, 41–42

Research questions of dissertation, 9–12
Risk factors, 4–5, 41, 48, 120–121

SABIC - Sample size Adjusted Bayesian Information Criterion, 27–28
Self-reported offending, 86–89
Sensitive period, 42–43
Social learning, 6, 22–23, 40–41
Specialisation in violence, 20–21
State dependency, 41–42
Stereotypes, 148

The Netherlands
    policy, 106–107, 122–123
Transfive Study
    description, 13–14

Author Index

Adler, M. J., 2, 162
Aebi, M., 159
Agnew, R., 43, 151
Agresti, A., 20, 151
Agresti, B. F., 20, 151
Aiken, L. S., 91, 151
Akers, R. L., 136, 151
Amato, P. R., 109, 151
Amlund-Hagen, K., 43, 162
Ananth, C. V., 16, 151
Apel, R., 1, 167
Asmussen, L., 43, 160
Asparouhov, T., 163
Avakame, E. F., 1, 19, 151

Bailey, J. A., 2, 151
Bandura, A., 6, 22, 23, 40, 151
Barnes, G. C., 1, 15, 36, 47, 77, 124, 142, 156
Baron, R. A., 148, 151
Baron, R. M., 5, 110, 152
Bartels, M., 158
Becker, H. S., 82, 152
Beckerman, A., 111, 152
Beichner, D., 83, 102, 166
Bell, R. Q., 140, 144, 152
Belsky, J., 140, 144, 152
Bender, D., 23, 161
Berk, L. E., 42, 152
Bernburg, J. G., 82, 85, 137, 152
Besemer, S., 43, 44, 46, 51, 57, 152
Besjes, G., 1, 152
Bijleveld, C. C. J. H., 1, 22, 36, 43, 57, 60, 77, 78, 106, 107, 109, 133, 152, 155, 158, 159, 165, 167
Bishop, D. M., 83, 84, 101, 152
Black, D. S., 6, 22, 23, 152
Blanden, J., 57, 123, 153
Bleske, A., 160
Bliesener, T., 23, 161

Blokland, A. A. J., 57, 60, 82, 125, 126, 153, 162, 163, 167, 168
Blonigen, D. M., 22, 153
Bloom, B., 108, 111, 153
Blumstein, A., 10, 14, 20, 60, 85, 123, 153, 164
Boivin, M., 153
Bornstein, M. H., 42, 153
Bouchard, T. J., 22, 153
Bouchard Jr, T., 158
Bouffard, J. A., 20, 153
Bouffard, L. A., 20, 153
Bowlby, J., 108, 111, 153
Bowles, S., 2, 153
Braithwaite, J., 123, 153
Brame, R., 20, 161, 164
Breen, R., 57, 123, 153
Brendgen, M., 6, 153
Brennan, P. A., 6, 23, 153, 164
Brennan, P. K., 84, 153
Bridges, G. S., 84, 153
Bukatko, D., 42, 153
Burke, J. D., 140, 164
Bursik, R. J., 65, 153
Bushway, S. D., 63, 154
Byrne, D., 148, 151

Cadoret, R. J., 6, 154
Capaldi, D. M., 1, 2, 20, 22–25, 47, 56, 111, 144, 145, 154, 159
Caspi, A., 1, 7, 154, 159, 160, 162
Catalano, R. F., 154, 156, 159
Caudy, M. S., 20, 166
Chapdelaine, A., 16, 154
Chaplin, R., 1, 154
Christiansen, K. O., 23, 154
Cohen, J. M., 10, 24, 153, 154
Coid, J. W., 156
Compas, B. E., 43, 154

Conger, R. D., 1, 19, 21, 85, 154, 165, 166
Connor-Smith, J. K., 43, 154
Cooperman, J. A., 165
Craig, I. W., 154, 160
Cressey, D. R., 6, 41, 166
Crick, N. R., 23, 35, 154
Crutchfield, R. D., 84, 153
Cukier, W., 16, 154

Daehler, M. W., 42, 153
Daly, K., 83, 154
Day, S., 106, 165
de Graaf, N. D., 41, 167
De Heer-de Lange, N., 1, 15, 159
Dean, C. W., 20, 161, 164
De Castro, B. O., 147, 154
DeGarmo, D., 22, 154
De Li, S., 85, 155
Delisi, M., 20, 168
Derks, E. M., 158
Devor, E., 6, 154
DiLalla, L. F., 6, 23, 144, 155
Dinovitzer, R., 107–109, 158
Dionne, G., 153
Dirkzwager, A., 107, 160
Dixon, J., 123, 155
Dodge, K. A., 23, 35, 154, 159
Downes, D., 13, 106, 107, 123, 155
D'Unger, A. V., 27, 64, 78, 155

Eckenrode, J., 44, 46, 155
Eckert, E., 158
Eddy, J. M., 108, 109, 155, 160
Edwardes, M. D. d., 16, 158
Eggleston, E. P., 64, 78, 155
Eisen, S., 165
Elliott, D. S., 87, 158
Enders, C. K., 28, 166
Engels, R. C., 1, 163
Eron, L. D., 21, 158
Esselstyn, T. C., 111, 157
Ezinga, M. A., 109–111, 125, 155

Farrington, D. P., 1, 3–8, 10, 13–15, 19–21, 23–25, 35–37, 40, 43, 46–48, 51, 56, 57, 60, 61, 68, 77, 81–89, 94, 101, 106–111, 120, 123, 124, 138, 139, 142, 145–147, 152, 155–157, 159, 161–166, 168
Feise, R., 141, 157
Felson, R. B., 21, 23, 157
Ferguson, T., 77, 157

Fergusson, D. M., 60, 157
Fidell, L. S., 48, 166
Field, A., 65, 91, 157
Finnegan, T. A., 156
Fisher, G., 36, 78, 157
Fishman, S. H., 111, 157
Fite, P. J., 140, 164
Flatley, J., 1, 154
Fligelstone, R., 20, 157, 166
Forgatch, M., 22, 154
Forrester, J. E., 16, 158
Francis, B., 20, 27, 34, 35, 157, 166
Frank, V., 153
Frazier, C. E., 83, 84, 101, 152
Freeman-Gallant, A., 1, 166
Frick, P. J., 6, 161
Friedman, S., 111, 157
Fuentes, A. I., 84, 168

Gabel, S., 111, 157
Gamoran, A., 2, 157
Garbarino, J., 43, 157
Garland, D. W., 126, 149, 157
Gartrell, J. W., 48, 160
Gelsthorpe, L., 36, 142, 158
Gibson, H. B., 87, 157
Gilliéron, G., 143, 159
Gintis, H., 2, 153
Giordano, P. C., 1, 19, 39, 59, 81, 136, 138, 140, 157
Girard, A., 153
Goldberg, J., 165
Goodman, L. A., 65, 157
Goodman, S. H., 43, 157
Gorman-Smith, D., 1, 77, 157
Gotlib, I. H., 43, 157
Gottesman, I. I., 6, 23, 144, 155
Gottfredson, M. R., 22, 41, 157, 158
Green, D. A., 123, 157, 158
Gregg, P., 57, 153
Grove, W., 6, 158
Gundry, G., 21, 156

Haapanen, R., 164
Haberman, S. J., 65, 158
Hagan, J., 83, 84, 107–109, 158
Hairston, C. F., 111, 158
Ham, M., 43, 160
Hanley, J. A., 16, 158
Harley, B., 42, 158
Harnett, L., 156
Harrington, D. P., 16, 160
Harris, J. R., 140, 145, 158
Hartnagel, T. F., 48, 160

Author Index

Hawkins, J. D., 2, 151, 154, 156, 159
Hay, D. A., 60, 167
Hearold, S., 22, 158
Hedderman, C., 36, 142, 158
Henderson, C. R., 155
Henry, D. B., 1, 157
Henry, S., 6, 160
Herbers, J. E., 2, 165
Herrnstein, R. J., 2, 168
Heston, L., 158
Hicks, B. M., 22, 153
Hill, K. G., 2, 151, 156, 158, 159
Hindelang, M. J., 87, 158
Hirschi, T., 22, 41, 87, 108, 157, 158
Hissel, S. C. E. M., 109, 138, 155, 158
Horwood, L. J., 60, 157
Hudziak, J., 6, 158
Huesmann, L. R., 21, 23, 158
Huizinga, D. H., 84, 87, 158
Hurt, K. B., 2, 165
Huschek, D., 159

Iacono, W. G., 22, 153
Iovanni, L., 82, 164
Ireland, T. O., 40, 43, 44, 46, 55, 159, 166

Jaffee, S. R., 1, 7, 109, 159
Janson, C.-G., 162
Jensen, P. S., 160
Jeong Kim, K., 1, 154
Johnson, B. T., 148, 151
Johnson, C., 165
Johnson, J. D., 84, 160
Johnston, D., 111, 159
Jolliffe, D., 1, 84, 87, 100, 156, 159
Jones, B. L., 63, 159
Juby, H., 109, 159
Junger, M., 87, 159
Junger-Tas, J., 100, 101, 159

Kaim-Caudle, P. R., 123, 159
Kalb, L. M., 1, 156
Kalidien, S. N., 1, 15, 159
Kalmuss, D., 22, 159
Kandel, E., 23, 161
Kazdin, A. E., 4, 37, 57, 146, 159, 160
Kemp, R. A. d., 1, 163
Kennon, S., 43, 162
Kenny, D. A., 5, 110, 152
Kerr, D. C., 1, 159
Kessler, R. C., 4, 159, 160
Killias, M., 143, 159
Kim, H. K., 1, 159

Kim-Cohen, J., 7, 160
Kissling, I., 143, 159
Kitzman, H., 155
Kjellstrand, J. M., 109, 160
Knight, K. E., 158
Knudsen, E. I., 42, 160
Kokko, K., 21, 23, 160
Kosterman, R., 156, 159
Kraemer, H. C., 4, 159, 160
Krahn, H., 48, 160
Krohn, M. D., 1, 4, 8, 63, 82, 85, 135, 137, 152, 154, 166
Krueger, R. F., 22, 153, 160
Kruttschnitt, C., 107, 158, 160
Kupfer, D. J., 4, 159, 160

Laird, N. M., 16, 160
Lambert, S., 1, 15, 36, 47, 77, 124, 142, 156
Land, K. C., 27, 60, 79, 155, 163
Lanier, M. M., 6, 160
Lanskey, C., 161
Larson, R., 43, 160
Laub, J. H., 46, 64, 68, 82, 100, 124, 155, 165
Lefkowitz, M. M., 21, 158
Lehoux, P. M., 165
Leiber, M. J., 84, 160
Lemert, E. M., 36, 42, 82, 108, 160
Lenneberg, E. H., 42, 160
Leve, L. D., 6, 154
Levy, F., 60, 167
Liang, K.-Y., 16, 17, 160, 168
Liefbroer, A. C., 2, 160
Lipsitz, S. R., 16, 160
Lizotte, A. J., 1, 166
Loeber, R., 1, 24, 48, 87, 106, 121, 156–158, 161
Loehlin, J. C., 22, 153
Lösel, F., 23, 35, 146, 161
Lovegrove, P. J., 1, 158, 166
Lykken, D. T., 158
Lyons, M., 165

Machin, S., 57, 153
Maguire, M., 36, 78, 161
Marcynyszyn, L. A., 155
Markson, L., 161
Marshall, I. H., 100, 101, 159
Martin, J., 154
Mason, D. A., 6, 161
Masten, A. S., 2, 165
Maxfield, M. G., 87, 161
Mazerolle, P., 20, 161, 164

McAra, L., 85, 102, 161
McCall, P. L., 27, 155
McClay, J., 154
McCord, J., 21, 22, 35, 161
McCutcheon, A. L., 17, 20, 26, 161
McGloin, J. M., 20, 161, 166
McLanahan, S., 109, 165
McVie, S., 85, 102, 161
Mednick, B. R., 6, 153
Mednick, S. A., 6, 23, 153, 161, 164
Messner, S. F., 48, 162
Michael, J., 2, 162
Micklewright, J., 149, 162
Mill, J., 154
Mitchell, O., 83, 84, 162
Moffitt, T. E., 1, 6–8, 43, 56, 60, 68, 77, 154, 159–163
Morris, P., 123, 162
Morrison, S., 87, 157
Muftic, L. R., 20, 153
Mulvey, E. P., 164
Murray, J., 4, 43, 51, 82, 84, 106, 107, 109–112, 124, 137, 138, 149, 152, 162
Murray, L., 109–111, 138, 162
Musterd, S., 57, 123, 162
Muthén, B. O., 26, 162, 163
Muthén, L. K., 26, 162
Myers, B. J., 43, 111, 162

Nagin, D. S., 11, 17, 27, 41, 59–61, 63, 64, 66, 78, 79, 125, 153, 155, 157, 159, 163, 164
Neapolitan, J. L., 48, 163
Negassa, A., 16, 158
Nelson, J. F., 84, 163
Neppl, T., 1, 154
Newcombe, R., 160
Nieuwbeerta, P., 1, 41, 60, 125, 126, 153, 163, 167, 168
Nijhof, K. S., 1, 163
Nylund, K. L., 163

Obradović, J., 2, 165
Oesterle, S., 2, 151
Offord, D. R., 4, 159, 160
Olsen, R. F., 4, 162
Olweus, D., 6, 21, 23, 163
Ormiston, 129, 146, 163
Osborn, S. G., 21, 35, 82, 156, 163
Osgood, D. W., 20, 37, 142, 163
Owen, L. D., 1, 2, 154, 159

Painter, K. A., 48, 89, 120, 156

Palloni, A., 84, 158
Pardini, D. A., 140, 144, 164
Paternoster, R., 20, 41, 82, 161, 163, 164
Patrick, C. J., 22, 153
Patterson, G. R., 2, 20, 22–25, 140, 144, 154, 164
Pears, K. C., 1, 2, 154, 159
Penfield, W., 42, 164
Perneger, T. V., 141, 164
Pérusse, 153
Peters, P. L., 165
Petersilia, J., 84, 164
Piquero, A. R., 14, 20, 23–25, 60, 64, 70, 79, 85, 123, 161, 164, 166
Platt, R. W., 16, 151
Pratt, T. C., 20, 83, 164, 166, 168
Pruitt, C. R., 83, 164
Pugh, G., 161
Pulkkinen, L., 21, 23, 160
Putnam, F. W., 44, 164

Raine, A., 6, 23, 153, 164
Rankin, J. H., 109, 167
Ray, J. V., 20, 166
Reid, J. B., 108, 155
Reiss, A. J., 6, 164
Research Development and Statistics Directorate, 15, 27, 31, 165
Rettew, D. C., 158
Rhee, S. H., 6, 165, 167
Ribeaud, D., 159
Rietveld, M. J. H., 158
Rivera, C. J., 82, 152
Roberts, L., 42, 164
Robins, L. N., 47, 56, 111, 165
Roeder, K., 63, 159
Ross, S., 36, 78, 157
Roth, J. A., 10, 153
Rowe, D. C., 1, 61, 77, 165
Ruiter, S., 41, 167
Rutter, M., 7, 43, 159, 162, 165, 166

Saltzman, H., 43, 154
Sampson, R. J., 46, 64, 68, 82, 100, 124, 155, 165
Savitz, D. A., 16, 151
Scaramella, L. V., 1, 85, 154, 166
Schmidt, L., 87, 156
Schreck, C. J., 20, 37, 142, 163
Schwartzman, A. E., 165
Scott, J. P., 42, 165
Sealock, M. D., 83, 84, 101, 165
Segal, N., 158
Sekol, I., 4, 109, 162

Serbin, L. A., 2, 165
Shaffer, A., 2, 165
Sharkey, P., 2, 165
Sherman, L. W., 36, 82, 108, 165
Shindledecker, R., 111, 157
Sigle-Rushton, W., 109, 165
Silva, P. A., 7, 160, 162
Simons, R. L., 85, 165, 166
Simpson, S. S., 83, 84, 101, 165
Skardhamar, T., 79, 165
Slotboom, A.-M., 106, 109, 155, 165
Slutske, W., 61, 165
Smarsh, T. M., 43, 162
Smith, C. A., 1, 40, 44, 46, 55, 159, 166
Smith, E., 155
Smith, K., 1, 154
Snyder, H. N., 156
Solon, G., 2, 166
Soothill, K., 20, 157, 166
Soteriou, N., 156
Souza, K. A., 161
Spohn, C., 83, 84, 102, 153, 166
Sroufe, L. A., 43, 166
Stack, D. M., 165
Stack, S. A., 6, 161
Steinhart, D., 108, 111, 153
Stewart, E. A., 85, 166
Stice, E., 4, 160
Stouthamer-Loeber, M., 1, 24, 87, 156, 161
Stuifbergen, J. A., 152
Sullivan, C. J., 20, 37, 142, 161, 166
Sussman, S., 6, 152
Sutherland, E. H., 6, 41, 166

Tabachnick, B. G., 48, 166
Taylor, A., 1, 159, 160
Theobald, D., 46, 68, 82, 124, 162, 166
Thomsen, A. H., 43, 154
Thornberry, T. P., 1, 4, 8, 19, 40, 41, 44, 46, 48, 55, 61, 63, 77, 121, 135, 154, 158, 159, 166
Tofighi, D., 28, 166
Tolan, P. H., 1, 157
Tollenaar, N., 126, 168
Tonry, M., 107, 133, 167
Tremblay, R. E., 3, 78, 79, 163, 167
True, W., 165
Tsuang, M., 165
Turner, R., 156

Unger, J. B., 6, 152

United Nations General Assembly, 147, 167

Van Beijsterveldt, C., 158
Van de Rakt, M. G., 1, 41, 46, 57, 61, 79, 80, 143, 167
Van der Geest, V. R., 43, 57, 60, 63, 82, 100, 137, 147, 152, 167
Van der Werff, C., 144, 167
Van Gaalen, R., 1, 152
Van Giezen, A., 106, 165
Van Kammen, W. B., 24, 87, 156, 161
Van Swaaningen, R., 13, 106, 107, 123, 155
Verbruggen, J., 57, 147, 167
Villettaz, P., 143, 159
Visher, C. A., 10, 153
Vondra, J., 140, 144, 152

Wadsworth, M. E., 43, 123, 154, 167
Walder, L. O., 21, 158
Waldman, I. D., 6, 60, 165, 167
Walmsley, R., 105, 167
Wang, W., 42, 158
Warr, M., 43, 108, 167
Webster-Stratton, C., 146, 167
Weiler, B. L., 87, 161
Weiss, J. G., 87, 158
Wells, L. E., 109, 167
Welsh, B. C., 37, 57, 123, 146, 157
Wermink, H. T., 126, 168
West, D. J., 6, 7, 13, 21, 35, 57, 77, 82, 85, 87, 94, 156, 157, 163, 168
West, S. G., 91, 151
Widom, C. S., 87, 161
Wientjes, J. A., 1, 163
Wiesner, M., 60, 168
Wijkman, M., 1, 22, 77, 133, 152
Williams, B., 160
Wilson, H., 77, 168
Wilson, J. Q., 2, 83, 164, 168
Windle, M., 60, 168
Wright, K. A., 20, 153, 168
Wu, B., 84, 168
Wu, C.-i., 165

Yang, C.-C., 28, 168
Young, J., 149, 168

Zedner, L., 1, 168
Zeger, S. L., 16, 17, 160, 168
Zielinski, D., 155